THE SAINT FOR SHALOM

How Pope John Paul II Transformed
Catholic-Jewish Relations
The Complete Texts 1979–2005

Presented by the Anti-Defamation League

*Compiled, Edited, and with Commentary
by Eugene J. Fisher and Leon Klenicki*

A Crossroad Herder Book
CROSSROAD • NEW YORK

2011

The Crossroad Publishing Company 370 Lexington Avenue, New York, NY 10017

Copyright © 2011 by the Anti-Defamation League

Printed in the United States of America

Library of Congress Cataloging-in-Publication Data

John Paul II, Pope, 1920–2005.
    The Saint for Shalom: How Pope John Paul II Transformed Catholic-Jewish Relations: The Complete Texts 1979–2005 / Pope John Paul II; with commentary and introduction by Eugene J. Fisher and Leon Klenicki, editors.
        p. cm.
    "A publication of the Anti-Defamation League."
    ISBN 0-8245-1544-7 (pb)
    1. Catholic Church—Relations—Judaism—Papal documents. 2. Judaism—Relations—Catholic Church—Papal documents. 3. John Paul II, Pope, 1920—Views on Judaism. I. Fisher, Eugene J. II. Klenicki, Leon. III. Anti-Defamation League. IV. Title.

    BM535.J583 1995
    261.2'6—dc20   95-22906
        CIP

A Note to the Reader

With the beatification of Pope John Paul II, the Anti-Defamation League is proud to offer this volume presenting his complete writings and statements on Judaism, the Jewish people, and the State of Israel. It is a story of the impact of *Nostra Aetate*, the 1965 Church declaration on the Jewish people, and of the pope's leadership in changing centuries-old attitudes toward Jews. It is especially significant for ADL that decades of interfaith dialogue offer us hope for the future.[1]

Abraham H. Foxman
National Director
Anti-Defamation League
June 2, 2011

---

1. The papal addresses cited in this collection are referred to by the dates on which they were delivered. The present volume includes texts contained in *Spiritual Pilgrimage, Texts on Jews and Judaism 1979–1995* edited by Eugene J. Fisher and Leon Klenicki (New York, Anti-Defamation League, 1995). Primary sources for papal texts and translations are the Information Service of the Pontifical Council for Christian Unity, *L'Osservatore Romano*, and Origins (Documentary Service of the Catholic News Service, Washington, D.C.).

Contents

INTRODUCTION

A COMMENTARY ON THE TEXTS

1979

1980

1982

1983

1986

1987

1988

1991

1992

1993

1994

1995

1998

1999

2000

2001

2002

2003

2004

2005

In the Footsteps of Pope John Paul II

Pope Benedict XVI

On this anniversary, as we look back over four decades of fruitful contacts between the Church and the Jewish People, we need to renew our commitment to the work that yet remains to be done. In this regard, from the first days of my Pontificate, and in a particular way during my recent visit to the Synagogue in Cologne, I have expressed my own firm determination to walk in the footsteps of my beloved predecessor Pope John Paul II. The Jewish-Christian dialogue must continue to enrich and deepen the bonds of friendship which have developed, while preaching and catechesis must be committed to ensuring that our mutual relations are presented in the light of the principles set forth by the Council.

—From the Vatican, October 26, 2005, Benedictus PP. XVI

An Appreciation

Cardinal William H. Keeler
Archbishop Emeritus of Baltimore

Pope John Paul II accomplished much to put Catholic-Jewish relations on the right footing. There was his long friendship with Jerzy Kluger, who was Jewish, and there is evidence from many corners about his friendship with Jewish people.

It is a point to be made that Leon Klenicki, who was Jewish, was present in Rome for the talks that were a breakthrough in the relationship between the Catholic Church and the Jewish people in 1987. His contributions I leave to others to recite.

The moment when Rabbi Klenicki and I were traveling back together from Rome was the moment in which I discovered that he was reading the psalms in the Hebrew scriptures and I was reading the psalms in the Latin of our breviary. This was something that I referred to at the service that we had jointly with the Jewish organization that he represented.

May the Lord bless our common efforts to end prejudice.

May, 2011

Foreword

Cardinal Stanisław Dziwisz
Archbishop of Krakow

The turnabout in Christian-Jewish relations that occurred after the Second Vatican Council was a response to the shock that humanity was going through in the twentieth century, becoming aware of the vast extent of suffering that can be brought by prejudices and hatred for other people. Aware of this, the Church wanted a more profound transformation of the minds and hearts of its sons and daughters with regard to their attitude toward Jews—a transformation at the level of theology and religious instruction.

The direction in which we are to go, the path toward full reconciliation and friendship between our communities, has been clearly marked by the declaration of the Second Vatican Council and the binding statements of the Magisterium of the Church. There is no retreat from this path, indicated by the Council and unambiguously endorsed by successive Popes and supported recently by the Holy Father Benedict XVI.

John Paul II, during his numerous meetings with the representatives of the Jewish community, often repeated that we are only at the beginning of our path of common aspiration to full reconciliation. It is only the span of time of two generations since we started deliberate and strong efforts to come nearer to each other. During his memorable 1986 visit to the Rome synagogue, John Paul II told the Chief Rabbi of Rome when they embraced each other, "We are like brothers who have found each other after a very long time." It is the situation in which we are today, owing to the magnanimity of God. Since we have found each other, we trust each other too little. We do not always feel like being together, as would be befitting for brothers.

For many Christians and Jews and for me personally, one of the most moving moments of the long pontificate of John Paul II was his visit in the Tent of Remembrance in Jerusalem, where at the ashes collected from the places where Jewish people were murdered, an eternal flame burns. He said during his pilgrimage, "We must work for a new era of reconciliation and peace between Jews and Christians. My visit is a pledge that the Catholic Church will do everything possible to ensure that this is not just a dream but reality" (March 23, 2000).

The wounds of time will not be healed in a day, but the path that John Paul II indicated for our time leads us to a new horizon. This voice of hope and determination is the source of inspiration to us in our efforts toward reconciliation. Let them ring in our ears!

Krakow, February 25, 2011

Preface

Most Reverend Timothy M. Dolan
Archbishop of New York
President of the United States Conference of Catholic Bishops

This new edition from the Anti-Defamation League completes the publication in their official English translation of the writings of Blessed John Paul II regarding the Church's relationship with the Jewish people. On the occasion of his beatification on May 1, 2011, in Rome by his successor, Pope Benedict XVI, this project is a fitting tribute to the man who many already call "John Paul the Great."

It is no exaggeration to state that Pope John Paul II helped to reconcile the Catholic Church and the Jewish people more than any pope since the time of St. Peter the Apostle (d. 64). Born and baptized as Karol Józef Wojtyła in 1920, John Paul II grew up with a love and respect for his Jewish friends and neighbors that would later inspire his entire priesthood, episcopacy, and pontificate. Indeed, under John Paul II, the teaching of the Second Vatican Council in its seminal document on the relationship of the Church to the Jews, *Nostra Aetate*, no. 4, found its most credible expression where it was most needed—in the shadow of the Holocaust. Condemning the anti-Judaism and anti-Semitism that gave rise to the extermination of millions of Jews in Europe, this pope once and for all clarified that one cannot be Christian and hate Jews.

This same message is suffused throughout all of John Paul's writings in this final volume. His extraordinary visit to Jerusalem and his unforgettable prayer at the Western Wall in 2000 typify both our need to repent of past wrongs, as well as to ask God for the grace of a new relationship with His chosen people:

> God of our fathers,
> you chose Abraham and his descendants
> to bring Your name to the nations:
> we are deeply saddened

by the behavior of those
who in the course of history
have caused these children of Yours to suffer
and asking Your forgiveness
we wish to commit ourselves
to genuine brotherhood
with the people of the Covenant.

John Paul II's legacy of embracing the Jewish people now lives on in the teachings of his successor, Pope Benedict XVI, who took as his own John Paul's now famous prayer, reaffirming its every word during his visit to the Great Synagogue of Rome in January of 2010. By doing so, Pope Benedict XVI made it clear that John Paul's life and example were not merely the personal concerns of an extraordinary pope but had now become the permanent expression of the entire Church.

On April 2, 2005, John Paul II died, a bridge of friendship to Christian and Jew alike. Only four years later, in April of 2009, Pope Benedict XVI would tell the Catholic world, "With you, I pray for the gift of beatification." Today, that prayer is answered.

May our reading of this last and complete edition of Blessed John Paul's writings on Jews and Judaism be an inspiration for us to follow in his example!

The Feast of the Divine Mercy, 2011

In Memory of Leon

Dr. Eugene J. Fisher
Distinguished Professor of Catholic-Jewish Studies
Saint Leo University

This is the last book of my dear friend, Rabbi Leon Klenicki, and the last on which we collaborated. I first met Leon in the spring of 1977, when he arrived in Detroit to oversee the Anti-Defamation League (ADL)'s section of the third National Workshop on Christian-Jewish Relations (NWCJR), of which I was the local chair representing the Archdiocese of Detroit. Jaunty, he came in energetically, wearing one of his signature hats. I instantly liked him, an effect he had on most people, I came to realize, including bishops and popes, for there was depth and substance beneath the jauntiness and ready wit.

When I came to Washington in the summer of 1977 to take over as director of the Secretariat for Catholic-Jewish Relations of the U.S. Conference of Catholic Bishops (USCCB), Leon was one of the first to seek me out and to welter me with ideas for projects. These were good ideas and excellent programs, I came to realize. Over the years Leon and I wrote together and coedited numerous books and articles for both the Catholic and Jewish press. Working through the dialogical, Catholic-Jewish process of creating these works is an intimate experience, not unlike a good marriage. We disagreed at times, as will happen in good marriages, but we were each deepened in our inner selves by the sharing, agreeing, disagreeing, and cocreating. Certainly I was, and I hope the same was true of him.

Leon was always open to new ideas and always had a bottom line of respect for the other and of demanding respect from the other for Jews and Judaism. He opposed defamation by creating an alternative to it, understanding, sharing, and delighting in difference. Jews and Catholics, while siblings, are not the same. The bottom line differences, while irreconcilable logically, can be understood to be as compatible, Leon knew, if only we reach within to the space where our specific creedal statements are touching upon the larger, transcendent truths we finite humans seek so inadequately to articulate.

One of Leon's favorite statements was that we Jews and Christians must go beyond tea and sympathy, to dig deeper, to penetrate, to encounter the other as both different and yet the same image and likeness of the one God, the God of Israel, we share. And so he did, bringing Jewish newspaper editors together with Catholic newspaper editors so that, instead of simply writing about the other, they could (as some still do) call each other, talk, and write more objective two-sided stories about current events and controversies between our communities. Likewise with editors and biblical and liturgical scholars.

Leon's was a life in dialogue, thankfully to some extent with me. Thankfully, also, he has a worthy successor, Rabbi Eric Greenberg, to carry on his work. Leon's work was seismic in the historic relationship between the Catholic Church and the Jewish People. His name, I am sure, will be for a blessing. And his work will benefit Catholics and Jews for generations to come.

August, 2011

Rabbi Leon Klenicki:
An Appreciation

Rabbi Eric J. Greenberg
Director of Interfaith Affairs
Anti-Defamation League

On my work desk, smothered with multicolored file folders and news reports, there is a stack of reference books that are essential to my job.

Glancing at the books' titles, a clear pattern emerges:

- *Toward a Theological Encounter*, edited by Rabbi Leon Klenicki
- *Issues in the Jewish-Christian Dialogue*, coedited by Rabbi Leon Klenicki
- *Dictionary of the Jewish-Christian Dialogue*, coedited by Rabbi Leon Klenicki
- *Biblical Studies: Meeting Ground of Jews and Christians*, coedited by Boadt, Kroner, and, oh yes, Rabbi Klenicki

Indeed, it is impossible to understand the significance of the profound changes in Christian-Jewish relations during the last decades of the twentieth century without reading the works of Rabbi Leon Klenicki, my predecessor and the longtime Director of Interfaith Affairs for the Anti-Defamation League.

Today, I am honored to be involved with the publication of Leon's final work, *The Saint for Shalom*—the complete texts of Pope John Paul II on Jews and Judaism, coedited with Leon's longtime collaborator and friend, Dr. Eugene Fisher.

As ADL's interfaith director, Leon was a pioneer in nurturing a new, positive relationship between the Catholic Church and the Jewish people after nearly two thousand years of tragedy. He was greatly influenced by such important Catholic thinkers as Jacques

Maritain. It is worth noting that Rabbi Klenicki and Pope John Paul II both wrote their theses on the same religious figure—St. John of the Cross.

Leon understood what it was like for Jews living in a country where anti-Semitism was rife and where the church was a source of that anti-Semitism. That is because he grew up in Argentina. He could relate to the individual happiness and pain that people in our community experience. For him, Catholic-Jewish relations were never simply an abstract endeavor but a human experience.

Leon personified ADL in that he believed in the need to speak out in the face of Christian anti-Semitism but, equally important, to educate Christian leaders for the long run. His favorite work was his interpretation of the Gospels for Christians, showing that it was not inevitable that churchgoers be exposed to anti-Jewish renditions of Christian scripture. This was always a priority for him, because he had understood the long-term impact of how biblical texts were interpreted.

He could talk to Jews and Christians with equal facility and ease. It was amazing to witness the depth of respect Catholic leaders showed Leon. This was because he was always honest with them, ready to criticize when necessary, to praise when appropriate, and always to be constructive in the relationship. One key part of his job was to help Christians understand their Jewish roots and to acknowledge that for Jews, the Covenant God made with Moses at Mount Sinai is eternal and irrevocable. But Leon also helped educate the Jewish community about Christians. He sought to deepen our understanding and highlight our commonalities, while acknowledging our differences.

Rabbi Klenicki met with Pope John Paul II on many occasions, in Rome and in the United States, and had held him in high regard. He met with Pope Benedict XVI when he was Cardinal Ratzinger, and he told the then-Cardinal about ADL educational programs on early Christianity and rabbinic Judaism and the presentation of Jews and Judaism that have sometimes been misunderstood and misused to promote anti-Semitism. Rabbi Klenicki also met with Cardinal Ratzinger, where they focused on the need for Catholics and Jews to reflect together on the theological meaning of the Holocaust.

I was privileged to know Leon in several capacities. When I was a newspaper reporter, he was a trusted news source. He soon became a confidante and most importantly a mentor and friend.

In 2008, Pope Benedict XVI honored Rabbi Klenicki with the highest award that can be given to a non-Catholic by the pope—the Knighthood of St. Gregory. He is one of only a handful of Jews to be so honored. Leon's acceptance speech summed up his profoundly optimistic future perspective on a historically tragic relationship. "Through our dialogue with each other, people of faith, as equals we can overcome the historical domain to enter into a dominion of sacredness," he said. "Let us build on this sacred relationship of Catholic to Jew and Jew to Catholic that God may light the world with understanding and blessing."

Shortly after Leon's death in January 2009, ADL held a memorial tribute for him. The venue, quite appropriately, was the Pope John Paul II Center in Washington, D.C., where Catholic and Jewish leaders gathered from around the country to pay their respects. Cardinal William H. Keeler, archbishop emeritus of Baltimore and longtime moderator of Catholic-Jewish Affairs for the United States Conference of Catholic Bishops, said of Leon, "This faithful son of Torah leaves behind more than thirty years of scholarship and leadership in interfaith relations. For the Catholic Church in the United States and Latin America, Leon was a pioneer in the promotion of a vision of Catholic-Jewish relations that drew inspiration from the Second Vatican Council and the vital streams of contemporary Jewish thought."

Two years after his passing, Leon's books are still all over my office. And now it is my great honor to make space for the latest one, *The Saint for Shalom*. I am proud and honored to carry on the work of our beloved teacher, colleague, and friend, Rabbi Leon Klenicki. May his memory be for a blessing.

September, 2011

Acknowledgments

We wish to extend our heartfelt thanks to Kenneth W. Orce and Martin L. Budd for providing us with the opportunity and support to create this book. As partners in this endeavor, they play a critical role in the work we do and the people we touch.

We also want to extend a special thanks to Abraham H. Foxman, national director of the Anti-Defamation League, for his leadership and vision in the creation of this project and in helping strengthen Jewish-Catholic relations for the last forty years.

Introduction

From Historical Mistrust to Mutual Recognition

RABBI LEON KLENICKI

FOR ALMOST TWO MILLENNIA, CHRISTIANS AND JEWS HAVE lived in the same universe, under the same sky. They are both in history, experiencing history. But they have seldom been together. To be in the same place does not necessarily imply togetherness, the sharing of a living presence of the other as a child of God. Although there are eloquent contemporary exceptions, Jews and Christians primarily have seen each other as objects—in many respects, as objects of contempt. The negative opinions of each other have, at times, translated this alienation into an enmity of word and action. Prejudice all too often still shapes the faith commitment, influencing the spiritual encounter and society itself.

This relationship of monologue, of seeing not the other but only one's own construct—or stereotype—of the other, has been undergoing a transformation since the last decades of the twentieth century. The focus now is on dialogue, a meeting of hearts, a prophetic encounter of faith. This encounter through dialogue is a reckoning of time past, of deeds, of what has been done and left undone. It is a moment of facing history. True dialogue between Jews and Christians is a process that entails a consideration of each other's faith commitment as part of God's design and way. It demands a critical examination by Christians of their traditional presentation of Jews and Judaism and by Jews of their attitudes toward Christianity. Dialogue means a reflection on the witnessing to each other and to the world that is respectful of each other's differences. Dialogue

1

necessitates a reckoning with centuries of one-sided teaching and centuries of memory. Christians have to overcome two thousand years of contempt for Israel's covenant with God, for Israel's mission in the world. Jews have to overcome two thousand years of memories, memories of the crusades, of ghettos, and of the wearing of special garments to identify their Jewish condition. They have to overcome memories of the present as well—memories of widespread Christian silence during, and even complicity in, the Holocaust, and of continuing Christian misunderstandings of the State of Israel and of the struggle of Jews for security in their ancient homeland.

Some two thousand years ago, during the first century in Christian chronology, two divinely appointed vocations were shaped out of a common heritage. It was, as Paul seems to portray it in the Epistle to the Romans, like the relationship between root and branches. The root is the word of God expressed in the Hebrew Bible from the first to the last book; the branches are rabbinic Judaism and Christianity. God's word, especially after the destruction of the temple by Roman troops in the year 70 CE (Common Era), was expanded into distinct yet related messages by these two great movements of faith.

Rabbinic Judaism, which developed from Pharisaism, was the in-depth process of understanding God's covenantal relationship after the destruction of the Jerusalem temple. Rabbinic Judaism built an inner temple that has lasted for centuries. In our time, this inner temple has suffered its greatest challenge by the devastating wind of the *Shoah*, the Holocaust committed by Nazi totalitarianism. The twentieth century marked a new time for Jews searching, once again, for the meaning of God, the presence of God in Jewish existence.

Christianity, the other branch that developed from the root of biblical Israel, expressed itself in the writings of the New Testament and related texts, conveying the mission of Jesus to humanity. Interestingly, it too finds the source of many of its doctrines and rituals in Pharisaic and Synagogue Judaism. Due to the impact of history, both branches have been fighting with each other for centuries up to our own days.

Christianity, especially after its alliance with Constantine, the fourth-century Roman emperor, became the established religion of the Roman Empire. That gave to Christian leaders the political power that enabled God's word to be spread through the then-known world. But it also opened Christians to the corruptive force of power. The alliance of secular power and ecclesiastical power in Christian history meant for the Jewish community numerous restrictions in its civil life. In the late Middle Ages, Jews were ordered to live in special quarters—the ghettos—and were forbidden to exercise the normal work and professions open to other citizens. Jews were forbidden to own or cultivate land or to engage in certain kinds of business activities and were, thus, pressed into the exercise of money-lending, which was not allowed to Christians. Jews were at the mercy of ecclesiastical leaders and secular kings. Often, mobs, incited by sermons and the Christian teaching of contempt—especially, it is sad to say, during Holy Week when the deicide charge would burst forth—would erupt into violence against the Jews.

The theological teaching of contempt accused the Jews of being the killers of Jesus and condemned them to eternal Diaspora. The teaching of contempt disqualified the covenant between God and Israel, arguing that it was superseded by a new covenant—the Christian testimony—with the coming of Jesus. In the Middle Ages, religious confrontations were called to debate theological points. Jews—rabbis and religious teachers—were obligated to explain biblical passages, such as references to Emanuel or to the suffering servant in Isaiah, which Christians saw as typological references to Jesus and his vocation. The confrontations generally ended in expulsion of the Jews from the city, the burning of sacred Hebrew books, or the imposition of more restrictions on the civil rights of the Jewish community.

In modern times, social changes introduced by the Industrial Revolution and modernity somewhat changed the picture. Jews were allowed to become citizens, with the same obligations as other citizens but, generally, not with the same advantages. Jews were "tolerated" but never fully accepted into European society. This lack of pluralism, of respect for the other as he or she is, transformed the theological anti-Judaism of Christian teaching into a new dimension. Modern social and racial anti-Semitism is a force that is trying to restrict Jewish rights; it threatens the very destruction of the Jewish community. The culmination of modern social anti-Semitism took place with the totalitarianism of Nazi Germany. The Holocaust was a devastating wind that took six million Jews to the gas chamber and to systematic murder. The Holocaust is one of the turning points in Jewish history, but it is also the greatest challenge to Christian commitment. The Holocaust occurred in the very heart of Western Christian civilization and was performed by a nation that had proclaimed for centuries its Christianity and had given to the world great Christian thinkers and theologians as well as the most sophisticated, diabolic murderers. The Holocaust entails for the Jewish people a rethinking of Jewish vocation and role in history. It also entails a Christian reckoning of Christian silence, indifference, and complicity, despite the heroic deeds of some Christians in saving Jewish lives.

The twentieth century marked for Jews and Christians a new moment. It was a time of vast spiritual change, of incredible scientific creativity, and of historical development. It was a time of great hope but, equally, a time of profound despair. Persecutions, murder, hunger, and lack of sensitivity over the situation of the vast majority of humanity are signs of a failure in our religious witnessing. For Jews and Christians, the twentieth century was the first century in proclaiming together God's covenant. For Jews, it was a rethinking of their commitment vis-à-vis tolerance and the nearly eternal danger of total destruction. Rethinking the meaning of the covenant and God's call signified a consideration of the diabolic forces that will always attempt to destroy the people of God. Totalitarianism in any form is an attempt to destroy God's covenant.

Today, Christians and Jews are, for the first time, together in history, together to discover for themselves their own proper vocations in a time of radical change. It is a time to look closely at each other, to overcome the teaching of contempt and memories, and to see the other as a part of the covenant of God. It is a new time of reckoning, renewal, and prophetic response.

The Second Vatican Council, in the 1960s, began a period of actualization and active awareness, of experience of God and of God's presence in the contemporary Christian historical context. It was called *aggiornamento* by Pope John XXIII. The Council initiated in the Church a process of inner renewal that entails respect for the other.

Pope John Paul II played a key role in expounding certain concepts and ideas for further reflection by the Catholic community. Indeed, he is the most active Pope ever in the pursuit of friendship and understanding between Jews and Catholics.

He demonstrated his interest and commitment to the Catholic-Jewish dialogue and the Jewish people in the documents published in this volume. He met with Jewish leaders wherever he traveled in the world. His interest deepened through the years both theologically and politically. This becomes clear in his New Testament comments made at the weekly audience. He was always careful to stress the unique value of the Hebrew Bible during these meetings at which he received visitors from around the world and which were reported in the press. In Germany, in 1980, he proclaimed the Jewish people as "the people of God, of the Old Covenant never revoked by God."

And in October 1997, John Paul II called a group of New Testament scholars to a meeting in Rome to discuss "the Roots of Anti-Judaism in the Christian Milieu." He told the participants that "erroneous and unjust interpretations of the New Testament regarding the Jewish people and their presumed guilt circulated for too long" and "contributed to a lulling of many consciences at the time of World War II." He pointed out that "anti-Semitism is without any justification and absolutely condemnable," echoing his previous condemnation of anti-Semitism as a sin.

Pope John Paul II found many opportunities to denounce the horror of the Holocaust. In June 1979 at Auschwitz he stopped at the stone in Yiddish. There he spoke of Jewish martyrdom, though the small monument set up by the Communists did not mention that Jews had died here but instead referred to the deaths of three million Europeans.

During his historic visit to Israel he prayed at Yad Vashem and met with Holocaust survivors. His heartfelt words and the emotional tone of his voice deeply moved the Israelis and Catholics and Jews everywhere.

In his first meeting with Catholic leadership after the fall of communism he devoted a whole page of this speech to Jews. He again referred to the Holocaust and Jewish suffering and asked the painful question that troubles so many of us: "Is it still possible to speak about God after Auschwitz?"

He took advantage of every opportunity to express his concern about Jews. For example, upon receiving the German ambassador to the Holy See on November 8, 1990, he said that "we should also mention the tragedy of the Jewish people. For Christians the heavy burden of guilt for the murder of the Jewish people must be an enduring call to repentance; thereby we can overcome every form of anti-Semitism and establish a new relationship with our kindred nation of the Old Testament."

His interest in establishing an ongoing theological conversation with Jewish people was expressed in his response to the first Israeli ambassador to the Holy See and on innumerable other occasions. His visit to Israel was a pilgrimage of peace, to a land that he considers sacred for religious people.

The Pope's prayers at the Western Wall were an expression of solidarity with the Jewish people and Judaism. The image of this frail elderly man in his pontifical robes placing a note in the Wall moved many in the world. The note was a copy of the prayer asking for forgiveness that he presented at the Holy See on March 12, 2000. The original prayer ended with a reference to Christ, which the Pope omitted from the text he left at the Wall.

The prayer said, "Let us pray that, in recalling the suffering endured by the people of Israel throughout history, Christians will acknowledge the sins committed by not a few of their number against the people of the covenant and the blessings, and in this way will purify their hearts."

Pilgrimage is part of the spirituality of Christianity and Judaism. Judaism calls pilgrimage "*Áliyah*" (going up). Since ancient days Jews were called upon to go to Jerusalem on three specific festivals:

Passover, Shavuot, and Sukkot (Exodus 23:17, 34:23; Deuteronomy 16:16; II Chronicles 8:13). Christian pilgrimage to Israel became a ritual from the fourth century on, their destinations were Jerusalem, Galilee, and Bethlehem.

Pope John Paul II's pilgrimage echoed the experience of centuries of journeys to the Middle East. But his visit brought a feeling of unity to all religious people. There was a sense of sacredness in his encounters with different faith communities, his prayers, and his visits to holy sites.

As in any relationship, there were moments of misunderstanding, when we were not happy with some of the pope's actions—his meetings with Arafat, Kurt Waldheim, and Assad, for instance. These incidents were upsetting but they do not diminish the magnitude of his efforts to have the Church acknowledge the validity of the Jewish people's covenant with God and their connection to the land of Israel.

[John Paul II] played a key role in expounding certain concepts and ideas for further reflection by the Catholic community. Along with the Church's fundamental probing of the mystery of God's people—Israel—two questions require the serious consideration and reflection of the Catholic people of God today. Pope John Paul II paid attention to both of them. One is the question of anti-Semitism and the Holocaust, and the other is the reality of the State of Israel.

The consideration of anti-Semitism was central to the Second Vatican Council's reckoning with the Jewish people in its declaration *Nostra Aetate* (1965). Its language, however, was seen by many to lack strength. In the words of *Nostra Aetate*, the Church "deplores anti-Semitism." The 1974 *Guidelines and Suggestions for Implementing the Conciliar Declaration* Nostra Aetate, No. 4 "condemn (as opposed to the very spirit of Christianity) all forms of anti-Semitism." Pope John Paul II taught that anti-Semitism is "sinful" for all Catholics. In such progressive interpretations, one can see the positive development of church teaching today.

The first edition of this collection was published by the United States Catholic Conference in cooperation with the Anti-Defamation League in 1987. It was widely used in interfaith meetings by ecumenical groups and dioceses throughout the United States and English-speaking countries. The volume was sent to Pope John Paul II by Archbishop John L. May, president of the National Catholic Council of Bishops. The book was warmly received by John Paul II. He wrote of his "profound gratitude" for what he felt was a "significant undertaking." The second edition of the book, published by Crossroad, won a national Jewish book award in 1995.

The following commentary and texts, it is hoped, will enable the reader to chart the extraordinary contributions made by Pope John Paul II to the historic dialogue between Jews and Catholics today. The spiritual pilgrimage undertaken by the pope on his way to the Synagogue of Rome, the first visit ever by a pope to a synagogue since the time of Peter, spanned centuries of mistrust. The story of that pilgrimage, here presented, is, we believe, an exciting one and one filled with profound courage and faith in the future.

As no other Pope in history has been, Pope John Paul II will be forever recognized as the Pilgrim of Shalom and the Apostle of Reconciliation to the whole world. Strong and vital, sick and frail, he visited innumerable countries, bringing with him a spirituality cherished by Catholics and much appreciated by those who were neither Catholic nor even Christian. Wherever he went, he preached the Word of God, sharing his experience of God's Presence, projecting the example of a committed religious life in an ideologically stormy and complicated spiritual time. It is hoped that his message of Shalom will inspire all the people of the Middle East and the world.[1]

---

1. This introduction, which appeared in the second edition of *Spiritual Pilgrimage*, was augmented with relevant writings from the late Rabbi Klenicki by his wife Myra Cohen Klenicki and Rabbi Eric Greenberg.

A Commentary on the Texts

Pope John Paul II's Pilgrimage of Reconciliation

Eugene J. Fisher, Ph.D.

THROUGH THE CHOICE OF THE NAME THAT WOULD MARK HIS pontificate, Pope John Paul II paid homage and made a commitment to all three of his immediate predecessors: John XXIII, who called the Second Vatican Council and who mandated that it address the ancient, long-neglected question of the Church's spiritual debt to Judaism; Paul VI, who implemented that mandate and who institutionalized it through the creation of the Holy See's Commission for Religious Relations with the Jews; and John Paul I, the "smiling pope," whose all too brief reign was marked by an appreciation for the "divine humor" of creation and a sense of abiding hope in humanity.

The declaration on the Jews, *Nostra Aetate*, 4, distilled in fifteen tightly worded Latin sentences the essence of the Second Vatican Council's major themes of biblical reappraisal, liturgical renewal, and the openness to the Spirit working in the world beyond the visible boundaries of the Church. Implementation of *Nostra Aetate*, then, can properly be seen as a "litmus test" for the success or failure of the Council's vision as a whole. How has Pope John Paul II fulfilled his commitment to his predecessors in the area of Catholic-Jewish relations, the area of the Church's ministry that embodies the most ancient and, some would say, potentially divisive issues posed to the Church by its own history?

Addresses and remarks by the pope on Judaism have been given on numerous occasions and in a remarkably wide range of locations

9

throughout the world. Virtually wherever the pope has traveled, there exists a Jewish community, whether large, as in the United States, or tragically small, as in the tiny remnant of the once-flourishing Jewish community of Poland. And, wherever the pope goes, he seeks out those communities to reach out to them in reconciliation and affirmation of the infinite worth of Judaism's continuing proclamation of the name of the One God in the world.

The papal talks discussed here represent those that have been officially printed. They provide a record of a profound spiritual pilgrimage for the pope and the Church, almost two millennia after the Church's birth as a Jewish movement in the land and among the people of Israel. In the thematic analysis that follows, I will argue that one can discern in the pope's addresses a growth and development in the pope's understanding of and appreciation for how "the Jews define themselves in the light of their own religious experience" (Prologue, 1974 *Guidelines* cited by the pope in his first address to representatives of Jewish organizations, March 12, 1979).

Perhaps more important, this development teaches us much about how the Church must reinterpret today its own understanding of its relationship to the Jewish people as "people of God."

The ongoing papal reconsideration and redefinition of ancient theological categories represent the fruits of a painstaking effort, support by the efforts of thousands of Catholics and Jews in dialogue throughout the world, as the pope has acknowledged ("Historic Visit to the Synagogue of Rome," April 13, 1986, no. 4), to articulate anew the mystery of the Church in the light of a positive articulation of the abiding mystery of Israel. The results, as the patient reader will discern, are as breathtaking as they have been painstaking.

Progress, in one sense, has been painfully slow since the Second Vatican Council. It is measured in small steps, a word uttered here to clarify an awkward phrase there; a slightly less ambiguous wording to replace a more ambiguous, potentially misleading theological formula; and so forth. But, the direction is clear, we believe, and the basic message starkly unambiguous: The Church is not alone in the world as "people of God." The Church is joined by the Jewish people in its proclamation of the oneness of God and the true nature of human history, which Jews and Christians alike pray daily and, through their prayers, proclaim universally (cf. 1985 Vatican *Notes*, II, 9–11). The following thematic categories serve to organize just some of these small steps and interventions by which the pope has sought to frame and to move forward the Church's side of historic dialogue between Catholics and Jews.

In assessing the major events of the year 1986 in the Diocese of Rome, the pope singled out his visit to "our elder brothers in the faith of Abraham in their Rome Synagogue" as his most significant action of the year. It will be remembered, he predicted, "for centuries and millennia in the history of this city and this church. I thank Divine Providence because the task was given to me" (*National Catholic News Service*, December 31, 1986).

1. The Spiritual Bond Between the Church and the Jewish People: The Special Relationship

The notion of a "spiritual bond" linking the Church and the Jewish people ("Abraham's stock") was central to *Nostra Aetate*. It has become a major theme of Pope John Paul II's own reflections on the subject over the years, one which he has consistently tried to probe and refine. In his first address to Jewish representatives, for example, he interpreted the conciliar phrase as meaning "that our two religious communities are connected and closely related at the very level of their respective identities" (March 12, 1979), and he spoke of "fraternal dialogue" between the two.

Using terms such as *fraternal* and addressing one another as *brothers* and *sisters*, of course, reflect ancient usage within the Christian community. They imply an acknowledgement of a commonality of faith, with liturgical implications. It was an ecumenical breakthrough, for example, when the Second Vatican Council and Pope Paul VI began the practice of addressing Orthodox and Protestant Christians in such terms. Pope John Paul II's extension of this terminology to Jews, therefore, is by no means accidental.

The relationship, he is saying, is not marginal to the Church. Rather, it reaches to the very essence of the nature of Christian faith itself, so that to deny it is to deny something essential to the teaching of the Church (cf. Vatican *Notes*, 1, 2). The spiritual bond with Jews, for the pope, is properly understood as a "sacred one, stemming as it does from the mysterious will of God" (October 28, 1985).

In bringing this lesson home, the pope has used startling and powerful language. In his important allocution to the Jewish community of Mainz, West Germany (November 17, 1980), for example, the pope likened the relationship to that between "the first and second part" of the Christian Bible (i.e., between the Hebrew Scriptures and the New Testament).

The dialogue between Catholics and Jews, therefore, is not a dialogue between past (Judaism) and present (Christianity) realities, as if the former had been "superseded" or "replaced" by the latter, as certain Christian polemicists would have it. "On the contrary," the pope made clear in Mainz, "it is a question rather of reciprocal enlightenment and explanation, just as is the relationship between the Scriptures themselves" (cf. *Dei Verbum*, 11).

In this vein, the pope has also moved to assist Catholics to formulate more sensitive biblical terminology. Instead of the traditional "Old Testament" and "New Testament," which might be understood to imply that the "old" has been abrogated in favor of the "new" (a false conclusion known from history as the Marcionite heresy), the pope, in his address to the Jews of Australia (November 26, 1986), has suggested the use of the terms, "the Hebrew Scriptures" and "the Christian Scriptures" as appropriate alternatives. Again, small changes can have major consequences in theological and sociological perception.

In the pope's view, so close is the spiritual bond between our two peoples of God that the dialogue is properly considered—unlike any other relationship between the Church and a world religion—to be "a dialogue within our Church" (Mainz, November 17, 1980). Interpreting *Nostra Aetate* during his visit to the Rome Synagogue, the pope brought these themes to a dramatic culmination:

> The Church of Christ discovers her "bond" with Judaism by "'searching into her own mystery" (*Nostra Aetate*, 4). The Jewish religion is not "extrinsic" to us, but in a certain way is "intrinsic" to our own religion. With Judaism, therefore, we have a relationship which we do not have

with any other religion. You are dearly beloved brothers and, in a certain way, it could be said that you are our elder brothers (Rome, April 13, 1986).

In a meditation on *Nostra Aetate, no. 4,* during the Angelus on January 14, 1996, the pope noted that "the Declaration devotes special attention to our Jewish brethren, with whom Christianity has a particularly close relationship. Indeed, Christianity had its beginnings in the religious experience of the Jewish people from whom came Christ according to the flesh."

Speaking to members of the Pontifical Biblical Commission on April 11, 1997, as they were beginning the process of developing a major statement on *The Jews and Their Scriptures in the Christian Bible* (1992), John Paul reaffirmed the relationship between the Scriptures and thus between God's People, Jews and Christians: "Since the 2nd Century the Church has been faced with the temptation to separate the New Testament completely from the Old . . . (which), according to Marcion, came from a god unworthy of the name because he was vindictive and bloodthirsty, while the New Testament revealed a God of reconciliation and generosity. The Church firmly rejected this error . . . Unfortunately, the Marcionite temptation is making its appearance again in our time. However what occurs most frequently is an ignorance of the deep ties linking the New Testament to the Old, an ignorance that gives some people the impression that Christians have nothing in common with Jews . . . The Christian must know that by belonging to Christ he has become 'Abraham's offspring' (Gal 3:29) and has been grafted onto a cultivated olive tree (cf. Rom 11:17–24), that is, included among the people of Israel to 'share the richness of the olive tree'" (Rom 11:17).

In addressing a symposium on "The Roots of Anti-Judaism," the pope underscored and explained the last point more fully: "That is why those who regard the fact that Jesus was a Jew and that his milieu was the Jewish world as mere cultural accidents, for which one could substitute another religious tradition from which the Lord's person could be separated without losing its identity, not only ignore the meaning of salvation history, but more radically challenge the very truth of the Incarnation" (Oct. 31, 1997).

In a general audience of April 28, 1999, oriented to preparing for the Jubilee Year 2000, which the pope notes is a Jewish notion, John Paul states that "In meditating on the mystery of Israel and its 'irrevocable calling (cf. *Insegnamenti* IX/1, 1968, p. 1028), Christians also explore the mystery of their own roots. In the biblical sources which they share with their Jewish brothers and sisters, they find the indispensable elements for living and deepening their own faith."

Finally, in a letter to the chief rabbi of Rome on the occasion of the 100th anniversary of the Rome Synagogue (May 22, 2004), John Paul brought together key several key themes: "Not only the Sacred Scriptures, which to a large extent we share, not only the liturgy but also very ancient art forms witness to the Church's deep bond with the Synagogue; this is because of that spiritual heritage which without being divided or rejected has been made known to believers in Christ and constitutes and inseparable bond between us and you, the people of the Torah of Moses, the good olive tree unto which a new branch was grafted (cf. Rom 11:17).

2. A Living Heritage

The phrase, "elder brothers," used here with caution, raises the question of how the pope has dealt with the sometimes awkward (for Christians) question of the Church's spiritual debt to Judaism. Traditionally, this debt has been acknowledged—as in medieval canon Law's exception allowing Jews freedom of worship (within certain limitations)—a right granted to no other religious group outside Christianity.

Yet the acknowledgment often came negatively. For many Christians over the ages, for example, the use of the term *elder brother* applied to the Jews would have conjured images of apologetic interpretations of the younger/elder brother stories of Genesis in which the younger brother takes over the heritage or *patrimony* of the elder (e.g., Esau and Jacob). The powerful imagery of the Gothic cathedrals of Europe is another example of this. Juxtaposed on either side of the portals of many medieval cathedrals is a statue of the Synagogue (portrayed in the physical form of a woman), her head bowed, holding a broken staff of the Law, with the tablets of the Ten Commandments slipping from her fingers, on the one side, and the Church, resplendently erect and triumphant on the other. The pairings symbolized for the medieval artists the passage of the Covenant from Judaism to Christianity.

Here, as in so many other ways, however, the pope has sought to reinterpret ancient apologetics and to replace negative images with positive affirmations. In his address to the Jewish community in Mainz, the pope cited a passage from a declaration of the Bishops of the Federal Republic of Germany, issued earlier that year, calling attention to "the spiritual heritage of Israel for the Church." He added to the citation, however, a single word that removed any possible ambiguity and opened up a new area of theological reflection, calling it "a *living* heritage, which must be understood and preserved in its depths and richness by us Catholic Christians" (November 17, 1980).

In March 1982, speaking to delegates from Episcopal conferences gathered in Rome from around the world to discuss ways to foster improved Catholic-Jewish relations, the pope confirmed and advanced this direction in his thought:

> Christians have taken the right path, that of justice and brotherhood, in seeking to come together with their Semitic brethren, respectfully and perseveringly, in the common heritage, a heritage that all value so highly. . . . To assess it carefully in itself and with due awareness of the faith and religious life of the Jewish people *as they are professed and practiced still today,* can greatly help us to understand better certain aspects of the life of the Church (March 6, 1982, italics added).

The "common spiritual patrimony" of Jews and Christians, then, is not something of the past but of the present. Just as the Church, through the writings of its doctors and saints and the statements of its councils, has developed a rich tradition interpreting and clarifying its spiritual heritage over the centuries, so has Judaism developed, through rabbinic literature and the Talmud, through Jewish philosophers and mystics, what was given to it in its founding by God, as explicitly stated in the 1985 Vatican *Notes*, VI. Today, then, the pope calls us to understand the "common spiritual patrimony" not only positively but assertively as a joint witness of God's truth to the world: "Jews and Christians are the trustees and witnesses of an ethic marked by the Ten Commandments in the observance of which man finds his truth and freedom" (Rome Synagogue, April 13, 1986). In the perspective of this renewed papal vision, one can imagine a new statue of the Synagogue on cathedrals, head held high in faithful observance of God's permanent covenant; and a new statue of the Church, with a look of saving humility mitigating the triumphal expression of the past. The two, while remaining distinct, would stand together to proclaim the divine truth that both share and yet interpret in unique ways.

In his 1997 address to the Pontifical Biblical Commission, cited earlier, the pope made clear that the fact that Jesus was a Jew "according to the flesh," also meant that he was a Jew religiously and in his spirituality: "It is impossible fully to express the mystery of Christ without reference to the Old Testament. Jesus' human identity is determined on the basis of his bond with the people of Israel . . . And this does not mean only a physical belonging. By taking part in the synagogue celebrations where the Old Testament texts were read and commented on, Jesus also came humanly to know these texts; he nourished his mind and heart with them. Thus he became an authentic son of Israel, deeply rooted in his own people's long history . . . To deprive Christ of his relationship with the Old Testament is therefore to detach him from his roots and to empty his mystery of all meaning . . . Christ would (be) like a meteor that falls by chance to earth devoid of any connection with human history . . . From her origins the Church has fully accepted Christ's insertion into the history of the People of Israel. She has regarded the Hebrew Scriptures as the perennially valid Word of God addressed to her as well as to the children of Israel. It is of primary importance to preserve and renew this ecclesial awareness." One might note, here, the pope's use of the term, "Hebrew Scriptures," a title better recognized among Jews than "Old Testament."

In his April 28, 1999, general audience defining the meaning of the Jubilee Year, John Paul affirms that first among all interreligious dialogue is that with the Jews (no. 1) and notes that despite "long and tormented history" of the relationship "there have been occasions of peaceful and constructive dialogue" from which both communities have learned, citing also "the vivid dialogical dimension strongly present in contemporary neo-Jewish literature, which has deeply influenced the philosophical and theological thought of the 20th century."

During his visit to Yad Vashem museum in Jerusalem on March 23, 2000, the pope stated that "Jews and Christians share an immense spiritual patrimony flowing from God's self-revelation." In a letter of January 25, 2002, sent to a Catholic-Jewish meeting organized by the European Jewish Congress, John Paul noted that "Jews and Christians are bound together because of their respective identities and should pursue that culture of dialogue that Martin Buber envisioned," modeling a Church activity on the thought of a Jewish philosopher. In his May 22, 2004, letter to Rabbi Riccardo di Segni celebrating the centenary of the Synagogue of Rome, John Paul, who was a philosopher himself, recommended the joint study of key Jewish philosophers, concluding with what I believe to be the first papal citation of a Talmudic text: "In the Middle Ages, some of your great thinkers, such as Yehuda ha-Levi and Moses Maimonides sought to examine how it would be possible to worship the Lord and serve suffering humanity together, thereby paving the way to peace. The great philosopher and theologian, well known to St. Thomas Aquinas, Maimonides of Cordoba (1138–1204), the eighth century of whose death we are commemorating this year, expressed the hope that better relations between Jews and Christians might lead "the whole world to unanimous adoration of God as has been said: 'I will change the speech of the peoples to a pure speech, that all of them may call on the name of the Lord and serve him with one accord' (Zeph 3:9)" (*Mishneh Toah*, Hilkhot Melakhim XI, 4, ed. Jerusalem, Mossad Harav Kook).

3. Permanent Validity of God's Covenant with the Jewish People

Underlying the previous considerations is a central message that Pope John Paul II has made his own wherever he has traveled. This message grows out of the Second Vatican Council, and what the pope has done is to make explicit what was implicit in the Council's teaching. Not only *Nostra Aetate* but the Dogmatic Constitution on the Church, *Lumen Gentium*, drew upon the strong affirmation of St. Paul in Rom. 11:28–29 when seeking to define the role of the Jewish people in God's plan of salvation, even after the time of Christ: "On account of their fathers, this people [the Jews] remains most dear to God, for God does not repent of the gifts He makes nor of the calls He issues" (*Lumen Gentium*, 16).

Logically, the conciliar affirmation means that Jews remain God's chosen people in the fullest sense ("most dear"). This affirmation, the pope teaches, is unequivocal and in no way diminishes the Church's own affirmation of its own standing as "people of God." In Mainz, the pope addressed the Jewish community with full respect as "the people of God of the Old Covenant, which has never been revoked by God," referring to Rom. 11:29, and emphasized the "permanent value" of both the Hebrew Scriptures and the Jewish community that witnesses to those Scriptures as sacred texts (November 11, 1980).

In meeting with representatives of Episcopal conferences, the pope stressed the present tense of Rom. 9:4–5 concerning the Jewish people, "who have the adoption as sons, and the glory and the covenants and the legislation and the worship and the promises" (March 6, 1982), while also affirming "the universal salvific significance of the death and resurrection of Jesus of Nazareth" (ibid.). The pope does not seek a superficial reconciling of these two great truths but affirms them both together, commenting: "This means that the links between the Church and the Jewish people are founded on the design of the God of the Covenant" (ibid.). Or, as the pope put it in addressing the Anti-Defamation League, "the respect we speak of is based on the mysterious spiritual link which brings us close together, in Abraham and, through Abraham, in God who chose Israel and brought forth the Church from Israel" (March 22, 1984).

Here there is not the slightest hint of supersessionism or of that subtler form of triumphalism that would envision Israel as having exhausted its salvific role in "giving birth" to Christianity. The mystery, in the pope's profound vision, lies much deeper than any such "either/or" theological dichotomies can reach. It is precisely such a "both/and" approach that the pope is calling Catholic scholars and educators to develop today. In the words of the *Ecumenical Aids* for the Diocese of Rome, the mystery (a term reserved for the sacraments and the deepest truths of the Catholic faith) encompasses "the people of God, Jews and Christians."

The pope's remarkable formulation in Australia distills years of theological development: "The Catholic faith is rooted in the eternal truths of the Hebrew Scriptures and in the irrevocable covenant made with Abraham. We, too, gratefully hold these same truths of our Jewish heritage and look upon you as our brothers and sisters in the Lord" (November 26, 1986).

The pope continued to expand and deepen this central theme over the years. In his January 14, 1996, meditation on *Nostra Aetate no. 4*, he said, "Sharing with Jews the part of Scripture called the Old Testament, the Church continues to take life from that same patrimony of faith, rereading it in the light of Christ. The inauguration of the times, accomplished by him with the new and eternal covenant, did not destroy the ancient root but opens it to a universal fruitfulness." Meeting with the Jewish community of Berlin on June 23, 1996, the pope emphasized the mission of the Jews to the world, including to the Church: "By their vocation and history the Jewish people were chosen in a special way to proclaim God's saving will to the entire human race (cf. *Dei Verbum* no. 16)."

In 1998, the Bishop of Rome, Karol Wojtyla, responded to a request from the Polish Church for a Prayer for the Jewish People. The prayer this extraordinarily poetic and literary pontiff wrote for use in his home country summarizes much of his overall understanding and hope for the Church's relationship with Jews. Following is the short version published by Catholic New Service on December 24, 1998:

> *God of Abraham, the prophets, Jesus Christ, in you everything is*
> *embraced,*
> *Toward you everything moves. You are the end of all things.*
> *Hear the prayers we extend for the Jewish People which—thanks to*
> *its forefathers—*

is still very close to you.

*Instill within it a constant, ever livelier desire to deepen your truth
and love.*

*Help it, as it yarns for peace and justice, to reveal to the world the
might of your blessing.*

*Succor it, that it may obtain respect and love from those who do not
yet understand*

the greatness of suffering it has borne, and those who, in solidarity

*and a sense of mutual care, experience together the pain of wounds
inflicted upon it.*

*Remember the new generations of Jewish youth and children, that,
unchangeably*

*faithful to you, they may uphold what is still the particular mystery
of their vocation.*

*Strengthen all generates that, thanks to their witness, humanity will
understand*

*that your salvific intention extends to all humankind, and that
you, God*

are for all nations the beginning and the final end. Amen

4. Catechetics and Liturgy

For the pope, it is not enough to rework the framework of Christianity's traditional understanding of Jews and Judaism. The renewed vision of the relationship needs to permeate every area of church life. In his address to representatives of bishops' conferences, for example, the pope stressed especially, "the case of [Catholic] liturgy, whose Jewish roots remain still to be examined in depth, and in any case should be known and appreciated by our faithful" (March 6, 1982). Regarding catechetics, he encouraged a major effort: "We should aim, in this field, that Catholic teaching at its different levels, in catechizing to children and young people, presents Jews and Judaism, not only in an honest and objective manner, free from prejudices and without any offenses, but also with full awareness of the heritage sketched above" (ibid.).

In his response to the International Conference of Christians and Jews, the pope noted that the "great common spiritual patrimony" shared by Jews and Christians rests on a "solid" foundation of "faith in a God . . . as a loving father . . . in a common basic liturgical pattern, and in a common commitment, grounded in faith, to all men and women in need, who are our 'neighbors' (cf. Lev. 19:18, Mark 12:32, and parallels)" (July 6, 1984). Catechesis and the liturgy itself, in other words, have as a primary goal making clear the "spiritual bond" that links the Church to the people Israel (cf. Vatican *Notes*, II, VI).

Also needing to be made clear to Catholic youth is the often tragic history of Christian-Jewish relations over the centuries: "The proper teaching of history is also a concern of yours [ICCJ's]. Such a concern is very understandable, given the sad and entangled common history of Jews and Christians—a history that is not always taught or transmitted correctly" (July 6, 1984). As Father Edward Flannery commented in his classic study of that history, *The Anguish of the Jews* (New York: Paulist Press, 1985), "those pages of history that Jews have committed to memory are the very ones that have been torn from Christian history books" (p. 1).

Finally, in his visit to Rome Synagogue, the pope added a note of urgency and even impatience to his encouragement to Catholic educators and homilists "to present always and everywhere, to ourselves and others, the true face of the Jews and of Judaism . . . at every level of outlook, teaching, and communication" (April 13, 1986), reminding "my brothers and sisters of the Catholic Church" that guidelines "are already available to everyone." In the 1974 *Guidelines and Suggestions for Implementating the Conciliar Declaration* Nostra Aetate, No. 4, and in the 1985 *Notes* issued by the Holy See's Commission for Religious Relations with the Jews, the pope concluded that "it is only a question of studying them carefully, of immersing oneself in their teachings, and of putting them into practice" (April 13, 1986).

In the General Audience of April 28, 1999, speaking of the "indispensable elements for living and deepening (our own Christian) faith," John Paul singled out the liturgy. "This can be seen, for example, in the liturgy. Like Jesus, whom Luke shows us as he opens the book of the prophet Isaiah in the synagogue of Nazareth (Lk 4:16ff), the Church draws from the liturgical wealth of the

Jewish people. She arranges the liturgy of the hours, the liturgy of the word and even the structure of her Eucharistic prayers according to the models of the Jewish tradition. A few great feasts like Easter and Pentecost recall the Jewish liturgical year (Pesach/Passover and Shavuoth—ed.) and are excellent occasions for remembering in prayer the people God chose and loves (cf. Rom 11:2). Today, dialogue means that Christians should be more aware of these elements which bring us closer together. Just as we take note of the 'covenant never revoked by God (cf. *Insegnamenti*, 1980, III/2, pp. 1272–1276), so we should consider the intrinsic value of the Old Testament (cf. *Dei Verbum*, no. 3)."

5. Condemnations of Anti-Semitism and Remembrances of the Shoah

A major theme that runs through the following addresses is the pope's deep abhorrence of anti-Semitism. This abhorrence is not simply theoretical. The pope lived under Nazism in Poland and experienced personally the malignancy of the ancient evil of Jew-hatred.

In his very first audience with Jewish representatives, the pope reaffirmed the Second Vatican Council's repudiation of anti-Semitism "as opposed to the very spirit of Christianity," and "which in any case the dignity of the human person alone would suffice to condemn" (March 12, 1979). The pope has repeated this message in country after country throughout the world.

And, in country after country, especially in Europe, the pope has called on Catholics to remember, "in particular, the memory of the people whose sons and daughters were intended for total extermination" (Homily at Auschwitz, July 7, 1979). From the intensity of his own experience, the pope is able to articulate both the *uniqueness* of the Jewish experience of the *Shoah* while at the same time revering the memory of all of Nazism's millions of non-Jewish victims. The pope would, it may be appropriate to say, agree unreservedly with the formulation of Elie Wiesel: "Not every victim of the Holocaust was a Jew, but every Jew was a victim."

Meeting with Jews in Paris (May 31, 1980), the pope made a point of mentioning the great suffering of the Jewish community of France "during the dark years of the occupation," paying homage to them as victims "whose sacrifice, we know, has not been fruitless." The pope went on to acknowledge that from the French Jewish survivors came the courage of "pioneers, including Jules Isaac" to engage in the dialogue with Catholics that led to *Nostra Aetate*. In Germany (November 17, 1980), the pope addressed the subject at some length. And, in his controversial homily at Otranto, he linked, for the first time, the Holocaust and the rebirth of a Jewish state in the land of Israel: "The Jewish people, after tragic experiences connected with the extermination of so many sons and daughters, driven by the desire for security, set up the State of Israel" (October 5, 1980, also see the following).

Speaking as a Pole and as a Catholic on the fortieth anniversary of the uprising and destruction of the Warsaw Ghetto, the pope termed "that horrible and tragic event" a "desperate cry for the right to life, for liberty, and for the salvation of human dignity" (April 25, 1983). On the twentieth anniversary of *Nostra Aetate*, the pope stated that "anti-Semitism, in its ugly and sometimes violent manifestations, should be completely eradicated." He called the attention of the whole Church to the mandate given in the 1985 Vatican *Notes* to develop Holocaust curricula in Catholic schools and catechetical programs: "For Catholics, as the *Notes* (no. 25) have asked them to do, to fathom the depths of the extermination of many millions of Jews during World War II and the wounds thereby inflicted on the consciousness of the Jewish people, theological reflection is also needed" (October 28, 1985).

In Australia, the pope recalled that "this is still the century of the *Shoah*" and intensified the Council's condemnation of anti-Semitism by declaring that "no theological justification could ever be found for acts of discrimination or persecution against Jews. In fact, such acts must be held to be sinful" (November 26, 1986).

In his 1987 address to the Jews of Warsaw, the pope probed the mystery even deeper, acknowledging the *priority* as well as uniqueness of Jewish suffering in the *Shoah*: "It was you who suffered this terrible sacrifice of extermination: one might say that you suffered it also on behalf of those who were likewise to be exterminated." From this, he derives the very significant theological insight that the Jewish witness to the *Shoah* is, for the Church as well as for all of humanity, a "saving warning," indeed a continuation "in the contemporary world" of the prophetic mission itself. The Church, in turn, is therefore called to listen to this uniquely Jewish proclamation and to unite its voice to that of the Jewish people in their continuing "particular vocation," one may say, to be a light to the nations.

The order of the pope's theological reflection on the *Shoah* is important. As he stated in his letter to Archbishop John L. May (August 8, 1987), an "authentic" approach first grapples with the "specific," and therefore specifically Jewish reality of the event. Only then, and with this continually in mind, he seems to be saying to us, can one begin to seek out its more "universal meaning."

In Miami, the pope spoke of the "mystery of the suffering of Israel's children," and he calls on Christians to learn from the "acute insights" of "Jewish thinkers" on the human condition and to develop in dialogue with Jews "common educational programs which . . . will teach future generations about the Holocaust so that never again will such a horror be possible. Never again!" (September 11, 1987). From "the suffering and martyrdom of the Jewish people," understood within the context of their "constant progression in faith and obedience to the loving call of God" over the centuries, then, our remembrance of the *Shoah* may lead to "even deeper hope, a warning call to all of humanity that may serve to save us all" (July 24, 1988, Vienna), a prophetic "prick of conscience" that may tell us "what message our century [can] convey to the next" (Mauthausen, June 24, 1988).

The challenge to Christian complacency and to Christian teaching in these statements, taken together, I believe, is both very clear and Pilgrimage very strong. Over the years, the pope has issued strong statements of condemnation of acts of terrorism against synagogues and Jewish communities, sending messages of sympathy for their victims. For example, he condemned the August 29, 1981 bomb-throwing attack on a synagogue in Vienna, Austria, as a "bloody and absurd act, which assails the Jewish community in Austria and the entire world," and warned against a "new wave of that same anti-Semitism that has provoked so much mourning throughout the centuries" (*NC News*, September 1, 1981).

During the October 7, 1985 seizure by Palestinian terrorists of the Italian cruise ship, *Achille Lauro*, the pope condemned what he called "this grave act of violence against innocent and defenseless persons," calling on the hijackers to "put an end to their deed": "It is not through recourse to violence that one finds a just solution to problems. I wish that the perpetrators of this rash act would understand this."

After the September 1986 attack on the Istanbul Synagogue, the pope expressed his "firm and vigorous condemnation" of the act and his "heartfelt thought to the victims . . . brothers gathered together in a place of prayer" (*L'Osservatore Romano*, September 22, 1986).

In his general audience of July 11, 1988, the pope summarized what to him was the essence of his trip to Austria in June of that year (see the section "Controversies and Dialogue," which follows on p. *xxxv*). The pope stressed that 1988 marked the fiftieth anniversary of the *Anschluss*, the annexation of Austria by Nazi Germany, "a traumatic event which left a tragic imprint on the history of Europe. . . . The dreadful years of Nazi terror caused millions of victims of many nations. A special measure of extermination was reserved, unfortunately, for the Jewish nation. This fact came to the fore in the meeting with the representatives of the Jewish community living in Austria" (*L'Osservatore Romano*, July 11, 1988, no. 28, p. 3).

Similarly, in his June 5, 1990 discourse to those preparing the 1991 European Synod of Bishops, the pope commented that: "the Second World War . . . with its immense cruelty, a cruelty that reached its most brutal expression in the organized extermination of the Jews . . . revealed to the European the other side of a civilization that he was inclined to consider superior to all others. . . . Perhaps in no other war in history has man been so thoroughly trampled on in his dignity and fundamental rights. An echo of the humiliation and even desperation caused by such an experience could be heard in the question often repeated after the war: How can we go on living after Auschwitz?" (Washington: *Origins*, Catholic News Service Documentary Service 20, no. 6 [1990] 92).

On September 26, 1990, in his annual Jasna Gora meditation celebrating the feast of Our Lady of Chestochowa, the pope spoke as a Pole to his fellow Poles, reminding them: "There is yet another nation, a particular people, the people of the Patriarchs, of Moses and the Prophets, the heirs of the faith of Abraham. . . . This people lived arm and arm with us for generations on that same land which became a kind of new homeland during the Diaspora. This people was afflicted by the terrible deaths of millions of its sons and daughters. First they were marked with special signs, then they were shoved into ghettos, isolated quarters. Then they were carried off to the gas chambers, put to death simply because they were the sons and daughters of this people. The assassins did all this in our land, perhaps to cloak it in infamy. However, one cannot cloak a land in infamy by the death of innocent victims. By such deaths the land becomes a sacred relic. The people who lived with us for many generations has remained with us after the terrible death of millions of its sons and daughters. Together we await the Day of Judgment and Resurrection" (Vatican City: Pontifical Council on Christian Unity: *Information Service*, no. 75, 4:172).

Indeed, in this period it appeared that the pope seldom missed a chance to remind Europeans of the *Shoah*. On November 8, 1990, when he received the first ambassador of the reunited Germany, he stated for the permanent record: "It was really the Second World War which came to an end on October 3 [with the unification] and made many people aware of what fate and guilt mean to all peoples and individuals. We think of the millions of people, most of them totally innocent, who died in that war. . . . For Christians the heavy burden of guilt for the murder of the Jewish people must be an enduring call to repentance; thereby we can overcome every form of anti-Semitism and establish a new relationship with our kindred nation of the Old Covenant. . . . Guilt should not oppress and lead to departure for conversion" (ibid.).

Several times that fall and winter, the pope cited the statement of the Thirteenth International Catholic-Jewish Liaison Committee meeting held in Prague with its call for Christian "*teshuvah* (repentance)" for anti-Semitism over the centuries and its statement that anti-Semitism is "a sin against God and humanity" (cited in ibid.,

4:172–178), in order to place that joint statement firmly within Catholic teaching.

In the late summer of 1991, John Paul II took another trip through the now-free countries of Eastern Europe. In informal remarks during his visit to his childhood home in Wadowice, Poland, he reminisced about his childhood friends, many of them Jewish. "In the school of Wadowice there were Jewish believers who are no longer with us. There is no longer a synagogue near the school. . . . Let us remember that we are near Auschwitz" (*Catholic News Service*, August 15, 1991).

On August 16, 1991 in Hungary, he met with representatives of that country's eighty thousand-member Jewish community. He struck the themes of *teshuvah*, repentance and reconciliation: "Thousands of the Jewish community [of Hungary] were imprisoned in concentration camps and progressively exterminated. In those terrible days the words of the prophet Jeremiah once more became a reality: 'In Ramah is heard the sound of moaning, of bitter weeping! Rachel mourns her children, she refuses to be consoled because her children are no more' [Jer. 31:15]. My thoughts go with deep respect to the great believers who even in those days of devastation—*yom shoah* in the words of Zephaniah [cf. 1:15]. . . . We are here now to adore the God of Israel, who this time, too, has stretched out his protecting hand over a blessed remnant of his people. How often this mysterious ransom has been repeated in your history! Sustained by its faith in the Lord, the Jewish people have preserved, even in their millenary dispersion, their identity, their rites, their tradition. . . . In the face of the risk of a resurgence and spread of anti-Semitic feelings, attitudes and initiatives, of which certain disquieting signs are to be seen today and of which we have experienced the most frightful results in the past, we must teach consciences to consider anti-Semitism and all forms of racism as sins against God and humanity" (*Origins* 21, no. 13 [September 5, 1991], p. 203).

Speaking to the Central Council of Jews of Berlin on June 23, 1996, the pope spoke to them of the beatification of two anti-Nazi priests, one of whom, the Rev. Bernard Lichtenberg, Provost of the Cathedral, was killed by the Nazis specifically for his frequent condemnations from the pulpit of the persecution of Jews. "Today the Church honors two priests, Karl Leisner and Bernard Lichtenberg . . . The provost Lichtenberg in particular became a witness to the dignity that God has given all humanity . . . (He) saw with his own eyes what men can do to their fellowmen when on November 9–10, 1938 he witnessed the terrible prelude to the pogrom (i.e. *Kristallnacht*—ed.). That evening, from the pulpit of St. Hedwig's Cathedral, he said: 'Outside, the temple is burning; that too is a house of God.' He started to pray publicly in the cathedral every evening 'for the persecuted non-Aryan Christians, for the Jews.' Denounced for these prayers, he was arrested on October 23, 1941. Two years later he died while being taken to the concentration camp in Dachau . . . Even if, as historians have shown, many priests and lay people were opposed to that regime of terror, this was still insufficient . . . They are an appeal to Christians and Jews to work together for the dignity of all humanity wherever it is still threatened today or threatened again. This includes, in particular, action against any form of anti-Semitism so that events such as the Shoah will never happen again." The pope also offered a special prayer at Lichtenberg's tomb:

> *"God our Father, your servant Bernard Lichtenberg . . . risked his*
>   *freedom and his life,*
> *defending those persecuted, especially the Jews.*
> *We beg you, Father of all, free the world from the evil of selfishness*
>   *and violence.*
> *Help us to follow the example of Bernard Lichtenberg."*

In his address to the symposium on the Roots of Anti-Judaism (October 31, 1997), the pope emphasized the necessity of a Church-wide "examination of conscience" especially with regard to the sins of Catholics during the second millennium. With regard to the Jews, "the (Second Vatican) Council's Declaration, *Nostra Aetate* laid the foundations for this and I myself, in exercising my Magisterium, have had occasion several times to speak on them. In fact, in the Christian world—I do not say on the part of the Church as such—erroneous and unjust interpretations of the New Testament regarding the Jewish people and their alleged culpability have circulated for too long, engendering feelings of hostility towards this people. They contributed to the lulling of consciences, so that when he wave of persecutions inspired by a pagan anti-Semitism, which in essence is equivalent to an anti-Christianity, swept across Europe . . . the spiritual resistance of many was not what humanity rightfully expected from the disciples of Christ." Here, the pope states strongly that his many statements on Catholic-Jewish relations were not casual or occasional utterances, but part of his central exercise of his Magisterium as the Supreme Pontiff, hence not something to be easily disregarded by subsequent generations. While maintaining a distinction between the anti-Jewish teachings of so many Christians over the centuries and modern racial anti-Semitism, he establishes as well a strong connection between them. It can be said that while the Christian teaching of contempt was not a sufficient cause for the spread of genocidal anti-Semitism in the twentieth century, leading to the Shoah (since other causes are also necessary to explain it), it was a necessary cause, without which that spread cannot be full explained. He also notes that, given the fact that Christianity is supported by its roots in biblical Judaism, anti-Semitism, properly understood, is also anti-Christian. Finally, he calls on the symposium, in the light of "a purification of memory" to show that "anti-Semitism has no justification and is absolutely reprehensible."

In his general audience of April 28, 1999, John Paul reflected on the importance of the document, *We Remember: A Reflection on the Shoah*, issued in March of that year, stating that the dialogue between Catholics and Jews concerning the "sorrowful and tragic events" of the Shoah, should become, as the document stated, a *"memoria futuri"* motiving both Peoples of God to work together "so that the seeds infected with anti-Judaism and anti-Semitism will never again take root in human hearts."

In his message on the sixtieth anniversary of the liberation of Auschwitz on January 15, 2005, the pope stated, with deep sorrow, "I bow my head before all those who experienced this manifestation of the *mysterium iniquitatem* . . . the millions of persons who, through no fault of their own, were forced to endure inhuman suffering and extermination and in the gas chambers . . . No one is permitted to pass by the tragedy of the Shoah. That attempt at the systematic destruction of an entire people falls like a shadow on the history of Europe and the whole world. It is a crime which will forever darken the history of humanity. May it serve, today and for the future, as a warning: there must be no yielding to ideologies which justify contempt for human dignity on the basis of race, color, language or religion."

6. Land and State of Israel

On December 30, 1993, representatives of the Holy See and the State of Israel signed in Jerusalem the *Fundamental Agreement* that would lead the way to full diplomatic "normalization" of relations between the two. On August 16, 1994, the Apostolic Pro-Nuncio, Archbishop Montezemolo, presented his credentials to President Chaim Weizman of the State of Israel as the first Ambassador of the Holy See to the Jewish State.

As the Fundamental Agreement acknowledged, this was not just a moment of international diplomacy between two tiny Mediterranean states. It was a theologically significant moment in the nearly two-millennia-long history of the relationship between the Jewish people and the Catholic Church. The preamble defines the significance with precision:

The Holy See and the State of Israel,

Mindful of the singular character and universal significance of the Holy Land;

Aware of the unique nature of the relationship between the Catholic Church and the Jewish people, and the historic process of reconciliation and growth in mutual understanding and friendship between Catholics and Jews . . .

Realizing that such Agreement will provide a sound and lasting basis for the continued development of their present and future relations . . .

Agree upon the following Articles. (December 30, 1993/16 Tevet 5754)

The pope's references to Israel over the years have been positive ones, as they have been positive as well toward the Palestinians as a people. This essentially supportive attitude was expressed as early as his apostolic letter, *Redemptionis Anno*, and was cited by him many times after that, such as in his address to American Jewish leaders in Miami (September 11, 1987):

> For the Jewish people who live in the State of Israel and who preserve in that land such precious testimonies of their history and faith, we must ask for the desired security and the due tranquility that is the prerogative of every nation and of progress for society. (April 20, 1984)

The implications for Catholic religious education preaching of this unambiguous papal affirmation of the right of the Jewish State to existence and security were drawn out in theological terms in the Holy See's 1985 *Notes on the Correct Presentation of the Jews and Judaism in Catholic Preaching and Teaching*. The *Notes* distinguished between land, people, and State of Israel, affirming each appropriately. In the process, the Vatican document gave a positive theological interpretation of the Diaspora as Israel's universal and "often heroic" witness to the world, thus neatly turning on its head the old "wandering Jew" canard that was so crucial to the ancient teaching of contempt against Judaism. "Witness," of course, is a powerful word in Catholic vocabulary. It is the meaning of the Greek word, *martyr*. The pope on many occasions has used the term witness to describe the Jewish people's ongoing role in God's plan of salvation. And he stresses especially the Jewish witness to the *Shoah*, as a "saving witness" continuing the line of Israel's biblical Prophets:

> The history of Israel did not end in the year A.D. 70. It continued, especially in a numerous Diaspora which allowed Israel to carry to the whole world a witness—often heroic—of its fidelity to the one God and to "exalt God in the presence of all the living" (Tobit 13:4), while preserving the memory of the land of their forefathers at the heart of their hope. [Passover Seder]

Christians are invited to understand this religious attachment, which finds its roots in biblical tradition, without, however, making their own any particular religious interpretation of this relationship.

The existence of the State of Israel and its political options should be envisaged not in a perspective which is in itself religious but in their reference to the common principles of international law.

Over the years the pope has increasingly expressed his deep concerns over and profound hopes for the Holy City: "Jerusalem, called to be a crossroads of peace, cannot continue to be the cause of discord and dispute. I fervently hope that some day circumstances will allow me to go as a pilgrim to that city which is unique in all the world, in order to issue again from there, together with Jewish, Christian and Muslim believers, [the] message of peace" (March 6, 1991). "What a blessing it would be if this Holy Land, where God spoke and Jesus walked, could become a special place of encounter and prayer for peoples, if the Holy City of Jerusalem could be a sign and instrument of peace and reconciliation" (January 11, 1992).

This is, again, language redolent with theological nuance in Catholic terms. "A sign and instrument of peace and reconciliation" is specifically *sacramental* language. It may be used to describe the nature of the sacrament of Eucharist (communion) itself! To use it of an earthly city, albeit one with a "heavenly" analogue according to both Jewish and Christian traditions, is breath takingly daring from one point of view. But it is accurate to Christian doctrine and belief. Catholic reverence for the Holy City of Jerusalem is not political. The Church claims no sovereignty there. But it does believe in the sacredness of the city with a belief rooted in the psalms that the Church prays daily. So the Church does—or should—have the means by which to understand and to affirm the Jewish people's "religious attachment" to the land of Israel and the city of Jerusalem.

Welcoming the then-new ambassador of Israel to the Holy See on April 10, 1997, the Holy Father conveyed his good wishes to its president, Ezer Weizman, and asked the ambassador to "assure him of my prayers for your country and for all the peoples of the Holy Land." Quoting the words of the 1993 *Fundamental Agreement*, he assured the ambassador also that "the Holy See and the Catholic Church as a whole are deeply committed to cooperating with the State of Israel 'in combating all forms of anti-Semitism and all kinds of racism and religious intolerance'," thus acknowledging the unique role of the Israeli State in preserving and safeguarding Jewish existence. "The spirit of that *Agreement*," he said, must be constantly at the forefront of all our efforts as we continue to travel together the road of mutual understanding, friendship, and cooperation.

The highlight of the pope's outreach to the people and the State of Israel, of course, came with his unprecedented pilgrimage to it in the Millennium Year 2000, a trip fraught with symbolism and evocations of the centuries.

7. Controversies and Dialogue

While the pontificate of John Paul II has been marked by the most solid and extensive advances in Catholic-Jewish relations, perhaps in the history of the Church, it has also seen some of the most vocal controversies between Catholics and Jews since the Second Vatican Council. These revolve, in retrospect not surprisingly, around the two key events of Jewish history in this century—and for many centuries: The Holocaust and the State of Israel. The substantive position of the pope on both of these issues has been stated already. A series of incidents with regard to the *Shoah* greatly increased our awareness of the fragility of the contemporary dialogue between our two communities.

The incidents to which I refer include the pope's meetings with Yasir Arafat and Kurt Waldheim, the beatification of Edith Stein, and—though the Holy See had nothing to do with the problem but only with its resolution—the Carmelite convent in the Auschwitz-Birkenau death camp complex. Each of these controversies has its specifics and, especially on the symbolic level for the Jewish perspective, commonalities with the others. Indeed, some Jewish commentators have perceived a rather ominous sort of pattern in these incidents: an attempt not so much to deny as to appropriate the Holocaust for the Church. Obviously, there is not space in this essay to go into a full exposition of why I believe such a pattern does not exist (always a tough case to prove in any event). With regard to the latter point, Rabbi Daniel Polish has published an excellent extended editorial in *Ecumenical Trends* (16:9 [October 1987], 153–55; cf. my response in the February 1988 issue, 24–28), for which he won an award from the Catholic Press Association. I have also gone into some detail on these matters in a feature article for the Catholic journal *SIDIC* (22, 1–2, Rome [1989], 10–15). Here, let it suffice for me to make just a few points to frame the situation, as it were, and to present what can be discerned of the pope's reaction to it all.

First, it needs to be said that in each of these events there has been, if one takes the time to look, a papal response. The Holy See's responses tend to address the substance of Jewish concerns, and do not always have an eye to what we in this country would call "media relations." In the meeting with Arafat, for example, the Vatican Secretariat of State on the day of the meeting issued a tersely worded statement defining the meeting as not intending to give any credence whatsoever to PLO claims, and that the pope was meeting with Arafat to express humanitarian concerns for the Palestinian people and to exhort him to eschew violence against Jews. The Catholic press picked this up, but neither the Jewish nor the secular media did much with it. The result was that, to this day, many Jews will speak of the pope "embracing" Arafat. He did not; the photo shows only a rather distant handshake, nothing like an "embrace" at all. Catholics, on the other hand, were rather satisfied that the pope, while meeting with Arafat, took the occasion to lambast him about PLO terrorism.

Likewise, those Catholics who read carefully the text of the pope's homily in beatifying Edith Stein know that, far from seeking to foster conversionism, as some have charged, the pope took the occasion to acknowledge the uniqueness of the *Shoah* for the Jews and to urge Catholics to greater sensitivity to the trauma suffered by the Jewish people. Again, the Catholic press tended to emphasize these healing elements of the pope's talks while the Jewish press expressed concern over what they saw as the possibility of a new wave of proselytism.

So, too, with the pope's visit to Austria in 1988. What the pope actually did and said during his meeting with the Jewish representatives in Vienna and later that same day in Mauthausen was reported very differently by and for our two communities. The point being made here is not to adjudicate between the two versions of John Paul II's pontificate that are emerging in the Jewish and Catholic communities, but simply to note the fact that they are two. Understood on their own, which is to say Catholic, terms, the pope's actions in these very authentically sensitive areas for Jews do not carry the symbolic weight or intent that the Jewish community appears to derive from them. For Catholics, the pope's meetings with Arafat and Waldheim did not in any way give credence to either figure as such; in the course of his pastoral work, the pope, like any priest, meets all sorts of unsavory characters, one may say, and like any head of state has meetings with numerous people of whom he may or may not personally approve.

But this said and (for the sake of the discussion) at least provisionally accepted by the reader of this paper, it needs also to be said that this is exactly the problem. Catholics do not understand sufficiently, I believe, the suffering and trauma that lie behind these largely symbolic (for Jews more so than for Catholics) actions on the part of the pope. The symbolism is very different on both sides. And while this pope, perhaps more than any other, is sensitive and open to Jews and Judaism, he acts, as in a very real sense he must act, as a Catholic. We need, then, both understanding of each other's symbolic referents (to Catholics, of course, much of what Jews have said about our Holy Father during these controversies is all but indistinguishable from the anti-Catholic bigotries of the old Protestant nativist movements in this country of the pre-ecumenical era) and a very real measure of mercy on and with each other's words and gestures. Too often, both sides tend to presume a negative intent when only a positive is meant.

One needs to recall also the extraordinary gestures of this pope not only in visiting and praying in the Great Synagogue of Rome in 1986, but equally remarkable during the summer of 1987 in inviting a group of Jewish leaders to visit with him at his summer residence outside Rome. What will history say of the record of this pope on Catholic-Jewish relations? Only history and the historians can say, of course. But I would urge historians to check all sides of all of these issues. The question, in terms of the judgment of history, is not just what a particular incident meant to Jews, however valid were Jewish concerns, but what it meant for Catholics (the latter factor being the more relevant when it comes to determining papal intent). More basically, Catholics and Jews need to develop the habit of listening to each other tell their version of such events to their own respective communities. It can be surprising and illuminating to discover that in many cases they will sound as if two different events involving entirely different people have occurred. But, I submit, the days when we had the luxury, if we ever did, to attempt to tell each our own versions of our common history in isolation from the other are, or should be, over. Nothing in the long run is more dangerous or more likely to lead us into problems than that. The stakes are too high today.

With this sense of the future-orientation of the enterprise of dialogue, I would like to conclude with some reflections on what the pope in his many reflections on the matter sees as the future, which is to say the goal of the relationship between the Church and the Jewish people.

8. A Vision for the Future: The Call to Joint Witness and Action in History

Central to the pope's vision of the Christian-Jewish relationship is the hope that it offers for joint social action and witness to the One God and the reality of the Kingdom of God as the defining point of human history. In his address in Mainz, the pope calls this "third dimension" of the dialogue a "sacred duty": "Jews and Christians, as children of Abraham, are called to be a blessing for the world [cf. Gen. 12:2ff] by committing themselves to work together for peace and justice among all peoples" (November 17, 1980).

Such joint action, for the pope, is far more than simple "good neighborliness." It is a fulfillment of what is essential to the mission of both Judaism and Christianity for, "certainly, the great task of promoting justice and peace [cf. Ps. 85:4], the sign of the messianic age in both the Jewish and Christian tradition, is grounded in its turn in the great prophetic heritage" (March 22, 1984). The possibility of a joint proclamation by word and deed in the world, which yet avoids "any syncretism and any ambiguous appropriation" (April 13, 1986), is seen by the pope as no less than a divine call: "The existence and providence of the Lord, our Creator and Saviour, are thus made present in the witness of our daily conduct and belief. This is one of the responses that those who believe in God and are prepared to 'sanctify his name' *[Kid-dush ha-Shem]* [cf. Matt. 6:9] can and should give to the secularistic climate of the present day" (April 19, 1985).

This way of collaboration "in service of humanity" as a means of preparing for God's Kingdom unites Jews and Christians on a level that, in a sense, can be said to be deeper than the doctrinal distinctions that divide us historically. "Through different but finally convergent ways we will be able to reach, with the help of the Lord, who has never ceased to love his people (Rom. 11:1), true brotherhood in reconciliation and respect and to contribute to a full implementation of God's plan in history" (March 6, 1982). That "full implementation" the pope defines in religious terms. It is a "society . . . . . where justice reigns and where . . . throughout the world it is peace that rules, the *shalom* hoped for by the lawmakers, Prophets, and wise men of Israel" (April 13, 1986). To use the words of the 1985 Vatican *Notes* to summarize Pope John Paul II's thoughts on Christian—Jewish relations, one can say that it is his vision that through dialogue:

> We shall reach a greater awareness that the people of God of the Ancient [Hebrew] Scriptures and the New Testament are tending toward a like end in the future: the coming or return of the Messiah—even if they start from two different points of view. Attentive to the same God who has spoken, hanging on the same word, we have to witness to one same memory and one common hope in Him who is the master of history. We must also accept our responsibility to prepare the world for the coming of the Messiah by working together for social justice, respect for the rights of persons and nations, and for social and international reconciliation. To this we are driven, Jews and Christians, by the command to love our neighbor, by a common hope for the Kingdom of God, and by the great heritage of the Prophets.

In the general audience of April 28, 1999, the pope stated that "the courageous witness of faith (of Jews over the centuries) should also mark the collaboration of Christians and Jews in proclaiming and realizing God's saving plan for all humanity . . . It is our duty to work together in promoting a human condition that more closely conforms to God's plan . . . to restore peace and social justice. Recognizing god's dominion over all creation (Lev 25), all believers are called to translate their faith into a practical commitment to protecting the sacredness of human life in all its forms and to defending the dignity of every brother and sister."

9. Papal Encyclicals

This updated edition of Pope John Paul II's many reflections on Catholic-Jewish relations contains also selections from several of his major encyclicals, chiefly his most recent, *Veritatis Splendor* (1993). These will illustrate how the Church's "first teacher" has attempted over the years to integrate into his overall teachings the insights he has derived from his contacts with Jewish leaders and his continuing meditation upon the meaning of Jewish tradition for Catholic thought.

In *Veritatis Splendor*, for example, the pope considers the relations between Law and Love within the dynamic of Catholic doctrine, which holds both to be central to a life of faith lived according to the Gospel. In this, he consciously breaks down old stereotypes that would hold the two—that is, God's Law as expressed in the Hebrew Scriptures and God's Law as expressed by Jesus, for example in the Beatitudes of the Sermon on the Mount—to be contradictory. The encyclical is excerpted at some length in these passages because the pope's creative model of how to turn an ancient "either/or" dichotomy into a more accurate "both/and" approach shows so well in practice what he meant in Mainz, Germany, when he said that the dialogue between Christians and Jews is at the same time a dialogue "within the Church," that is, within its Scriptures and how they are most authentically to be understood today.

Such a renewed model of positive reinforcement between the Scriptures offers hope for even richer spiritual and theological fruits in the future, as the dialogue itself matures to enable serious joint theological reflection by Jewish and Catholic thinkers working together on these ageless themes of Jewish and Christian belief.

In his Apostolic Letter, *Tertio Millennio Adveniente*, "On Preparing for the Jubilee Year 2000," the Holy Father urged interreligious and especially Catholic-Jewish and Catholic-Muslim observances:

"52. Recalling that 'Christ . . . by the revelation of the mystery of the Father and his love, fully reveals man to man himself and makes his supreme calling clear',(34) two commitments should characterize in a special way the third preparatory year: *meeting the challenge of secularism and dialogue with the great religions*. With regard to the former, it will be fitting to broach the vast subject of the *crisis of civilization*, which has become apparent especially in the West, which is highly developed from the standpoint of technology but is interiorly impoverished by its tendency to forget God or to keep him at a distance. This crisis of civilization must be countered by *the civilization of love*, founded on the universal values of peace, solidarity, justice and liberty, which find their full attainment in Christ.

"53. On the other hand, as far as the field of religious awareness is concerned, the eve of the Year 2000 will provide a great opportunity, especially in view of the events of recent decades, for *interreligious dialogue*, in accordance with the specific guidelines set down by the Second Vatican Council in its Declaration *Nostra Aetate* on the relationship of the Church to non-Christian religions. In this dialogue the Jews and the Muslims ought to have a pre-eminent place. God grant that as a confirmation of these intentions it may also be possible to hold *joint meetings* in places of significance for the great monotheistic religions. In this regard, attention is being given to finding ways of arranging historic meetings in places of exceptional symbolic importance like Bethlehem, Jerusalem and Mount Sinai as a means of furthering dialogue with Jews and the followers of Islam, and to arranging similar meetings elsewhere with the leaders of the great world religions. However, care will always have be taken not to cause harmful misunderstandings, avoiding the risk of syncretism and of a facile and deceptive irenicism."

10. Millennium Year 2000

One of the most significant highlights of the Jubilee Year 2000 was the Day of Pardon, March 12, 2000 (the first day of Lent), in which the pope participated in a Liturgy of Repentance in St. Peter's Basilica. The "confession of sins against the people of Israel" was one of a short list of millennial sins of Christians over the ages for which the pope asked God's forgiveness in the name of the universal Church. In each, an appropriate Cardinal of the Curia began the petition. In the case of sins against the Jews, this was Cardinal Edward Idris Cassidy, president of the Commission for Religious Relations with the Jews: "Let us pray that, in recalling the sufferings endured by the people of Israel throughout history, Christians will acknowledge the sins committed by not a few of their number against the people of the Covenant and the blessings, and in this way will purify their hearts." John Paul then asked for God's forgiveness. The prayer, it turned out, was the same one which he placed in the Kotel (Temple wall) in Jerusalem later that same month!

John Paul II's pilgrimage to the Holy Land, and to the State of Israel, was a highlight not only of his pontificate but a seminal moment in the long relationship between Jews and Christians. It was a healing moment of reconciliation and hope in which the head of the Catholic Church reached out to the Jewish people in their ancient homeland into which they had been ingathered and as a people reborn anew after the devastation of the Shoah, many of them survivors or children of survivors of the death camps.

The Holy Father's first official visit, on March 23, appropriately, was to the Sephardi and Ashkenazi chief rabbis of Israel. He came to them, he said, "with deep respect" and characterized it as "a uniquely significant meeting," which he hoped would lead to further contacts deepening "the historical and theological relationship between our respective religious heritages." Speaking "personally," he said, "I have always wanted to be counted among those who work, on both sides, to overcome old prejudices and to secure ever wider and fuller recognition of the spiritual patrimony shared by Jews and Christians." He challenged both peoples to "work together to build a future in which there will be no more anti-Judaism among Christians or anti-Christian sentiment among Jews. There is so much that we can do together for peace, for justice, for a more human and fraternal world."

In meeting with the president of Israel later that day, he noted, "You represent Jewish memory, reaching beyond the recent history of this land to your people's unique journey through the centuries and millennia. I come as one whose Christian memory reaches back through the two thousand years since the birth of Jesus in this very land . . . We must work for a new era of reconciliation and peace between Jews and Christians. My visit is a pledge that the Catholic Church will do everything possible to ensure that this is not just a dream but a reality . . . My pilgrimage is a journey of hope: the hope that the 21st century will lead to a new solidarity among peoples of the world, in the conviction that development, justice and peace will not be attained unless they are attained for all."

At Yad Vashem, the memorial museum to the victims of the Holocaust, the pope met with a group of Polish-Jewish survivors and embraced them. He spoke of his "friends and neighbors" who perished in the *Shoah*. "Here as at Auschwitz and many other places in Europe, we are overcome by the echo of the heart-rending laments of so many. Men, women and children cry out to us from the depths of the horror that they knew. How can we fail to heed their cry? No one can forget or ignore what happened. No one can diminish its scale . . . The world must heed the warning that comes from the victims of the Holocaust and from the testimony of the survivors. Here at Yad Vashem the memory lives on, and burns itself into our souls."

Finally, as he was leaving Jerusalem on March 26, he stopped at the Western Wall and, like thousands of Jews before him, he placed a prayer in a crack between its ancient stones: "God of our fathers, you chose Abraham and his descendants to bring your name to the Nations. We are deeply saddened by the behavior of those who in the course of history have caused these children of yours to suffer, and asking your forgiveness we wish to commit ourselves to genuine brotherhood with the people of the Covenant."

1979

Audience for Representatives of Jewish Organizations

March 12, 1979

Jewish Perspectives on Dialogue

On March 12, Pope John Paul II received in audience representatives of Jewish organizations in Rome for meetings of the International Jewish Liaison Committee. Philip Klutznick, president of the World Jewish Congress, spoke on behalf of the Jewish delegation. In the address that follows, he said that the pope had developed a special understanding during World War II of the demonic consequences of hatred directed to the Jews in Poland. He also discussed the problem of Soviet Jewry and the importance of "the covenant of the land" to Jewish people.

"Peace, peace be unto you, and peace be to your helpers" [1 Chron. 12:18].

With these words from Holy Scripture we convey to you our sincere good wishes for the success of your pontificate and offer our heartfelt prayers for the welfare of the millions of Catholic faithful throughout the world.

This is an important occasion in the long and often difficult history of the relations between the Catholic Church and the Jewish people. This history was profoundly affected by the Second Vatican Council and by subsequent events.

With *Nostra Aetate*, promulgated by the Vatican Council in 1965, and the guidelines of 1974 which amplified the teachings of the conciliar document, the church embarked on a profound examination of its relationship to Judaism. The establishment of the Commission for Religious Relations with the Jews and the formation of the International Catholic-Jewish Liaison Committee served to encourage a fraternal dialogue based on mutual respect. The result has been a significant improvement in Catholic—Jewish understanding and friendship, based on the affirmation of a shared reverence for sacred Scripture, the condemnation of anti-Semitism, support of religious liberty and joint social action.

Judaism and the Catholic Church share in the belief that authentic faith compels religious people to be vitally concerned for the welfare of individuals and societies. God is not indifferent to man's Injustice toward his fellow man. We have noted with admiration that in areas of the world where grave violations of religious liberty and of other human rights exist, the Catholic Church has courageously upheld the values which flow from our common conviction that human beings are not accidental appearances on the cosmic scene but creations of God whose dignity stems from the divine image implanted by the creator. As a people that has known suffering, and impelled by the moral teachings of our faith, we are committed to the alleviation of human misery and injustice wherever they may be found.

Your Holiness, Poland, your country of origin, was a great center of Jewish culture for over a thousand years. This great epoch in Jewish history came to a tragic end during World War II when most of European Jewry was destroyed, victims of the most virulent anti-Semitism. Your Holiness experienced firsthand the demonic consequences of religious and racial hatred which resulted in the immense human suffering of World War II and culminated in the Holocaust of European Jewry. Therefore, you have a special understanding of the importance of eradicating the spiritual sickness that is anti-Semitism and of combating prejudice in all its forms.

Anti-Semitism is a disease which can be dormant and then reappear in new and insidious guises. That is why the Jewish community has been so concerned with the problem of Soviet Jewry.

We dedicate ourselves again to the struggle for human rights and fundamental freedoms for all persons and to the cause of religious liberty. Jews will work together with Catholics and others in the common search for social justice and peace.

The guidelines implementing *Nostra Aetate* invite Christians to learn by what essential traits Jews define themselves in the light of their religious experience. In the Jewish self-understanding, the bond of people of the covenant to the land is fundamental. In the long history of the Jewish people, few events have been experienced with as much pain as the Exile, the separation of the people from the land promised by God. Never, during this separation, have the people of Israel lost hope in the fulfillment of the divine promise.

Much progress in the relations of the Catholic Church and the Jewish people has been made since the Second Vatican Council.

At meetings of the liaison committee we have welcomed the progressive elimination of references unfavorable to Jews and Judaism from Catholic teaching materials and the removal of unfavorable stereotypes from Jewish teaching materials.

We trust that during your pontificate these principles will be reaffirmed and further progress will be made in advancing mutual esteem between our faith communities.

The members of the International Jewish Committee for Interreligious Consultations—consisting of the World Jewish Congress, the Synagogue Council of America, including the Union of American Hebrew Congregations, the American Jewish Committee, the Anti-Defamation League—and the Israel Jewish Council for Interreligious Consultations—reiterate their good wishes for the success of the tasks before you. May we together contribute to the world of which Isaiah [32:16–17] spoke when he said:

> Then justice will dwell in the wilderness and righteousness abide in the fruitful field. And the effect of righteousness will be peace, and the result of righteousness quietness and trust forever.

Response of the Pope

In the address that he delivered at this meeting, the pope spoke of fra-
ternal dialogue and collaboration with the Jews and pledged to do ev-
erything in his power for the peace of that land "which is holy for you
as for us."

Dear Friends:

It is with great pleasure that I greet you, presidents and representatives of the Jewish world organizations, and in that capacity
forming with the representatives of the Catholic Church the international liaison committee. I greet also the other representatives of
various national Jewish committees who are here with you. Four
years ago, my predecessor, Paul VI, received in audience this same
international committee and told them how he rejoiced that they
had decided to meet in Rome, the city which is the center of the
Catholic Church [cf. *Address* of January 10, 1975].

Now you have also decided to come to Rome, to greet the new
pope, to meet with members of the Commission for Religious Relations with the Jews, and thus to renew and give a fresh impulse to
the dialogue which for the past years you have had with authorized
representatives of the Catholic Church. This is indeed, therefore,
an important moment in the history of our relations, and I am
happy to have the occasion to say a word myself on this subject.

As your representative has mentioned, it was the Second Vatican
Council with its declaration *Nostra Aetate, No. 4,* that provided the
starting point for this new and promising phase in the relationship
between the Catholic Church and the Jewish religious community.
In effect, the Council made very clear that, "while searching into
the mystery of the Church," it recalled "the spiritual bond linking
the people of the New Covenant with Abraham's stock" [*Nostra
Aetate*, 4]. Thus it understood that our two religious communities
are connected and closely related at the very level of their respective
religious identities. For the beginning of [the Church's] faith and
election are already found among the patriarchs, Moses and the
Prophets," and "therefore she cannot forget that she received the
revelation of the Old Testament through the people with whom

God in his inexpressible mercy deigned to establish the ancient covenant" [ibid.]. It is on the basis of all this that we recognize with utmost clarity that the path along which we should proceed with the Jewish religious community is one of fraternal dialogue and fruitful collaboration.

According to this solemn mandate, the Holy See has sought to provide the instruments for such dialogue and collaboration and to foster their realization both here at the center and elsewhere throughout the Church. Thus, the Commission for Religious Relations with the Jews was created in 1974. At the same time, the dialogue began to develop at several levels in the local churches around the world and with the Holy See itself. I wish to acknowledge here the friendly response and goodwill, indeed the cordial initiative, that the church has found and continues to find among your organizations and other large sections of the Jewish community.

I believe that both sides must continue their strong efforts to overcome the difficulties of the past, so as to fulfill God's commandment of love, and to sustain a truly fruitful and fraternal dialogue that contributes to the good of each of the partners involved and to our better service of humanity.

The guidelines you have mentioned, whose value I wish to underline and reaffirm, indicate some ways and means to obtain these aims. You have rightly wished to stress a point of particular importance: "Christians must therefore strive to acquire a better knowledge of the basic components of the religious tradition of Judaism; they must strive to learn by what essential traits the Jews define themselves in the light of their own religious experience" [Prologue, *Guidelines and Suggestions for Implementing the Conciliar Declaration* Nostra Aetate, No. 4, Vatican Commission for Religious Relations with the Jews, December 1, 1974]. Another important reflection is the following: "In virtue of her divine mission, and her very nature, the Church must preach Jesus Christ to the world [*Ad Gentes*, 2]. Lest the witness of Catholics to Jesus Christ should give offense to Jews, they must take care to live and spread their Christian faith while maintaining the strictest respect for religious liberty in line with the teaching of the Second Vatican Council [*Dignitatis Humanae*]. They will likewise strive to understand the difficulties which arise for the Jewish soul—rightly imbued with an extremely high, pure notion of the divine transcendence—when faced with the mystery of the incarnate Word" [*Guidelines*, 1]

These recommendations refer, of course, to the Catholic faithful, but I do not think it is superfluous to repeat them here. They help us to have a clear notion of Judaism and Christianity and of their true mutual relationship. You are here, I believe, to help us in our reflections on Judaism. And I am sure that we find in you, and in the communities you represent, a real and deep disposition to understand Christianity and the Catholic Church in its proper identity today, so that we may work from both sides toward our common aim of overcoming every kind of prejudice and discrimination.

In this connection, it is useful to refer once more to the Council declaration, *Nostra Aetate*, and to repeat what the guidelines say about the repudiation of "all forms of anti-Semitism and discrimination," "as opposed to the very spirit of Christianity," but "which in any case the dignity of the human person alone would suffice to condemn" [*Guidelines*, Prologue]. The Catholic Church therefore clearly repudiates in principle all such violations of human rights wherever they may occur throughout the world. I am, moreover, happy to evoke in your presence today the dedicated and effective work of my predecessor Pius XII on behalf of the Jewish people. And on my part I shall continue with divine help in my pastoral ministry in Rome—as I endeavored to do in the See of Cracow—to be of assistance to all who suffer or are oppressed in any way.

Following also in particular in the footsteps of Paul VI, I intend to foster spiritual dialogue and to do everything in my power for the peace of that land which is holy for you as it is for us, with the hope that the city of Jerusalem will be effectively guaranteed as a center of harmony for the followers of the three great monotheistic religions of Judaism, Islam, and Christianity, for whom the city is a revered place of devotion.

I am sure that the very fact of this meeting today, which you have so kindly asked to have, is in itself an expression of dialogue and a new step toward that fuller mutual understanding which we are called to achieve. By pursuing this goal we are all sure of being faithful and obedient to the will of God, the God of the patriarchs and Prophets. To God, then, I would like to turn at the end of these reflections. All of us, Jews and Christians, pray frequently to him with the same prayers, taken from the Book which we both consider to be the word of God. It is for him to give to both religious communities, so near to each other, that reconciliation and effective love which are at the same time his command and his gift [cf. Lev. 19:18; Mark 12:30]. In his sense, I believe, each time that Jews recite the *Shema Israel,* each time that Christians recall the first and second great Commandments, we are, by God's grace, brought nearer to each other.

As a sign of understanding and fraternal love already achieved, let me express again my cordial welcome and greetings to you all with that word so rich in meaning, taken from the Hebrew language, which we Christians also use in our Liturgy: Peace be with you. *Shalom. Shalom!*

Homily at Auschwitz

June 7, 1979

Two former Nazi concentration camps were the setting for a dramatic appearance by Pope John Paul II at Auschwitz. He paid tribute on June 7 to the millions killed at the camps and made special reference to the Jewish martyrs, citing also Father Maximilian Kolbe, Edith Stein, and others. In this homily the pope awakens the remembrance of millions of victims of the tragic slaughter. (Oswiecim was known during World War II by its German name Auschwitz.)

I have come and I kneel on this Golgotha of the modern world, on these tombs, largely nameless like the great Tomb of the Unknown Soldier. I kneel before all the inscriptions that come one after another bearing the memory of the victims of Oswiecim in the languages: Polish, English, Bulgarian, Romany, Czech, Danish,

French, Greek, Hebrew, Yiddish, Spanish, Flemish, Serbo-Croat, German, Norwegian, Russian, Romanian, Hungarian, and Italian.

In particular, I pause with you dear participants in this encounter, before the inscription in Hebrew. This inscription awakens the memory of the people whose sons and daughters were intended for total extermination. This people draws its origin from Abraham, our father in faith [cf. Rom. 4:12], as was expressed by Paul of Tarsus. The very people who received from God the Commandment, "thou shalt not kill," itself experienced in a special measure what is meant by killing. It is not permissible for anyone to pass by this inscription with indifference.

Address to the Jewish Community—Battery Park

October 3, 1979

When Pope John Paul II revisited New York's Battery Park on October 3, he commented that the Jewish and Christian communities were closely related at the level of their respective religious identities, which can be the source of fraternal dialogue and collaboration.

I address a special word of greeting to the leaders of the Jewish community whose presence here honors me greatly. A few months ago, I met with an international group of Jewish representatives in Rome. On that occasion, recalling the initiatives undertaken following the Second Vatican Council under my predecessor, Paul VI, I stated that "our two communities are connected and closely related at the very level of their respective religious identities," and that on this basis "we recognize with utmost clarity that the path along which we should proceed is one of fraternal dialogue and fruitful collaboration" [*L'Osservtore Romano*, March 12–13, 1979].

I am glad to ascertain that this same path has been followed here in the United States by large sections of both communities and their respective authorities and representative bodies. Several common programs of study, mutual knowledge, a common determination to reject all forms of anti-Semitism and discrimination, and various forms of collaboration for human advancement, inspired by our common biblical heritage, have created deep and permanent links between Jews and Catholics. As one who in my homeland has shared the suffering of your brethren, I greet you with the word taken from the Hebrew language: *Shalom*! Peace be with you.

1980

Address to a Group from the British Council of Christians and Jews: General Audience

March 19, 1980

I am pleased to offer a special word of greeting to members of the Council of Christians and Jews coming from various parts of the British Isles. I am aware that the purpose of your association is to strive to overcome prejudice, intolerance, and discrimination, and to work for the betterment of human relations. I wish to express my cordial encouragement of your praiseworthy aims, and I gladly invoke upon all of you abundant divine blessings.

Meeting with Jews in Paris

May 31, 1980

While in France the pope met with representatives of the Jewish community on May 31. He paid tribute to the pioneers such as Jules Isaac, who opened the way to the present active stage of dialogue and collaboration between the Church and Judaism. He called for a deepening of these relationships, so that, united by the biblical ideal, Jews and Christians might work together for a society free of discrimination and a world at peace.

Dear Brothers:

It is a joy for me to receive the representatives of the numerous and vigorous Jewish community of France. This community has, indeed, a long and glorious history. It is necessary to recall here the theologians, exegetes, philosophers, and personages of public life who have distinguished it in the past and still distinguish it. It is true also, and I make a point of mentioning it, that your community suffered a great deal during the dark years of the occupation and the war. I pay homage to these victims whose sacrifice, we know, has not been fruitless. It was from there that there really began, thanks to the courage and decision of some pioneers, including Jules Isaac, the movement that has led us to the present dialogue and collaboration, inspired and promoted by the declaration *Nostra Aetate* of the Second Vatican Council.

This dialogue and this collaboration are very much alive and active here in France. This makes me happy. Between Judaism and the Church, there is a relationship, as I said on another occasion to Jewish representatives, a relationship "at the very level of their respective religious identities" [*Address* of March 12, 1979]. This relationship must be further deepened and enriched by study, mutual knowledge, religious education on both sides, and the effort to overcome the difficulties that still exist. That will enable

us to work together for a society free of discriminations and prejudices, in which love and not hatred, peace and not war, justice and
not oppression, may reign. It is toward this biblical ideal that we
should always look, since it unites us so deeply. I take advantage of
this happy opportunity to reaffirm it to you again and to express to
you my hope of pursuing it together.

Remarks to the Jewish Community in São Paulo

July 3, 1980

*On July 3, representatives of the Jewish community in São Paulo, Bra-
zil, heard Pope John Paul adverting to the religious frictions of the past
but stressing the interfaith cooperation, especially of Jewish—Christian
leadership and present-day friendships, as well as the bonds that unite
the Church with the descendants of Abraham in Brazil.*

I am very happy to be able to greet you, the representatives of the
Jewish community of Brazil, which is so vibrant and active in Sao
Paulo, in Rio de Janeiro, and in other cities. And I thank you from
the bottom of my heart for your great friendliness in wanting to
meet with me on the occasion of this apostolic journey to the great
Brazilian nation. For me, it is a happy opportunity to show and to
tighten the bonds that link the Catholic Church and Judaism here
in Brazil, and reaffirm in this way the importance of the relations
that are developing between us.

As you know, the declaration *Nostra Aetate* of the Second Vatican
Council, in its fourth paragraph, reaffirms that in scrutinizing its
own mystery the Church "remembers the bond that unites it with
the descendants of Abraham." In this way, the relation between
the Church and Judaism is not external to the two religions: it is

something that is based on the distinctive religious heritage of both, on the very origins of Jesus and the Apostles, and in the environment within which the early Church grew and developed.

In spite of this, our respective religious identities have divided us, at times grievously, through the centuries. This should not be an obstacle to our now respecting this same identity, wanting to emphasize our common heritage, and in this way to cooperate, in light of this same heritage, for the solution of problems which afflict contemporary society, a society needing faith in God, obedience to his holy Laws, active hope in the coming of his kingdom.

I am very pleased to know that this relationship of cooperation already exists here in Brazil, especially through Judeo-Christian brotherhood. Thus, Jews and Catholics strive to deepen the common biblical heritage without, however, trying to conceal the differences which separate us, and in this way a renewed mutual knowledge can lead to a more adequate presentation of each religion in the teaching of the other. Upon this solid base, cooperation for the benefit of concrete man, promotion of his rights, not rarely trod upon, of his just participation in the pursuit of the common good, without exclusiveness or discrimination, can be built up, as it is now being built.

These, moreover, are some of the points brought to the attention of the Catholic community by the *Guidelines and Suggestions for Implementing the Conciliar Declaration* Nostra Aetate, No. 4 published by the Holy See's Commission for Religious Relations with the Jews in 1974, as well as by the corresponding paragraphs of the final document of the Conference of Puebla [1110, 1123].

This will make the valuable spiritual patrimony that joins Jews and Christians vibrant and effective for the good of all. This I desire with all my heart. And this will hopefully be the fruit of this brotherly encounter with the representatives of the Jewish community of Brazil.

Homily at Otranto, Italy

October 5, 1980

On Sunday, October 5, the Holy Father concluded his pilgrimage to Otranto with the celebration of Mass on the Hill of the Martyrs, commemorating the five hundredth anniversary of Blessed Antonio Primoldo and his eight hundred companions. The pope delivered the following homily:

Prayer for the Middle East

At the same time, we cannot close our eyes to particularly delicate situations that have developed there and still exist. Harsh conflicts have broken out; the Middle East is pervaded by tensions and strife, with the ever-incumbent risk of the outbreak of new wars. It is painful to note that conflicts have often taken place following the lines of division between different confessional groups, so that it has been possible for some people, unfortunately, to feed them artificially by appealing to the religious sentiment.

The terms of the Middle East drama are well known: The Jewish people, after tragic experiences connected with the extermination of so many sons and daughters, driven by the desire for security, set up the State of Israel. At the same time the painful condition of the Palestinian people was created, a large part of whom are excluded from their land. These are facts that are before everyone's eyes. And other countries, such as Lebanon, are suffering as a result of a crisis which threatens to be a chronic one. In these days, finally, a bitter conflict is in progress in the neighboring region, between Iraq and Iran.

Gathered here today, at the tombs of the Martyrs of Otranto, let us meditate on the words of the liturgy, which proclaims their glory and their power in the Kingdom of God: "They will govern nations and rule over peoples, and the Lord will reign over them forever." Therefore in union with these martyrs, we present to the

One God, to the Living God, to the Father of all men, the problems of peace in the Middle East and also the problem, which is so dear to us, of the rapport and real dialogue with those with whom we are united—in spite of the differences—by faith in one God, the faith inherited from Abraham. May the spirit of unity, mutual respect, and understanding prove to be more powerful than what divides and sets in opposition.

Lebanon, Palestine, Egypt, the Arabian Peninsula, Mesopotamia nourished for millennia the roots of traditions sacred for each of the three religious groups. There again, for centuries, Christian, Jewish, and Islamic communities lived together on the same territories; in those regions, the Catholic Church boasts communities outstanding for their ancient history, vitality, variety of rites, and their own spiritual characteristics.

Towering high over all this world, like an ideal center, a precious jewel-case that keeps the treasures of the most venerable memories, and is itself the first of these treasures, is the Holy City, Jerusalem, today the object of a dispute that seems without a solution, tomorrow—if people only want it!—tomorrow a crossroads of reconciliation and peace.

Yes, we pray that Jerusalem, instead of being, as it is today, the object of strife and division, may become the meeting point towards which the eyes of Christians, Jews, and Moslems will continue to turn, as to their own common hearth; round which they will feel as brothers, no one superior, no one in the debt of others; towards which pilgrims, followers of Christ, or faithful of Mosaic Law, or members of the community of Islam, will continue to direct their steps.

Address to the Jewish Community—West Germany

November 17, 1980

Pope John Paul II spoke to representatives of the Jewish community on November 17 at Mainz, West Germany. He pointed out that an address such as this is not merely a matter of correcting a false religious view of the Jewish people but is, above all, "a question of the dialogue between the two religions which, with Islam, can give to the world the belief in one ineffable God who speaks to us and which, representing the entire world, wish to serve him."

Shalom! Ladies and Gentlemen, Dear Brothers and Sisters!

I thank you for your friendly and sincere words of greeting. This meeting was a deep need for me in the framework of this apostolic journey, and I thank you for fulfilling it. May God's blessing accompany this hour!

1. If Christians must consider themselves brothers of all men and behave accordingly, this holy obligation is all the more binding when they find themselves before members of the Jewish people! In the *Declaration on the Relationship of the Church with Judaism* in April of this year, the bishops of the Federal Republic of Germany put this sentence at the beginning: "Whoever meets Jesus Christ, meets Judaism." I would like to make these words mine, too. The faith of the Church in Jesus Christ, the son of David and the son of Abraham [cf. Matt. 1:1], actually contains what the bishops call in that declaration "the spiritual heritage of Israel for the Church" [11], a living heritage, which must be understood and preserved in its depth and richness by us Catholic Christians.

2. The concrete brotherly relations between Jews and Catholics in Germany assume a quite particular value against the grim background of the persecution and the attempted extermination

of Judaism in this country. The innocent victims in Germany and elsewhere, the families destroyed or dispersed, the cultural values or art treasures destroyed forever, are a tragic proof of where discrimination and contempt of human dignity can lead, especially if they are animated by perverse theories on a presumed difference in the value of races or on the division of men into men of "high worth," "worthy of living," and men who are "worthless," "unworthy of living." Before God all men are of the same value and importance.

In this spirit, during the persecution, Christians likewise committed themselves, often at the risk of their lives, to prevent or relieve the sufferings of their Jewish brothers and sisters. I would like to express recognition and gratitude to them at this moment. And also to those people who, as Christians, affirming they belonged to the Jewish people, traveled along the *via crucis* of their brothers and sisters to the end—like the great Edith Stein, called in her religious institute Teresa Benedicta of the Cross, whose memory is rightly held in great honor.

I would further like to mention also Franz Rosenzweig and Martin Buber, who, through their creative familiarity with the Jewish and German languages, constructed a wonderful bridge for a deeper meeting of both cultural areas.

You yourselves stressed, in your words of greeting, that in the many efforts to build up a new common life with Jewish citizens in this country, Catholics and the Church have made a decisive contribution. This recognition and the necessary collaboration on your part fills me with joy. For my part, I wish to express grateful admiration also for your initiatives in this connection, including the recent foundation of your Heidelberg University.

3. The depth and richness of our common heritage are revealed to us particularly in friendly dialogue and trusting collaboration. I rejoice that, in this country, conscious and zealous care is dedicated to all this. Many public and private initiatives in the pastoral, academic, and social field serve this purpose, as on very solemn occasions such as the recent one at the *Katholikentag* in Berlin. Also an encouraging sign was the meeting of the International Committee between the Roman Catholic Church and Judaism in Regensburg last year.

It is not just a question of correcting a false religious view of the Jewish people, which, in the course of history, was one of the causes that contributed to misunderstanding and persecution, but above all of the dialogue between the two religions which—with Islam— gave the world faith in the one, ineffable God who speaks to us, and which desire to serve him on behalf of the whole world.

The first dimension of this dialogue, that is, the meeting between the people of God of the Old Covenant, never revoked by God [cf. Rom. 11:29], and that of the New Covenant, is at the same time a dialogue within our Church, that is to say, between the first and the second part of her Bible. In this connection, the directives for the application of the conciliar declaration *Nostra Aetate* say: "The effort must be made to understand better everything in the Old Testament that has its own, permanent value . . . since this value is not wiped out by the later interpretation of the New Testament, which, on the contrary, gave the Old Testament its full meaning, so that it is a question rather of reciprocal enlightenment and explanation" [11].

A second dimension of our dialogue—the true and central one—is the meeting between present-day Christian Churches and the present-day people of the Covenant concluded with Moses. It is important here "that Christians—to continue the post-conciliar directives—should aim at understanding better the fundamental elements of the religious tradition of Judaism, and learn what fundamental lines are essential for the religious reality lived by the Jews, according to their own understanding" [Introduction]. The way for this mutual knowledge is dialogue. I thank you, venerated brothers and sisters, for carrying it out, you too, with that "openness and breadth of spirit," with that "tact" and with that "prudence" which are recommended to us Catholics by the above-mentioned directives. A fruit of this dialogue and an indication for its fruitful continuation is the declaration of German bishops quoted at the beginning "on the relationship between the Church and Judaism" in April of this year. It is my eager desire that this declaration should become the spiritual property of all Catholics in Germany!

I would also like to refer briefly to a third dimension of our dialogue. The German bishops dedicate the concluding chapter of their declaration to the tasks which we have in common. Jews and

Christians, as children of Abraham, are called to be a blessing for the world [cf. Gen. 12:2 ff.], by committing themselves together for peace and justice among all men and peoples, with the fullness and depth that God himself intended us to have, and with the readiness for sacrifices that this goal may demand. The more our meeting is imprinted with this sacred duty, the more it becomes a blessing also for ourselves.

4. In the light of this promise and call of Abraham's, I look with you to the destiny and role of your people among the peoples. I willingly pray with you for the fullness of *Shalom* for all your brothers in nationality and in faith, and also for the land to which Jews look with particular veneration. Our century saw the first pilgrimage of a pope to the Holy Land. In conclusion, I wish to repeat Paul VI's words on entering Jerusalem: "Implore with us, in your desire and in your prayer, respect and peace upon this unique land, visited by God! Let us pray here together for the grace of a real and deep brotherhood between all men, between all peoples! . . . May they who love you be blessed. Yes, may peace dwell in your walls, prosperity in your palaces. I pray for peace for you. I desire happiness for you" [cf. Ps. 122:6–9].

May all peoples in Jerusalem soon be reconciled and blessed in Abraham! May he, the ineffable, of whom his creation speaks to us: he, who does not force mankind to goodness, but guides it: he, who manifests himself in our fate and is silent; he, who chooses all of us as his people; may he guide us along his ways to his future!

Praised be his Name! Amen.

Address to Delegates to the Meeting of Representatives of Episcopal Conferences and Other Experts in Catholic-Jewish Relations: Commission for Religious Relations with the Jews

March 6, 1982

Dear Brothers in the Episcopate and in the Priesthood, Sisters, Ladies and Gentlemen:

From different parts of the world we are here assembled in Rome to see where we stand regarding the important questions of relations between the Catholic Church and Judaism. And the importance of this problem is also underlined by the presence among you of representatives of the Orthodox Churches, of the Anglican Communion, of the Lutheran World Federation, and of the World Council of Churches, whom I am particularly happy to greet and to thank for their collaboration.

I express equally my gratitude to all of you who are here, bishops, priests, religious and lay men and women. Your presence here, just as your involvement in pastoral activities or in the domain of biblical and theological research, reveals to what extent the relations between the Catholic Church and Judaism touch on different aspects of the life and activities of the Church.

And this, one can easily understand. The Second Vatican Council said in effect in its declaration on the relations between the Church and the non-Christian religions [*Nostra Aetate*, 4]: "As this Sacred Synod searches into the mystery of the Church, it recalls the spiritual bond linking the people of the New Covenant with Abraham's stock." And I myself have had an opportunity to say so on more than one occasion: "our two religious communities are connected and closely related at the very level of their religious identities" [cf. *Address*, March 12, 1979, to the representatives of Jewish Organizations and Communities]. Indeed, and it is again the very text of the declaration [*Nostra Aetate*, 4], "the Church of Christ acknowledges that, according to the mystery of God's saving design, the beginnings of her faith and her election are already found among the patriarchs, Moses and the Prophets. . . . The Church, therefore, cannot forget that she received the revelation of the Old Testament through this people. . . . Also the Church ever keeps in mind the words of the Apostle about his kinsmen 'who have the adoption as sons, and the glory and the covenants and the legislation and the worship and the promises, who have the fathers, and from whom is Christ according to the flesh' [Rom. 9:4–5], the son of the Virgin Mary."

This means that the links between the Church and the Jewish people are founded on the design of the God of the Covenant and—as such—have necessarily left their traces in certain aspects of the institutions of the Church, particularly in her liturgy.

Certainly, since the appearance, two thousand years ago, of a new branch from the common root, relations between our two communities have been marked by the misunderstandings and resentments with which we are familiar. And if, since the day of the separation, there have been misunderstandings, errors, indeed offenses, it is now our task to leave these behind with understanding, peace, and mutual respect. The terrible persecutions suffered by the Jews in different periods of history have finally opened the eyes of many and appalled many people's hearts. Christians have taken the right path, that of justice and brotherhood, in seeking to come together with their Semitic brethren, respectfully and perserveringly, in the common heritage that all value so highly. Should it not be pointed out, especially to those who remain skeptical, even hostile, that this reconciliation should not be confused with a sort of religious relativism, less still with a loss of identity? Christians, for their part, profess their faith unequivocally in the universal salvific significance of the death and resurrection of Jesus of Nazareth.

Yes, the clarity and affirmation of our Christian identity constitute an essential basis if we are to have real, productive, and durable ties with the Jewish people. In this sense, I am happy to know that you dedicate much effort in study and prayer together, the better to grasp and formulate the sometimes complex biblical and theological problems which have arisen because of the very progress of Judeo? Christian dialogue. Work that is of poor quality or lacking in precision would be extremely detrimental to dialogue in this field. May God allow Christians and Jews really to come together, to arrive at an exchange in depth, founded on their respective identities, but never blurring it on either side, truly searching the will of God the Revealer.

Such relations can and should contribute to a richer knowledge of our own roots, and will certainly cast light on some aspects of the Christian identity just mentioned. Our common spiritual patrimony is very large.

To assess it carefully in itself and with due awareness of the faith and religious life of the Jewish people as they are professed and practiced still today, can greatly help us to understand better certain aspects of the life of the Church. Such is the case of liturgy whose Jewish roots remain still to be examined in depth, and in any case should be better known and appreciated by our faithful. The same is true of the history of our institutions which, since the beginning of the Church, have been inspired by certain aspects of the synagogue community organization. Finally, our common spiritual patrimony is particularly important when we turn to our belief in only one God, good and merciful, who loves men and is loved by them [cf. Wisd. of Sol. 24:26], Lord of history and of the destinies of men, who is our Father and who chose Israel, "the good olive tree onto which have been grafted the wild olive branches, those of the gentiles" [*Nostra Aetate*, 4; cf. also Rom. 11:17–24].

This is why you yourselves were concerned, during your sessions, with Catholic teaching and catechesis regarding Jews and Judaism. On this particular point, as on many others, you have been guided and encouraged by the *Guidelines and Suggestions for Implementing the Conciliar Declaration* Nostra Aetate, No. 4, published by the Commission for Religious Relations with the Jews [see chapter 3]. We should aim, in this field, that Catholic teaching at its different levels, in catechesis to children and young people, presents Jews and Judaism, not only in an honest and objective manner, free from prejudices and without any offenses, but also with full awareness of the heritage we have sketched above.

It is ultimately on such a basis that it will be possible to establish—as we know is happily already the case—a close collaboration toward which our common heritage directs us, in service of man and his vast spiritual and material needs. Through different but finally convergent ways we will be able to reach, with the help of the Lord who has never ceased to love his people [cf. Rom. 11:1], this true brotherhood in reconciliation and respect and to contribute to a full implementation of God's plan in history.

I am happy to encourage you, dear brothers and sisters in Christ, to continue on the path that has begun, using discernment and trust and at the same time with great faithfulness to the Church's Magisterium. In such a way you will render the Church a great service which flows from her mysterious vocation. This should contribute to the good of the Church itself, of the Jewish people, and of the whole of humanity.

Addresses to Religious Leaders in Portugal

May 14, 1982

Lisbon

During his 1982 visit to Portugal, the pope gave new proofs of his respect for non-Christian religious traditions. On May 14, at Lisbon, speaking to a group of Jews, Christians, and Moslems, he affirmed that: "Abraham, our common ancestor, teaches all of us, Christians, Jews and Moslems, to follow this way of mercy and love."

Gentlemen and my Brothers:

1. I am grateful for the respectful words and for the good wishes that have been addressed to me, and I wish to greet the representatives of the Christian, the Jewish, and the Islamic communities here present, expressing to all of them fraternal respect and esteem. To be able to affirm today, together, faith in one God, creator of all things, living, almighty, and merciful, would be enough in itself to make this meeting a pleasure for me; I am happy that this opportunity to bear witness, which is at the same time homage and an act of submission to our God, has been offered to us.

We are united in some way by faith and by a commitment, similar in many ways, to demonstrate by good works the consistency of our respective religious positions; and also the desire that, honoring as Lord the Creator of all things, our example may serve to help others in the search for God, in the opening toward transcendence, in recognition of the spiritual value of the human person, and, at times, in the identification of the foundation and permanent source of man's rights. This—we well know—is the condition in which criteria of esteem for the human being may exist, which are not limited to "practical usefulness," but which may safeguard his intangible dignity. In addition to this, as far as Christians are concerned, common faith in Christ the Savior is a special reason for unity and witness.

2. Contemporary society seems to us to be heedless of, or even inclined on a wide scale to "prescind" from, God and religion, and to be greatly absorbed in the earthly and material dimensions of man and life: Admirable progress in all fields secure great benefits, but they seem to encourage in some people a reversal and substitution of values. By recognizing and proclaiming spiritual and religious values, we can certainly bring about and guide a general vital insight and, among persons in normal situations, a certain conceptual glimmer of the reality of a subsisting Creator.

On the other hand, there is always room for human solidarity in the fidelity to the religion we embrace since, convinced as we are of the good which belief in God constitutes for us, the desire to share this good with others is spontaneous. In all respects, we can make ourselves a symbol of the Almighty: he who for many is the "unknown God"; for others, he is erroneously symbolized by temporal powers, inexorably marked by their transience and frailness.

3. Our contacts, dialogue, and appreciation for the undeniable treasures of every religion's spirituality, Christian community, and, when it is possible, common prayer, can lead to the convergence of efforts to avert the illusion of building a new world without God, and the vanity of a purely anthropocentric humanism. Without the religious dimension and, even worse, without religious freedom, man is impoverished or cheated of one of his basic rights. And we all wish to avoid this impoverishment of man.

So, when motivated also by human solidarity, we pass from prayer, from obedience to the commandments and from the observance of justice, to concretely living our religious adherence aiding the search for God, we are contributing to the good of our neighbor and to the common good of humanity. And this can be verified:

- through personal honesty and discipline of habits in private and public life, halting the advance of the slackening of moral principles and those of justice, as well as ethical permissiveness;

- in respect for life and for the family and its values, fostering the uplifting, in humanity and dignity, of our fellow men and the consolidation of the irreplaceable bases for harmonious living together in society;
- by reverence for the authentic meaning and generous practice of human work, and with courageous and knowledgeable social and political participation, seeking the well-being of everyone and the building of societies and the world, always more in accord with the plans and decrees of God, throughout the world, since only in this way can there be a more just, peaceful world imbued with brotherly love.

4. As you know, I have come to Portugal in pilgrimage, primarily to celebrate God's mercy. Within me is the deep conviction that the merciful God wishes to see this characteristic more clearly reflected in the entire human family: authentic mercy seems to me something which is indispensable to giving shape and solidity to relations among men, inspired by the deepest respect for all that is human and for brotherhood.

In effect, Christians are exhorted to imitate the Lord Jesus, model of mercy. Judaism also considers mercy a fundamental commandment. And Islamism, in its profession of faith, attributes this trait to God. And Abraham, our common ancestor, teaches everyone—Christians, Jews, and Muslims—to follow this way of mercy and of love.

May I be allowed to conclude my remarks by lifting up my spirit in a prayer to the merciful God:

> *O Ineffable One, of whom all creation speaks,*
> *O Almighty One, who never forces, but only invites and guides*
>   *mankind toward good,*
> *O Compassionate One, who desires mercy among all men: may*
>   *he always guide us along his paths, fill our hearts with his love,*
>   *with his peace and joy, and bless us!*

May 15, 1982

Sameiro

Then, on May 15, at Sameiro in the Archdiocese of Braga, the pope spoke of Jesus:

Born during the night at Bethlehem, the son of Mary thus entered into the spiritual inheritance of Israel—of his people.

Pastoral Visit to Great Britain

May 31, 1982

Manchester

On the occasion of his 1982 visit to Great Britain, the pope twice met with leaders of the Jewish Community. On May 31, during his visit to Manchester, he was welcomed by the vice-president of the Jewish Board of Deputies of Britain, Lionel Kopelowitz, who spoke to him in Polish. Following an address by the chief rabbi of Great Britain, Sir Emmanuel Jakobovits, the pope replied ex tempore.

The chief rabbi's speech, although very brief, was most comprehensive in the way in which it looked realistically both at the various aspects of the unhappy past of Jewish—Christian relations and also at the warmth of the present situation from the time of Pope John XXIII.

Chief Rabbi Sir Emmanuel Jakobovits welcomed the pope:

The pope's visit to this country, although officially of a pastoral nature, is a historical event of significance far beyond Catholic friends. British Jews join their fellow citizens in warmly greeting you not only as the world's most widely acclaimed spiritual leader, but as a charismatic personality of rare distinction, deeply respected for his vision, dynamic qualities, and human virtues.

These ecumenical aspirations, while primarily of inter-Christian concern, are of course of profound interest to Jews as well, much more so since the papacy had often been a cause of conflict and suffering in the long history of the Jewish people and, happily, past tragic relations have lately been reversed, notably by the enlightened policies of Catholic-Jewish reconciliation pioneered by Pope John XXIII, a momentous turning point to which the late Cardinal Heenan gave such powerful momentum.

As Pope John Paul II, you have maintained and further promoted this interfaith understanding, yourself hailing from a country in which you witnessed and shared the supreme agony of the Nazi Holocaust, including the massacre of three million Polish Jews.

Your election aroused special interest among the Jewish people. Also of particular relevance to Jews are the as yet unpredictable consequences of the religious stirring within the Communist world sparked by the Catholic revival in Poland under your spell.

These consequences may well eventually alleviate the bonds of more than three million Soviet Jews among the repressed religious communities. In the U.S.S.R. and her satellite countries, as senior progenitors of the Judeo-Christian heritage which nurtured Western civilizations, the Jewish people watched with profound gratification your immense efforts to reassert the moral and spiritual values we have in common against the disruptive inroads of violence, the blighting depression of materialism, and the despiritualized secularization which threatens everything we have built up over the ages and may even endanger human survival itself.

Whilst enormous strides have been made in defending Jewish—Christian harmony, some items on our common agenda still remain to be resolved. They include the elimination of the last vestiges of religious prejudices against Jews and some residual Christian hesitations in accepting the State of Israel as the fulfillment of millennial Jewish dreams.

We seek understanding for our love of Jerusalem, a city holy to three faiths because Jews first sanctified it as their capital five thousand years ago.

This anxious time, when our country is sadly once again at war with significant loss of life in defense of freedom and the rule of law, we pray with special fervor that your visit may contribute to the advancement of reconciliation and peace, inspiration and the blessing of rededication to the noblest ides of human brotherhood.

The Holy Father replied:

I should first say that I followed your speech with great interest, and I pondered the arguments you included in this speech. My answer is rather brief and not so full of arguments as your speech, but I am very grateful for your having put all these questions in your speech.

It is a joy for me to extend my fraternal greetings this morning to you, leading members of the Jewish community. Particularly I greet the chief rabbi of the Commonwealth, Sir Emmanuel Jakobovits, together with other distinguished colleagues. On the occasion of my visit to Britain, I wish to express my personal sentiments of esteem and friendship for all of you. At the same time, I wish to reiterate the full respect of the Catholic Church for the Jewish people throughout the world. In the spirit of the Second Vatican Council, I recall the desire of the Church to collaborate willingly with you in the great cause of mankind, knowing that we have a common tradition that honors the sanctity of God and calls us to love the Lord our God with all our heart and with all our soul.

I extend cordial greetings to all those whom you represent.

June 1, 1982

Scotland

And on the following day in Scotland, during the course of a meeting with various religious leaders, the pope included the following reference to its Jewish community:

I am happy to greet also the representatives of the Jewish community in Scotland, who, through their presence here, symbolize the profound spiritual links which unite our two religious communities so closely together.

Pastoral Visit to Spain

November 3, 1982

Address to Leaders of the Jewish Community, Madrid

Gentlemen:

Shalom! Peace be to you and all the members of the Jewish religious community in Spain.

First of all, I want to tell you how much I appreciate your readiness to come to meet me during my pastoral visit to this country. This significant gesture of yours is a proof that the fraternal dialogue, which seeks to improve knowledge and mutual esteem between Jews and Catholics, which was promoted and warmly recommended by the Second Vatican Council in its declaration *Nostra Aetate* [4], is continuing and becoming more widespread, notwithstanding inevitable difficulties.

We have a common spiritual heritage; the People of the New Testament, that is to say the Church, feels itself and is spiritually bound to the stock of Abraham, "our father in the faith."

I pray to God that the Jewish and Christian tradition, founded on the Word of God, which has so profound an awareness of the dignity of the human person made in the image of God [cf. Gen. 1:26], will lead us to fervent worship and love of the one true God; and that this will be translated into effective action on behalf of men, each man and every man.

Shalom! May God, the Creator and Savior, bless you and your community.

1 9 8 3

Address on the Fortieth Anniversary of the Warsaw Ghetto Uprising

April 13 and 25, 1983

On April 25, the pope received in audience a Jewish delegation from the Simon Wiesenthal Center, Los Angeles, returning from ceremonies commemorating the fortieth anniversary of the Warsaw Ghetto Uprising in Poland. The following is the text of the pontiff's address:

Dear Friends:

I extend a warm greeting to all the members of the delegation organized by the Simon Wiesenthal Center of Los Angeles. I am very pleased to welcome you to the Vatican today and in this way to further the continuing religious dialogue between Judaism and the Catholic Church. Such meetings as ours deepen bonds of friendship and trust and help us to appreciate more fully the richness of our common heritage as people who believe in the one Lord and God who has revealed himself to man.

As Christians and Jews, as children of Abraham, we are called to be a blessing for the world [cf. Gen. 12:2ff] especially by our witness in faith to God, the source of all life, and by our commitment to work together for the establishment of true peace and justice among all peoples and nations. Taking up the way of dialogue and mutual collaboration, we deepen bonds of friendship and trust among ourselves and offer to others a sign of hope for the future.

I am happy to know that your itinerary has included a visit to Poland to commemorate the fortieth anniversary of the Warsaw

Ghetto uprising. Just recently, speaking of that horrible and tragic event of history, I said: "It was a desperate cry for the right of life, for liberty, and for the salvation of human dignity. . . . Paying homage to the memory of these innocent victims, we pray: May the Eternal God accept this sacrifice for the well-being and the salvation of the world."

May God bless you and your families with harmony and peace. May he bless you with the fullness of *shalom*.

Some days previously, on April 13, at his general audience, the pope made allusion to his pilgrimage to Auschwitz in 1979 in the following terms:

During my pilgrimage to Auschwitz in June 1979, standing before the stone engraved in Hebrew characters, which is dedicated to the victims of this death camp, I spoke the following words:

> This inscription calls to mind the people whose sons and daughters were destined for total extermination. This people traces its beginnings back to Abraham, the father of our faith [cf. Rom. 4:12] as expressed by Paul of Tarsus. This same people, which had received from God the commandment: "Thou shalt not kill" has felt in itself in a special way what it means to be killed. No one, passing in front of this stone, can remain indifferent to its message.

Today, I want to call those words to mind again, remembering with all the Church in Poland and the whole Jewish people the terrible days of the uprising and of the destruction of the Warsaw Ghetto forty years ago (from April 19 to the middle of July 1943). It was a desperate cry for the right to life, for liberty, and for the salvation of human dignity.

Pastoral Visit to France

August 15, 1983

Address to Catholics of Lourdes

The pope does not always reserve his comments on Catholic-Jewish relations for official meetings with Jewish delegations. Often, as in this excerpt from a major address to French Catholics in Lourdes, he will remind the Catholic community of its responsibility for dialogue. The present excerpt stands for many similar ones that might have been chosen.

IV. And now, I give my cordial greeting and good wishes to these who, *without being Catholic*, share the *Christian faith*. With you we desire to correspond better to the will of Christ and actively to pursue the road to unity. I am sure also that faith in the one God can be a powerful leaven of harmony and collaboration among Christians, Jews, and Muslims in the struggle against the prejudices and suspicions that ought to be overcome.

In the same spirit of respect and friendship, I do not hesitate to address the inhabitants of this country who are *nonbelievers*, or who are troubled by doubt regarding the faith. We often have in common a loyal dedication to the same humanitarian causes, the concern for justice, fellowship, peace, respect for human dignity, and help to the most disadvantaged. I extend my best wishes to you and to your families.

For all of them as well as for the believers, I wish to add this. In tenaciously acting throughout the world for the respect of religious liberty, the Church of today is clearly aware of taking the lead in a necessary combat for the human person, for the most basic human liberty, for the defense of all the other basic liberties. I know that this land of France is singularly committed to such a struggle for liberty and human dignity. The Church, therefore, is more attentive than others to the respect that every honest step toward this end deserves.

Pastoral Trip to Austria

September 10, 1983

"Europe Vespers," Vienna

A highlight of the pope's 1983 trip to Austria was the celebration of the "Europe Vespers," reflecting Vienna's unique role as a crossroad between East and West. The pope reflected on the historic role of the city on both Christian-Jewish and Christian-Muslim relations. In the seventeenth century, the city successfully resisted the last great Muslim invasion of Europe, marking the end of an era. In a different and tragic way, the destruction of the Jewish community of Vienna symbolizes the end of another era in European history:

3. . . . The history of Europe is marked by discord not only in the sphere of states and politics. *Schisms* have divided also the one Church of Jesus Christ. In conjunction with political interests and social problems, these have resulted in bitter fighting, in the oppression and expulsion of dissenters, in repression and intolerance. As heirs to our forbears, we also place this guilt-ridden Europe under the Cross. For in the Cross is our hope.

5. . . . A special legacy of the decisive events of 1683 to the Christian Churches is above all the cause of religious peace—peace between the heirs of Abraham and unity among the brothers of Jesus Christ. The disciples of Mahomet, who then besieged your capital city, now live in your midst and many of them may serve as a model for us in their devout worship of the One God. The fate of the Jewish community, once so fruitfully integrated into the nations of Europe, now so tragically decimated, admonishes us to seize every opportunity for promoting human and spiritual understanding, so that we can stand before God together, and to serve humanity in his spirit. The rift among Christians, so fateful in its impact in 1683, also on the political level, now constitutes an opportunity, even a challenge, to move forward toward a community united in prayer and charitable service.

1984

Address to the
Anti-Defamation League

March 22, 1984

Dear Friends:

I am very happy to receive you here in the Vatican. You are a group of national and international leaders of the well-known Jewish association, based in the United States, but active in many parts of the world, including Rome itself, the Anti-Defamation League. You are also closely related with the Commission for Religious Relations with the Jews, founded ten years ago by Paul VI for the purpose of fostering relations, at the level of our respective faith commitment, between the Catholic Church and the Jewish community.

The mere fact of your visit to me, for which I am grateful, is in itself a proof of the constant development and deepening of such relations. Indeed, when one looks back to the years before the Second Vatican Council and its declaration *Nostra Aetate* and tries to encompass the work done since, one has the feeling that the Lord has done "great things" for us [cf. Luke 1:49]. Therefore we are called to join in a heartfelt act of thanksgiving to God. The opening verse of Psalm 133 is appropriate: "How good and pleasant it is when brothers dwell in unity."

Because, my dear friends, as I have often said since the beginning of my pastoral service as successor of Peter, the Galilean fisherman [cf. *Address*, March 12, 1979], the encounter between Catholics and Jews is not a meeting of two ancient religions each going its own way, and not infrequently, in times past, in grievous and painful conflict. It is a meeting between "brothers," a dialogue, as I said to the representatives of the German Jewish Community in Mainz

[November 17, 1980], "between the first and the second part of the Bible." And as the two parts of the Bible are distinct but closely related, so are the Jewish people and the Catholic Church.

This closeness is to be manifested in many ways. First of all, in the deep respect for each other's identity. The more we know each other, the more we learn to assess and respect our differences.

But then, and this is the great challenge we are called to accept: Respect does not mean estrangement, nor is it tantamount to indifference. On the contrary, the respect we speak of is based on the mysterious spiritual link [cf. *Nostra Aetate*, 4] which brings us close together, in Abraham and, through Abraham, in God who chose Israel and brought forth the Church from Israel.

This "spiritual link," however, involves a great responsibility. Closeness in respect implies trust and frankness, and totally excludes distrust and suspicion. It also calls for fraternal concern for one another and the problems and difficulties with which each of our religious communities is faced.

The Jewish community in general, and your organization in particular, as your name proclaims, are very much concerned with old and new forms of discrimination and violence against Jews and Judaism, ordinarily called anti-Semitism. The Catholic Church, even before the Second Vatican Council [cf. S. Congregation of the Holy Office, March 3, 1928; Pius XI to a group of Belgian radio-journalists, September 6, 1938] condemned such ideology and practice as opposed not only to the Christian profession but also to the dignity of the human person created in the image of God.

But we are not meeting each other just for ourselves. We certainly try to know each other better and to understand better our respective distinct identity and the close spiritual link between us. But, knowing each other, we discover still more what brings us together for a deeper concern for humanity at large: in areas, to cite but a few, such as hunger, poverty, discrimination wherever it may be found and against whomever it may be directed, and the needs of refugees. And, certainly, the great task of promoting justice and peace [cf. Ps. 85:4], the sign of the messianic age in both the Jewish and the Christian tradition, grounded in its turn in the great prophetic heritage. This "spiritual link" between us cannot fail to help us face the great challenge addressed to those who believe that God cares for all people, whom he created in his own image [cf. Gen. 1:27].

I see this at the same time as a reality and as a promise of the dialogue between the Catholic Church and Judaism, and of the relations already existing between your organization and the Commission for Religious Relations with the Jews and with other institutions in some local Churches.

I thank you again for your visit and for your commitment to the goals of dialogue. Let us be grateful to our God, the Father of us all.

Apostolic Letter of John Paul II

Redemptionis Anno

April 20, 1984

To understand the pope's message in this letter, one needs to understand it as a spiritual challenge, and not merely as a political statement. Likewise, one needs to read it within the context of the many statements on Christian—Jewish relations and the Middle East issued by the Holy See and bishops' conferences throughout the world since the promulgation almost two decades ago by the Second Vatican Council of the now-famous declaration on the Jews, Nostra Aetate, 4.

These statements, too numerous to be listed here, tell the story of a true teshuvah, *a turning on the part of Christianity regarding its understanding that acknowledges with respect and affirmation how the Jewish people views itself as a people. The letter, dated April 20, 1984 (Good Friday), follows:*

Revered Brothers and Beloved Sons:
 Health and Apostolic Blessing.
 As the Jubilee Year of Redemption draws to a close, my thoughts go to that special land which is located in that place where Europe,

Asia, and Africa meet and in which the Redemption of the human race was accomplished "once and for all" [Rom. 6:10; Heb. 7:27, 9:12, 10:10].

It is a land which we call holy, indeed the land which was the earthly homeland of Christ who walked about it "preaching the gospel of the kingdom and healing every disease and every infirmity" [Matt. 4:23].

This year especially I was pleased to be touched by the same sentiment and the same joy as my predecessor, Pope Paul VI, when he visited the Holy Land and Jerusalem in 1964.

Although I cannot be there physically, I nevertheless feel that I am spiritually a pilgrim in that land where our reconciliation with God was brought about, to beg the Prince of Peace for the gift of redemption and of peace which is so earnestly desired by the hearts of people, families, and nations—in a special way by the nations which inhabit this very area.

I think especially of the city of Jerusalem, where Jesus, offering his life, "has made us both one, and has broken down the dividing wall of hostility . . . bringing the hostility to an end" [Eph. 2:14, 16].

Before it was the city of Jesus the Redeemer, Jerusalem was the historic site of the biblical revelation of God, the meeting place, as it were, of heaven and earth, in which more than in any other place the word of God was brought to men.

Christians honor her with a religious and intent concern because there the words of Christ so often resounded, there the great events of the Redemption were accomplished: the Passion, Death, and Resurrection of the Lord. In the city of Jerusalem the first Christian community sprang up and remained throughout the centuries a continual ecclesial presence despite difficulties.

Jews ardently love her and in every age venerate her memory, abundant as she is in many remains and monuments from the time of David who chose her as the capital, and of Solomon who built the Temple there. Therefore, they turn their minds to her daily, one may say, and point to her as the sign of their nation.

Muslims also call Jerusalem "holy," with a profound attachment that goes back to the origins of Islam and springs from the fact that they have their many special places of pilgrimage and for more than a thousand years have dwelt there, almost without interruption.

Besides these exceptional and outstanding testimonies, Jerusalem contains communities of believers full of life, whose presence the peoples of the whole world regard as a sign and source of hope—especially those who consider the Holy City to be in a certain way their spiritual heritage and a symbol of peace and harmony.

Indeed, insofar as she is the homeland of the hearts of all the spiritual descendants of Abraham who hold her very dear, and the place where, according to faith, the created things of earth encounter the infinite transcendence of God, Jerusalem stands out as a symbol of coming together, of union, and of universal peace for the human family.

The Holy City, therefore, strongly urges peace for the whole human race, especially for those who worship the one, great God, the merciful Father of the peoples. But it must be acknowledged that Jerusalem continues to be the cause of daily conflict, violence, and partisan reprisals.

This situation and these considerations cause these words of the Prophet to spring to the lips: "For Zion's sake I will not keep silent, and for Jerusalem's sake I will not rest, until her vindication goes forth as brightness, and her salvation as a burning torch" [Isa. 62:1].

I think of and long for the day on which we shall all be so "taught by God" [John 6:45] that we shall listen to his message of peace and reconciliation. I think of the day on which Jews, Christians, and Muslims will greet each other in the city of Jerusalem with the same greeting of peace with which Christ greeted the disciples after the resurrection: "Peace be with you" [John 20:19].

The Roman pontiffs, especially in this century, have witnessed with an ever-anxious solicitude the violent events which have afflicted Jerusalem for many decades, and they have followed closely with watchful care the declarations of the United Nations which have dealt with the fate of the Holy City.

On many occasions the Holy See has called for reflection and urged that an adequate solution be found to this difficult and complex situation. The Holy See has done this because she is concerned for peace among peoples no less than for spiritual, historical, and cultural reasons of a nature eminently religious.

The entire human race, and especially the peoples and nations who have in Jerusalem brothers in faith—Christians, Jews and Muslims—have reason to feel themselves involved in this matter and to do everything possible to preserve the unique and sacred character of the city. Not only the monuments or the sacred places, but the whole historical Jerusalem and the existence of religious communities, their situation and future cannot but affect everyone and interest everyone.

Indeed, there should be found, with goodwill and farsightedness, a concrete and just solution by which different interests and aspirations can be provided for in a harmonious and stable form, and be safeguarded in an adequate and efficacious manner by a special statute internationally guaranteed so that no party could jeopardize it.

I also feel it an urgent duty, in the presence of the Christian communities, of those who believe in the One God and who are committed to the defense of fundamental human values, to repeat that the question of Jerusalem is fundamental for a just peace in the Middle East. It is my conviction that the religious identity of the city and particularly the common tradition of monotheistic faith can pave the way to promote harmony among all those who in different ways consider the Holy City as their own.

I am convinced that the failure to find an adequate solution to the question of Jerusalem, and the resigned postponement of the problem, only compromise further the longed-for peaceful and just settlement of the crisis of the whole Middle East.

It is natural in this context to recall that in the area two peoples, the Israelis and the Palestinians, have been opposed to each other for decades in an antagonism that appears insoluble.

The Church, which looks at Christ the Redeemer and sees his image in the face of every man, invokes peace and reconciliation for the people of the land that was his.

For the Jewish people who live in the State of Israel and who preserve in that land such precious testimonies to their history and their faith, we must ask for the desired security and the due tranquility that is the prerogative of every nation and condition of life and of progress for every society.

The Palestinian people, who find their historical roots in that land and who, for decades, have been dispersed, have the natural right in justice to find once more a homeland and to be able to live in peace and tranquility with the other peoples of the area.

All the peoples of the Middle East, each with its own heritage of spiritual values, will not be able to overcome the tragic events in which they are involved—I am thinking of Lebanon so sorely tried—unless they discover again the true sense of their history which through faith in the One God, calls them to live together peacefully in mutual cooperation.

I desire, therefore, to draw the attention of politicians, of all those who are responsible for the destiny of peoples, of those who are in charge of international organizations, to the plight of the city of Jerusalem and of the communities who live there. In fact, it escapes no one that the different expressions of faith and of culture present in the Holy City can and should be an effective aid to concord and peace.

On this Good Friday, when we solemnly recall the Passion and Death of the Savior, we invite you all, revered brothers in the Episcopate and all priests, men and women religious, and the faithful of the whole world, to include among the special intentions of your prayers the petition for a just solution to the problem of Jerusalem and the Holy Land, and for the return of peace to the Middle East.

As this Jubilee Year of Redemption draws to a close, a year which we have celebrated with great spiritual joy whether in Rome or in all dioceses of the universal Church, Jerusalem has been the ideal goal, the natural place to which we direct our thoughts of love and thankfulness for the great gift of the Redemption which the Son of Man accomplished for all people in the Holy City.

And since the fruit of the Redemption is the reconciliation of man with God and of every man with his brothers, we ought to pray that also in Jerusalem, in the Holy Land of Jesus, those who believe in God may find reconciliation and peace after such sorrowful divisions and strife.

This peace proclaimed by Jesus Christ in the name of the Father who is in heaven thus makes Jerusalem the living sign of the great ideal of unity, of brotherhood, and of agreement among peoples according to the illuminating words of the Book of Isaiah: "Many peoples shall come and say: 'Come, let us go up to the mountain of the Lord, to the house of the God of Jacob; that he may teach us his ways and that we may walk in his paths'" [Isa. 2:3].

Finally, we gladly impart our apostolic blessing.

Given in Rome at St. Peter's on Good Friday, 20 April 1984, the sixth year of our pontificate.

Pastoral Visit to Switzerland

June 14, 1984

Address to Representatives of the Jewish Community in Fribourg

Late in the afternoon of Thursday, June 14, the Holy Father met representatives of the Israelite Federation under the leadership of Mr. Robert Braunshweig, president of the Swiss Federation of the Israelite Community. The meeting took place in the residence of the Bishop of Fribourg. Pope John Paul II addressed the group as follows:

Dear Gentlemen and Beloved Brothers:

It is assuredly a joy for me to meet the representatives of the Swiss Federation of Jewish Communities. It is always so in the course of my apostolic voyages around the world, at least whenever it is possible to do so.

I do not need to go on at length about the importance of such encounters. Making for a certain deepening of our faith and allowing us to avail ourselves of our common biblical patrimony, such encounters contribute to reducing the prejudices and even the barriers that still exist between Christians and Jews. How can Christians, on their part, remain indifferent to the problems and dangers that concern you, if not in Switzerland, at least in numerous regions of the world? From another perspective, the teaching of the Christian Churches must take into account the result of researches done with regard to this common heritage and to the foundations of Christianity in the biblical tradition. Therein lies a way toward the strengthening of our dialogue. In this regard, I am grateful to the representatives of the Jewish Federation for having spoken positively about the Institute for Judeo-Christian Research at the Department of Catholic Theology in Lucerne.

I would also have liked, dear gentlemen and brothers, to speak with you about a fundamental problem, that of peace. The biblical *shalom*, with which it is customary to greet one another in the countries of the East, does it not contain an appeal to our responsibility? In fact, we are all invited to work ardently for the goal of peace. For its part, the Apostolic See continually endeavors to promote a peace based on justice, respect for the rights of all, and suppression of the sources of enmity, to begin with those which are hidden in the heart of man. It unceasingly advises the paths of dialogue and negotiation.

On the principle, it bears neither prejudices nor reservations toward any people. It would like to be able to manifest to all its solicitude, to aid the development of one and all, at the level of liberty, understood in its most authentic sense as on the place of interior and exterior concord, and of the true goods capable of furthering every person and every society.

Therein lies an ideal that can be much advanced by a persevering dialogue and active and fruitful collaboration between Jews and Christians. Allow me to close this brief fraternal meeting with the salutation you like so well: *Shalom aleijim.* It goes out from my heart to all of you who have come to meet with me but also to your families, to the Jewish communities in Switzerland, to all of them dispersed throughout the world, and to all men of goodwill.

To the Executive Committee of International Council of Christians and Jews

July 6, 1984

On Friday morning, July 6, in the Vatican, a delegation of the Executive Committee of the International Council of Christians and Jews was received in a thirty-minute private audience by Pope John Paul II.

In his capacity as president of the ICCJ, Dr. Victor C. Goldbloom addressed the pope on behalf of the delegation:

Remarks of Dr. Victor Goldbloom

Your Holiness:

In expressing the gratitude of the International Council of Christians and Jews for the privilege of this audience, I would like to say an introductory word to identify the ICCJ. It has existed for a considerable number of years in somewhat various forms. At present it is composed of seventeen national member organizations, all in the Western world; but it is significant that in the last four years we have been able to bring to our meetings a number of people, Christians and Jews, from Eastern Europe: from Czechoslovakia, from East Germany, and from Hungary.

If we continue to meet, year after year, in this fashion, it is because of the friendship, the understanding, and the trust which continue to grow between us. It is also because anti-Semitism, and other forms of hatred, including anti-Catholicism, are still unfortunately present in the world. But it is also because we share a sense of historic opportunity, the opportunity to set aside the antagonisms of the past and live together in peace.

For some years now, notably since (and as a result of) the Second Vatican Council, we have been experiencing a new era in Christian—Jewish relations, an era of undeniable progress.

Jews and Christians alike have reason to be grateful for the leadership which the Church has given in this work, leadership manifested by yourself and your recent predecessors; by Cardinal Bea; by Cardinal Willebrands; by Cardinal Etchegaray, whose remarkable statement we regard as a landmark and a beacon; by Monsignor Jorge Mejia, whose attendance at ICCJ meetings is greatly appreciated and whose intellectual contributions to our work are exceptionally valuable; by Dr. Eugene Fisher, both administratively and educationally; and by many, many more.

It has been a reciprocal learning process, and one of the most significant lessons we have derived from it is that the growth of harmony, understanding, and mutual respect has in no way diminished the religious integrity and vitality of Judaism or of Christianity— quite the contrary—nor weakened the commitment of any Jews or of any Christian to his or her faith and tradition.

What is deeply appreciated is the readiness of the Church, under your leadership, to review liturgy, to revise catechism, to reassess and reinterpret history, to recognize that teachings and policies in the past have erected barriers and indeed led to persecutions.

What is also deeply appreciated is the sense of mutual respect and equal partnership which pervades today's relationships.

Our dialogue has become not only a conversation about Judaism and Christianity, about Jews and Christians, but also a sharing of common concerns: *for* peace, *against* violence, *against* fanaticism, *against* curtailments of human rights and religious freedoms, *against* injustice and inequality and discrimination, *for* cooperation and decency and human dignity. Christian-Jewish dialogue is building a foundation for working together on behalf of humanity.

Our concern for peace extends throughout the world; it has a particular focus on the Middle East. We mourn every life that has been lost, Christian or Jewish or Muslim; and we pray that the State of Israel and its neighbors may come to live in security, in recognition, and in fruitful rather than hostile relations. We invoke your leadership toward these ends.

We renew our gratitude for the privilege of this audience. Knowing you at a distance, we have admired your courageous initiatives and have valued your contributions to Christian—Jewish understanding.

Meeting you now in person, we take encouragement from you in the continuation of our work.

That encouragement emboldens us to express a particular hope. We submit with respect, and with great appreciation for the statements you have made and the positions you have taken, that it is not enough for pronouncements to be made at the highest level; they must be heard and heeded in every parish as well.

We ask you therefore to continue the leadership you have manifested in Christian-Jewish relations. We ask you, in so doing, to reinforce the work of the Vatican Commission on Relations with the Jews: to upgrade the commission; to give it more scope, initiative, and authority. We also hope earnestly for the day when every diocese will have a person responsible for the dissemination of new understanding among its clergy and laity, for liaison with the Jewish community wherever it exists, in the State of Israel and throughout the world, and for the educational and practical implementation, at the grassroots level, of the statements and positions and decisions which derive from your initiative.

For all of this, we ask God's blessing upon you.

The Pope's Response

(The headline in the Vatican newspaper read: "The pope to the International Council of Christians and Jews: The peace of the "world must be built through the elimination of prejudice and the pursuit of dialogue.")

Dear Friends, Mr. President, and Members of the Executive Committee of the International Council for Christians and Jews:

1. I thank you, Mr. President, for the kind words of greeting with which you have now presented to me the aims, the tasks, and the concerns of the International Council of Christians and Jews. And I thank you also, members of the Executive Committee, for your kindness in visiting the pope on the occasion of your international

colloquium, to be held at Vallombrosa next week. Welcome to this house where the activities of those who promote the dialogue between Christians and Jews and are personally engaged in it are closely followed and warmly encouraged. Indeed, it is only through such a meeting of minds and hearts, reaching out to our respective faith communities, and also perhaps to other faith communities, as you try to do with Islam, that both Jews and Christians are able to profit from their "great common spiritual patrimony" [cf. *Nostra Aetate*, 4] and to make it fruitful for their own good and the good of the world.

2. Yes, a "great common spiritual patrimony" which should be, in the first place, brought to the knowledge of all Christians and all Jews and which embraces not only one or the other isolated element but a solid, fruitful, rich common religious inheritance: in monotheism; in faith in a God who as loving father takes care of humankind and chose Abraham and the Prophets and sent Jesus into the world; in a common basic liturgical pattern and in a common consciousness of our commitment, grounded in faith, to all men and women in need, who are our "neighbors" [cf. Lev. 19:18a, Mark 12:32, and parallels].

This is why you are so much concerned with religious education on both sides, that the images which each of us projects of the other should be really free of stereotypes and prejudices, that they should respect the other's identity, and should in fact prepare the people for the meetings of minds and hearts just mentioned. The proper teaching of history is also a concern of yours. Such a concern is very understandable, given the sad and entangled common history of Jews and Christians—a sad history which is not always taught or transmitted correctly.

3. There is again the danger of an always active and sometimes even resurgent tendency to discriminate between people and human groups, enhancing some and despising others, a tendency which does not hesitate at times to use violent methods.

To single out and denounce such facts and stand together against them is a noble act and a proof of our mutual brotherly commitment. But it is necessary to go to the roots of such evil, by education, especially education for dialogue. This, however, would not be enough if it were not coupled with a deep change in our heart, a real spiritual conversion. This also means constantly reaffirming common religious values and working toward a personal religious commitment in the love of God, our Father, and in the love of all men and women [cf. Deut. 6:5, Lev. 19:18, Mark 12:28–34]. The Golden Rule, we are well aware, is common to Jews and Christians alike.

In this context is to be seen your important work with youth. By bringing together young Christians and Jews, and enabling them to live, talk, sing, and pray together, you greatly contribute toward the creation of a new generation of men and women, mutually concerned for one another and for all, prepared to serve others in need, whatever their religious profession, ethnic origin, or color.

World peace is built in this modest, apparently insignificant and limited, but in the end, very efficient, way. And we are all concerned for peace everywhere, among and within nations, particularly in the Middle East.

4. Common study of our religious sources is again one of the items of your agenda. I encourage you to put to good use the important recommendation made by the Second Vatican Council in its declaration *Nostra Aetate, No. 4*, about "biblical and theological studies," which are the source of "mutual understanding and respect." In fact, such studies, made in common, and altogether different from the ancient "disputation," tend to the true knowledge of each religion, and also to the joyful discovery of the "common patrimony" I spoke of at the beginning, always in the careful observance of each other's dignity.

May the Lord bless all your endeavors and repay you with the blessedness which Jesus proclaimed, in the tradition of the Old Testament, for those who work for peace [cf. Matt. 5:9, Ps. 37 (36):37].

1985

To the American Jewish Committee

February 15, 1985

*1985 marked the anniversary of the Second Vatican Council's decla-
ration on the Jews, Nostra Aetate, 4. Consequently, there were many
exchanges and colloquia not only in Rome but around the world. In
the United States, for example, there were some seventy different celebrations in at least forty states. The American Jewish Committee was
involved in organizing a number of these events on the Jewish side, as
was the Anti-Defamation League and other Jewish groups. This out-
pouring in itself, we feel, indicates the great strides that have been taken
in improving relations in the years since the Second Vatican Council.
The first of the Roman events was the reception of a delegation from the
American Jewish Committee. The pope took the occasion to reaffirm
Nostra Aetate in the strongest language, language normally reserved for
describing the Scriptures themselves. The talk is, thus, an important
indication of the Church's ongoing commitment to the dialogue.*

Statement by Howard I. Friedman
President, American Jewish Committee

Your Holiness:

It is with warm sentiments of esteem and respect that I express
the heartfelt greetings of *shalom*, of peace and well-being, to you
on behalf of this delegation of leaders of the American Jewish
Committee.

We regard this audience with Your Holiness as a particularly auspicious occasion in the history of the Catholic Church and the

Jewish people. We meet with you to acknowledge the anniversaries of two climactic events:

First, 1985 marks the fortieth anniversary of the end of World War II and the defeat of the demonic ideology of Nazism, whose core was racial and religious anti-Semitism, Second, 1985 commemorates the twentieth anniversary of the ending of the Second Vatican Council and its adoption of the historic declaration *Nostra Aetate.*

As the Nazi trauma appalled us with despair over human evil, so the twentieth anniversary of the close of the Second Vatican Council inspires all of us with hope and promise for a more humane future. The adoption of the Vatican *Declaration on Non-Christian Religions,* on December 28, 1965, marked a decisive turning point in the nearly two-thousand-year encounter between the Catholic Church and the Jewish people.

We wish to acknowledge the act of justice and service to truth represented by that declaration, and your own moving pronouncements calling for mutual respect and collaboration between Catholics and Jews in common service to humanity. It is no exaggeration to state that as a result of these far-reaching pronouncements, and the practical actions they have inspired, greater progress in improved Catholic-Jewish relations has taken place during the past two decades than in the past two millennia.

The American Jewish Committee takes special pride in this encouraging process, for we were privileged to have been intimately involved, through collaboration with the late Augustine Cardinal Bea and his secretariat, throughout the Second Vatican Council. We have helped implement numerous concrete actions that have resulted in significant improvement in relations between the Catholic and Jewish peoples in the United States and in other parts of the world. Yet much remains to be done. We pledge our continued cooperation in helping further Catholic-Jewish solidarity and friendship. We sincerely hope that the forthcoming Synod of Bishops you have called will give further impetus in this direction.

As a pioneering human relations agency, the American Jewish Committee has shared Your Holiness's vision of upholding human dignity by vigorously advocating the universality of civil and political liberties—and, in particular, religious liberty—for all peoples everywhere, especially those in oppressive totalitarian societies.

At this moment, we are actively engaged in close cooperation with Catholic Relief Services and other relief agencies in seeking to relieve the suffering, hunger, and deprivation of millions of fellow human beings in Ethiopia, and in Africa generally. That life-saving collaboration between the Catholic and Jewish peoples, in service to an anguished humanity, is the latest testimony to the new spirit made possible by the Second Vatican Council.

Your Holiness, American Jewish Committee leaders come to this audience with you after a ten-day intensive mission in Israel. We have met with Israeli Jews, Christians, and Muslims, with Palestinian Arabs, with government leaders and ordinary people. Everywhere, we have found a great yearning for peace, for coexistence, for an end to conflict, violence, and terrorism. We know that these goals are dear to the heart and mind of Your Holiness.

Our visit to Israel has reinforced our conviction that the primary obstacle to peace in the area is the ongoing illusion of most of Israel's neighbors that somehow, without formal recognition by other states of Israel's sovereign legitimacy, her continued existence can be undermined.

Nothing would contribute more to peace in the area than the dispelling of that illusion. That is why the extension of full recognition throughout the civilized world is so vital.

We appreciate deeply your clear grasp of that reality as expressed in your apostolic letter, *Redempticnis Anno,* which emphasized the Church's de facto recognition of the State of Israel and the deep ties between the Jewish people and the city of Jerusalem in these words:

> For the Jewish people who live in the State of Israel, and who preserve in that land such precious testimonies to their history and their faith, we must ask for the desired security and the due tranquility that is the prerogative of every nation and condition of life and of progress for every society. . . .
>
> Jews ardently love her [Jerusalem], and in every age venerate her memory, abundant as she is in many remains and monuments from the time of David who chose her as the capital, and of Solomon who

built the Temple there. Therefore, they turn their minds to her daily, one may say, and point to her as the sign of their nation.

Your Holiness, we recognize the complexity of the problems involved, but we dare to hope that the spirit that inspired your apostolic letter will lead to steps that will formalize the diplomatic ties between the Holy See and the State of Israel and her people.

Such a historic act, we believe, would be a watershed event in Catholic—Jewish relations. It would help create the sense of reality which is indispensable to peace. We would consider it a happy development and confirmation of the decisions of the Second Vatican Council. Above all, it would be an act of profound spiritual and ethical significance in advancing the cause of world peace.

May God bless you and strengthen the work of your hands.

Statement of the Pope

Dear Friends:

It is a great pleasure for me to receive this important delegation of the American Jewish Committee, headed by your president, and I am grateful to you for this visit. You are most welcome in this house, which, as you know, is always open to members of the Jewish people.

You have come here to celebrate the twentieth anniversary of the conciliar declaration *Nostra Aetate*, on the relation of the Church with non-Christian religions, the fourth section of which deals at length with the Church's relation with Judaism.

During my recent pastoral visit to Venezuela, I received some representatives of the Jewish community there, in an encounter which has now become a normal feature of so many of my pastoral visits around the world. On that occasion, in response to the greeting address of Rabbi Pynchas Brener, I said that "I wish to confirm, with utmost conviction, that the teaching of the Church proclaimed during the Second Vatican Council in the declaration *Nostra Aetate* . . . remains always for us, for the Catholic Church, for the Episcopate . . . and for the pope, a teaching which must be followed—a teaching which it is necessary to accept not merely as something fitting, but much more as an expression of the faith, as an inspiration of the Holy Spirit, as a word of the Divine Wisdom" [*L'Osservatore Romano*, January 29, 1985].

I willingly repeat those words to you who are commemorating the twentieth anniversary of the declaration. They express the commitment of the Holy See, and of the whole Catholic Church, to the content of this declaration, underlining, so to speak, its importance.

After twenty years, the terms of the declaration have not grown old. It is even more clear than before how sound the declaration's theological foundation is and what a solid basis it provides for a really fruitful Jewish—Christian dialogue. On the one hand, it places the motivation of such a dialogue in the very mystery of the Church herself and, on the other hand, it clearly maintains the identity of each religion, closely linking one to the other.

During these twenty years, an enormous amount of work has been done. You are well aware of it, since your organization is deeply committed to Jewish—Christian relations, on the basis of the declaration, on both the national and international levels, and particularly in connection with the Holy See's Commission for Religious Relations with the Jews.

I am convinced, and I am happy to state it on this occasion, that the relationships between Jews and Christians have radically improved in these years. Where there was ignorance and therefore prejudice and stereotypes, there is now growing mutual knowledge, appreciation, and respect. There is, above all, love between us, that kind of love, I mean, which is for both of us a fundamental injunction of our religious traditions and which the New Testament has received from the Old [cf. Mark 12:28–34; Lev. 19:18]. Love involves understanding. It also involves frankness and the freedom to disagree in a brotherly way where there are reasons for it.

There is no doubt that much remains to be done. Theological reflection is still needed, notwithstanding the amount of work already done and the results achieved thus far. Our biblical scholars and theologians are constantly challenged by the word of God that we hold in common.

Education should more accurately take into account the new insights and directives opened up by the Council and spelled out in the subsequent *Guidelines and Suggestions for Implementing the Conciliar Declaration* Nostra Aetate, No. 4, which remain in force. Education for dialogue, love and respect for others, and openness toward all people are urgent needs in our pluralistic societies, where everybody is a neighbor to everybody else.

Anti-Semitism, which is unfortunately still a problem in certain places, has been repeatedly condemned by the Catholic tradition as incompatible with Christ's teaching and with the respect due to the dignity of men and women created in the image and likeness of God. I once again express the Catholic Church's repudiation of all oppression and persecution, and of all discrimination against people—from whatever side it may come—"in law or in fact, on account of their race, origin, color, culture, sex, or religion" [*Octogesima Adveniens*, 23].

In close connection with the preceding, there is the *large field of cooperation* open to us as Christians and Jews, in favor of all humanity, where the image of God shines through in every man, woman, and child, especially in the destitute and those in need.

I am well aware of how closely the American Jewish Committee has collaborated with some of our Catholic agencies in alleviating hunger in Ethiopia and in the Sahel, in trying to call the attention of the proper authorities to this terrible plight, still sadly not solved, and which is therefore a constant challenge to all those who believe in the one true God, who is the Lord of history and the loving Father of all.

I know also your concern for the peace and security of the Holy Land. May the Lord give to that land, and to all the peoples and nations in that part of the word, the blessings contained in the word *shalom*, so that, in the expression of the Psalmist, "justice and peace may kiss" [cf. Ps. 85:11].

The Second Vatican Council and subsequent documents truly have this aim: that the sons and daughters of Abraham—Jews, Christians, and Muslims [cf. *Nostra Aetate*, 3]—may live together and prosper in peace. And may all of us love the Lord our God with all our heart, and with all our soul, and with all our strength [cf. Deut. 6:5].

Thank you again for your visit.

Shalom!

Angelicum Colloquium on *Nostra Aetate*

April 19, 1985

The colloquium addressed here by the Holy Father was organized, on the Jewish side, by the Anti-Defamation League and held at the Dominican House of Study in Rome, commonly known as the Angelicum. The papers from the colloquium were published in Face to Face: An Interreligious Bulletin, published by ADL in New York.

Remarks at the Papal Audience
Rabbi Ronald B. Sobel

Your Holiness:

We of the Anti-Defamation League have come to Rome to participate in a scholarly colloquium at the Pontifical University of St. Thomas Aquinas, marking and celebrating the twentieth anniversary of the promulgation of *Nostra Aetate*. It is fitting and proper that we do so, not only we of the Anti-Defamation League, but the theology faculty at the university itself, the Friars of the Atonement, the members of SIDIC, and others, both Jews and Catholics, all in cooperation with the Commission of the Holy See for Religious Relations with the Jews. It is altogether fitting and proper that this celebration should have taken place here in Rome within the setting of one of the more important academic institutions of the Church, for no occasion of celebration is truly worthy or inherently authentic unless joined to and accompanied by forthright, honest, dispassionate scholarship. Thus, we have come to Rome to celebrate and evaluate.

Though we are not unaware that what has transpired between the Jewish people and the Church in the past twenty years is but the beginning of a process that will lead, God willing, into the long and distant future, we are, nevertheless, fully cognizant that the past two decades have been witness to nothing less than a modern miracle, a miracle wherein, within a period of one score years, two thousand years of our previous relationship have been reversed. Truly, this is God's doing. In the past twenty years we, His children, both Jew and Catholic, have come to realize and thus have begun to learn that theological differences, proud and decisive, need not be barriers to love and understanding; that in a world of many currents and crosscurrents Judaism and Christianity are not so much on opposite sides of the fence as we are on the same side; that though we shall never share some of the same theological convictions, we do share many of the same human dreams; that though we shall prove the mystery of God each in our own way, according to the demands of our own traditions and the dictates of our own consciences, we view our world today with the same anguish and the events of our time with the same apprehension.

Your Holiness, together we see the same darkness. Together we see and understand those forces of irreligion that are addressed not to the dignity of the spirit but to the degradation of the soul. Together we share the conviction that bigotry and prejudice, born of hatred and nurtured in the failure to respect each other's commitments, can no longer be tolerated, not now, not anywhere, not at any time. Therefore, Your Holiness, we applaud with gratitude each and every one of your many pronouncements, made from here in the Vatican and elsewhere in the world, against all those demonic forces that would enslave rather than liberate, that would destroy rather than create.

It was with particular gratification, Your Holiness, that the Jewish people noted that in your Easter Message to the City and to the World, you made reference, with deep sensitivity, to the unparalleled inhumanity of Nazi brutality against the Jewish people. We shall never forget this, and it is and shall remain a source of comfort to us to know that you shall help the world to remember as well. Yesterday was *Yom Hashoah*, the day in our Jewish religious calendar set aside for remembrance of the Holocaust and to commemorate the martyrdom of our six million. Therefore, during our colloquium yesterday, Catholics and Jews together set aside a time to commemorate and to meditate. And in the time that we set aside, how could we forget that out of the ashes of Auschwitz rose the miracle of Israel? In and through our dialogue, we look forward to the day when Rome and Jerusalem, this Eternal City and the place where heaven touches earth, will embrace in the fullness of fraternal love and recognition.

Yes, the dialogue has begun and much has been accomplished: *Nostra Aetate* in 1965; the Guidelines for its implementation in 1974; the devoted leadership of Cardinal Willebrands, Monsignor Mejia, and many others throughout the Catholic world; the work of some Episcopal conferences and national commissions for relations between Christians and Jews. Much has been done, but much more needs to be done. The dialogue is not equal in all places. We continue to hear from some pulpits in Latin America echoes of the teaching of contempt; in Oberammergau we are witness to themes that have been repudiated by the Church.

But we are grateful and remain hopeful, for if we continue what we have begun it may be that history will record that thirty-three centuries after the Exodus and two thousand years after Calvary, both Christians and Jews allowed their hearts to be opened to God in new and wondrous ways.

Statement of the Pope

Dear Friends:

I am happy to greet you in the Vatican on the occasion of the colloquium which you have called together to commemorate the twentieth anniversary of the conciliar declaration *Nostra Aetate*, on the relation of the Church with non-Christian religions, and particularly the section of it dealing with her relations with Judaism.

It is indeed a remarkable occasion, not only because of the commemoration in itself, but also because it happens to bring together Catholics, other Christians, and Jews, through the collaboration of the theological faculty of the Pontifical University of St. Thomas Aquinas, the Anti-Defamation League, the Centro Pro Unione, and the Service International de Documentation Judéochrétienne

(SIDIC). The Holy See's Commission for Religious Relations with the Jews has also agreed to give you its assistance and participation.

In this gathering of such important institutions for the purpose of celebrating *Nostra Aetate*, I see a way of putting into practice one of the main recommendations of the declaration, where it says that "since the spiritual patrimony common to Christians and Jews is . . . so great, this Sacred Synod wishes to foster and recommend that mutual understanding and respect which is the fruit above all of biblical and theological studies, and of brotherly dialogues" [*Nostra Aetate*, 4].

Your colloquium is one of those "brotherly dialogues," and it will most certainly contribute to that "mutual understanding and respect" mentioned by the Council.

Jews and Christians must get to know each other better. Not just superficially as people of different religions, merely coexisting in the same place, but as members *of such* religions which are so closely linked to one another [cf. *Nostra Aetate*, 4]. This implies that Christians try to know as exactly as possible the distinctive beliefs, religious practices, and spirituality of the Jews, and conversely that the Jews try to know the beliefs and practices and spirituality of Christians.

It is in this context that I note the reference of your program to the catastrophe which so cruelly decimated the Jewish people, before and during the war, especially in the death camps. I am well aware that the traditional date for such a commemoration falls about now. It is precisely an absence of faith in God and, as a consequence, of love and respect for our fellow men and women, which can easily bring about such disasters. Let us pray together that it will never happen again, and that whatever we do to get to know each other better, to collaborate with one another and to bear witness to the One God and to his will, as expressed in the Decalogue, will help make people still more aware of the abyss which mankind can fall into when we do not acknowledge other people as brothers and sisters, sons and daughters, of the same heavenly Father.

Jewish—Christian relations are never an academic exercise. They are, on the contrary, part of the very fabric of our religious commitment and our respective vocations as Christians and as Jews.

For Christians, these relations have special theological and moral dimensions because of the Church's conviction, expressed in the document we are commemorating, that "she received the revelation of the Old Testament through the people whom God in his inexpressible mercy deigned to establish the ancient Covenant, and draws sustenance from the root of that good olive tree into which have been grafted the wild olive branches of the Gentiles" [cf. Rom. 11:17–24 (*Nostra Aetate*, 4)]. To commemorate the anniversary of *Nostra Aetate* is to become still more conscious of all these dimensions and to translate them into daily practice everywhere.

I earnestly hope for this and pray that the work of your organizations and institutions in the field of Jewish—Christian relations will be ever more blessed by the Lord, whose name is forever to be praised: "Great is the Lord and highly to be praised" [Ps. 145:3].

Such seems to be the proper way to dispel prejudices, but also to discover, on the Christian side, the deep Jewish roots of Christianity, and, on the Jewish side, to appreciate better the special way in which the Church, since the days of the Apostles, has read the Old Testament and received the Jewish heritage.

Here we are already in what we Christians call a *theological* field. I see in the program of your colloquium that you are dealing with proper theological subjects. I believe this to be a sign of maturity in our relations and a proof that the thrust and practical recommendations of *Nostra Aetate* really do inspire our dialogues. It is hopeful and refreshing to see this done in an encounter commemorating the twentieth anniversary of the declaration.

Common theological studies cannot in fact be envisaged if there is not, on each side, a large measure of mutual trust and deep respect for each other—trust and respect which can only profit and grow from such studies.

You have also faced the question of Jewish and Christian spirituality in the present secularistic context. Yes, in our days one can sometimes have the sad impression of an absence of God and his will from the private and public lives of men and women. When we reflect on such a situation and its tragic consequences for mankind, deprived of its roots in God and therefore of its basic moral orientation, one can only be grateful to the Lord because we believe in him, as Jews and Christians, and we both can say, in the words of Deuteronomy: "Hear, O Israel, the Lord our God is one God" [Deut. 6:4].

But gratitude soon turns into a commitment to express and publicly profess that faith before the world and to live our lives according to it, so that "men may see our good words and give glory to our Father who is in heaven" [Matt. 5:16].

The existence and the providence of the Lord, our Creator and Savior, are thus made present in the witness of our daily conduct and belief. And this is one of the responses that those who believe in God and are prepared to "sanctify his name" [cf. Matt. 6:9] can and should give to the secularistic climate of the present day.

A commemorative colloquium thus easily becomes a point of departure for a new and strong dedication, not only to ever deeper relations between Jews and Christians in many fields, but also to what man needs most in the present world: a sense of God as a loving Father and of his saving will.

Address to the International Catholic-Jewish Liaison Committee on the Twentieth Anniversary of *Nostra Aetate*

October 28, 1985

The twelfth meeting of the International Catholic—Jewish Committee took place on October 28–30 at the offices of the Secretariat for Promoting Christian Unity of the Holy See. The event was timed to coincide with the twentieth anniversary of the Second Vatican Council's decla-

ration on the relationship between the Church and the Jewish people, Nostra Aetate, No. 4. That document, whose Latin title, taken from its opening words, means "In Our Times," was promulgated on October 28, 1965, by Pope Paul VI together with the 2, 221 Council fathers.

The International Liaison Committee was founded in 1970 as a means of implementing the Council's call for the institution of ongoing dialogue between the Church and the Jewish people after centuries of mistrust and often tragic conflict. The committee is composed of representatives of the Holy See's Commission for Religious Relations with the Jews and of the International Jewish Committee for Interreligious Consultations (IJCIC). IJCIC is composed of the World Jewish Congress, the Synagogue Council of America, the American Jewish Committee, the Israel Jewish Council for Interreligious Consultations, and B'nai B'rith.

Highlighting the event was an audience with Pope John Paul II on the afternoon of October 28. Cardinal Johannes Willebrands, president of the Holy See's Commission, introduced the Liaison Committee to the pope, who had met previously with its members. Rabbi Mordecai Waxman, chairman of IJCIC, hailed Nostra Aetate and subsequent papal statements as documents that revolutionized Christian-Jewish relations and created new opportunities for dialogue. Rabbi Waxman pointed out that the creation of the State of Israel was likewise a revolution in Jewish history that calls for new thinking by both Catholics and Jews.

The pope, for his part, reaffirmed the Church's commitment to Nostra Aetate and the uniqueness of the sacred "link" between the Church and the Jewish people, which he called one of "parentage, a relationship which we have with that religious community alone"

The full text of the pope's address follows.

Dear Friends:

Twenty years to the day after the promulgation of the declaration *Nostra Aetate* by the Second Vatican Council, you have chosen Rome as the venue of the twelfth session of the International Liaison Committee between the Catholic Church, represented by the Holy See's Commission for Religious Relations with the Jews, and the International Jewish Committee on Interreligious Consultations.

Ten years ago, in January 1975, you also met in Rome for the tenth anniversary of the promulgation of the same document. The declaration, in effect, in its fourth section deals with the relations between the Catholic Church and the Jewish religious community.

It has been repeatedly said that the content of this section, while not too long nor unduly complicated, was epoch making and that it changed the existing relationship between the Church and the Jewish people and opened quite a new era in this relationship.

I am happy to affirm here, twenty years later, that the fruits we have reaped since then—and your committee is one of them—prove the basic truth of these assertions. The Catholic Church is always prepared with the help of God's grace to revise and renew whatever in her attitudes and ways of expression happens to conform less with her own identity, founded upon the word of God, the Old and the New Testament, as read in the Church. This she does, not out of any expediency nor to gain a practical advantage of any kind, but out of a deep consciousness of her own "mystery" and a renewed willingness to translate it into practice. The declaration affirms, with great precision, that it is while delving into this "mystery" that she, the Church, "remembers the spiritual link" between herself and "Abraham's stock."

It is this "link," which the declaration goes on to explain and illustrate, that is the real foundation for our relation with the Jewish people—a relation which could well be called a real "parentage" and which we have with that religious community alone, notwithstanding our many connections with other world religions, particularly with Islam, and which the declaration appropriately elaborates in other sections. This "link" can be called a "sacred" one, stemming as it does from the mysterious will of God.

Our relations since that historic date could only improve, deepen, and branch out in different aspects and levels in the life of the Catholic Church and of the Jewish community. In this connection, as you are well aware, as far back as 1974 the Holy See took the initiative to create a Commission for Religious Relations with the Jews and also published, through that same commission, two further documents intended for the application of the declaration to many fields of the Church's life: the 1974 *Guidelines* and the very recent *Notes on the Correct Presentation of the Jews and Judaism in Catholic Preaching and Teaching*.

Both documents are a proof of the Holy See's continued interest in and commitment to this renewed relationship between the

Catholic Church and the Jewish people, and to drawing from it all practical consequences.

Regarding the above-mentioned document, the *Notes* published last June, I am sure that they will greatly help toward freeing our catechetical and religious teaching of a negative or inaccurate presentation of Jews and Judaism in the context of the Catholic faith. They will also help to promote respect, appreciation, and indeed love for one and the other, as they are both in the unfathomable design of God, who "does not reject his people" [Ps. 94:14; Rom. 11:1]. By the same token, anti-Semitism in its ugly and sometimes violent manifestations should be completely eradicated. Better still, a positive view of each of our religions, with due respect for the identity of each, will surely emerge, as is already the case in so many places.

To understand our documents correctly and especially the conciliar declaration, a firm grasp of Catholic tradition and Catholic theology is certainly necessary. I would even say that for Catholics, as the *Notes* [25] have asked them to do, to fathom the depths of the extermination of many million Jews during World War II and the wounds thereby inflicted on the consciousness of the Jewish people, theological reflection is also needed. I therefore earnestly hope that study of and reflection on theology will become more and more a part of our exchanges for our mutual benefit even if, quite understandably, some sections of the Jewish community may still have some reservations about such exchanges. However, deep knowledge of and respect for each other's religious identity seem essential for the reaffirmation and strengthening of the "link" the Council spoke about.

The International Liaison Committee which you form is, in itself, proof and practical manifestation of this "link." You have met twelve times since 1971 and, despite the normal difficulties of adjustment and even some occasional tensions, you have achieved a rich, varied, and frank relationship. I see here present both representatives of many local churches and of several local Jewish communities. Such large representations gathered in Rome for the twentieth anniversary of *Nostra Aetate* is itself consoling and promising. We have really made much headway in our relations.

In order to follow along the same path, under the eyes of God and with his all-healing blessing, I am sure you will work with ever greater dedication, for constantly deeper mutual knowledge, for even greater interest in the legitimate concerns of each other, and especially for collaboration in the many fields where our faith in one God and our common respect for his image in all men and women invite our witness and commitment.

For the work which has been done I give thanks with you to the Lord our God and, for what you are still called to do, I offer my prayers, and I am happy to reaffirm the commitment of the Catholic Church to this relationship and dialogue with the Jewish community. May the Lord help your goodwill and your personal and institutional commitment to this important task.

Statement by Rabbi Mordecai Waxman, Chairman of the International Jewish Committee on Interreligious Consultations, during Audience with Pope John Paul II

Your Holiness:

October 28, 1965, was both a historic and revolutionary date. It marked a turning away from eighteen centuries often characterized by both misunderstanding and persecution, toward a dialogue in which we explored our common spiritual roots and confronted our disagreements frankly but in a spirit of mutual understanding and respect.

In the ensuing years, the Episcopates in the United States, Latin America, and Europe have made the spirit of *Nostra Aetate* their own, carried its doctrines even further, and sought to translate them into modes of action and behavior.

Your Holiness personally has given great depth to the dialogue and evoked a warm response from Jews and, indeed, from many Catholics throughout the world through your own statements. These included your declaration in Mainz in 1980 in which you affirmed: "The people of God of the Old Covenant [which] was never repudiated by God. . . ." That was supplemented by your statement in Rome in 1982 that we pursue "diverse but, in the end, convergent paths with the help of the Lord."

There is a Hebrew proverb that says, "*D'vorim hayotzim min halev, nichnasim el ha-lev* (Words which come from the heart, speak to the heart)." The warmth with which you have spoken today of our common spiritual heritage, our common concerns, and our common goals enables us, in turn, to speak from the heart.

We appreciated, in *Nostra Aetate* and in the declarations which have flowed from it, the ability of a great faith to examine itself and to chart new directions.

The repudiation of the false teachings—responsible for so much hatred and persecution—that all Jews, then and now, were responsible for the death of Jesus, encouraged Jews everywhere to feel that there was a new spirit in the Christian world. We have noted with distress, lapses from time to time into the old and repudiated language by some Catholic authorities. Nonetheless, the wide acceptance of the new approach in the Catholic world has been for us a source of hope.

The further recognition in *Nostra Aetate* and in the *Guidelines* that the Jewish religious tradition has continued to evolve and grow through the centuries to the present day and has much to contribute to our world, and the assertion that every effort must be made to understand Judaism "in its own terms," as it sees itself, made dialogue possible.

But, in these same years, the Jewish people have been undergoing a profound transformation of our own. The Nazi Holocaust shook us to the core of our being. The creation of the State of Israel restored us as a factor in history but, even more, restored us religiously and spiritually. For the third time in Jewish history, the pattern of exile and redemption was reenacted. The implications are incalculable, but we are confirmed in biblical belief that the Covenant with the land established by the God of Abraham and his descendants endures, even as the Covenant of the Torah abides. It said to us in the words of the Torah portion read this week throughout the Jewish world that "Abraham still stands before the Lord."

We are deeply moved by the knowledge that Your Holiness has testified to this truth through your apostolic letter in April 1984:

For the Jewish people who live in the State of Israel and who preserve in that land such precious testimonies to their history and their faith, we must ask for the desired security and the due tranquility that is the prerogative of every nation and condition of life and of progress for every society.

Thus, a renewed Jewish people, restored to Jerusalem and to human dignity, can engage in dialogue with the Catholic Church, confident that we have spiritual riches to cherish and to share, aware that we both have a common obligation to engage in *Tikkun Olam*— the improvement and perfecting of our world. On this anniversary of *Nostra Aetate*, we are conscious that much of its vision has yet to be translated into reality and universal acceptance. But we look forward to the creation of structures and programs which will translate our dialogue into actions which will move the hearts of the members of our respective faiths in the joint quest for universal peace, for social justice and human rights, and for upholding the dignity of every human being created in the Divine image.

Your Holiness, in recognition of the common spiritual heritage we share and in consideration of the fact that the Catholic and Jewish world are commemorating the 850th anniversary of the birth of one of our greatest figures, we wish to present you with a copy of the beautiful Kaufman manuscript of the *Code of Maimonides*. With it, we offer the hope that the final line of the *Code* will be fulfilled through our continuing dialogue which shall, with God's will, grow in depth and understanding so that "the earth may be filled with the knowledge of the Lord as the waters cover the sea."

Historic Visit to the Synagogue of Rome

April 13, 1986

On Sunday, April 13, the Holy Father made his historic visit to the Synagogue in Rome. After an address of welcome by Prof Giacomo Saban, president of the Jewish Community of Rome, Chief Rabbi Elio Toaff then spoke. In reply, the Holy Father gave the following address:

Address by the Pope

Dear Chief Rabbi of the Jewish Community in Rome,
Dear President of the Union of Italian Jewish Communities,
Dear President of the Community in Rome,
Dear Rabbis,
Dear Jewish and Christian Friends and Brethren taking part in this historic celebration.:

1. First of all, I would like, together with you, to give thanks and praise to the Lord who stretched out the heavens and laid the foundations of the earth [cf. Isa. 51:16] and who chose Abraham in order to make him father of a multitude of children, as numerous "as the stars of heaven and as the sand which is on the seashore" [Gen. 22:17; cf. Isa. 15:5]—to give thanks and praise to him because it has been his good pleasure, in the mystery of his Providence, that this evening there should be a meeting in this, your "Major Temple," between the Jewish community which has been living in this city since the times of the ancient Romans and the bishop of Rome and universal pastor of the Catholic Church.

I likewise feel it is my duty to thank the chief rabbi, Professor Elio Toaff, who from the first moment accepted with joy the idea that I should make this visit, and who is now receiving me with great openness of heart and a profound sense of hospitality; and in addition to him I also thank all those members of the Jewish community in Rome who have made this meeting possible and who in so many ways have worked to ensure that it should be at one and the same time a reality and a symbol.

Many thanks therefore to you all.

Todâ rabbâ (Many thanks).

2. In the light of the word of God that has just been proclaimed and that lives forever [cf. Isa. 30:8], I would like us to reflect together—in the presence of the Holy One, may he be blessed! (as your liturgy says)—on the fact and the significance of this meeting between the bishop of Rome, the pope, and the Jewish community that lives and works in this city which is so dear to you and to me.

I had been thinking of this visit for a long time. In fact, the chief rabbi was kind enough to come and see me in February 1981, when I paid a pastoral visit to the nearby parish of San Carlo ai Catenari. In addition, a number of you have been more than once to the Vatican, on the occasion of the numerous audiences that I have been able to have with representatives in Italian and world Jewry, and still earlier, in time of my predecessors, Paul VI, John XXIII, and Pius XII. I am likewise well aware that the chief rabbi, on the night before the death of Pope John, did not hesitate to go to St. Peter's Square; and accompanied by members of the Jewish faithful, he mingled with the crowd of Catholics and other Christians, in order to pray and keep vigil, as it were bearing witness, in a silent but very effective way, to the greatness of soul of that pontiff, who was open to all people without distinction, and in particular to the Jewish brethren.

The heritage that I would now like to take up is precisely that of Pope John, "who on one occasion, as he passed by here—as the chief rabbi has just mentioned—stopped the car so that he could bless the crowd of Jews who were coming out of this very temple. And I would like to take up his heritage at this very moment, when

I find myself not just outside, but, thanks to your generous hospitality, inside the Synagogue of Rome.

3. This gathering in a way brings to a close, after the pontificate of John XXIII and the Second Vatican Council, a long period which we must not tire of reflecting upon in order to draw from it the appropriate lessons. Certainly, we cannot and should not forget that the historical circumstances of the past were very different from those that have laboriously matured over the centuries. The general acceptance of a legitimate plurality on the social, civil, and religious levels has been arrived at with great difficulty. Nevertheless, a consideration of centuries-long cultural conditioning could not prevent us from recognizing that the acts of discrimination, unjustified limitation of religious freedom, oppression also on the level of civil freedom in regard to the Jews were, from an objective point of view, gravely deplorable manifestations. Yes, once again, through myself, the Church, in the words of the well-known declaration *Nostra Aetate* [4], "deplores the hatred, persecutions, and displays of anti-Semitism directed against the Jews at any time and by anyone." I repeat: "by anyone."

I would like once more to express a word of abhorrence for the genocide decreed against the Jewish people during the last war, which led to the *Holocaust* of millions of innocent victims.

When I visited in June 1979, the concentration camp at Auschwitz and prayed for the many victims from various nations, I paused in particular before the memorial stone with the inscription in Hebrew and thus manifested the sentiments of my heart: "This inscription stirs the memory of the people whose sons and daughters were destined to total extermination. This people has its origin in Abraham, who is our father in faith [cf. Rom. 4:12], as Paul of Tarsus expressed it. Precisely this people, which received from God the commandment, "Thou shalt not kill," has experienced in itself to a particular degree what killing means. Before this inscription it is not permissible for anyone to pass by with indifference" [*Insegnamenti*, 1979, p. 1484].

The Jewish community of Rome, too, paid a high price in blood.

And it was surely a significant gesture that in those dark years of racial persecution the doors of our religious houses, of our churches, of the Roman seminary, of buildings belonging to the Holy See and of Vatican City itself were thrown open to offer refuge and safety to so many Jews of Rome being hunted by their persecutors.

4. Today's visit is meant to make a decisive contribution to the consolidation of the good relations between our two communities, in imitation of the example of so many men and women who have worked and who are still working today, on both sides, to overcome old prejudices and to secure ever wider and fuller recognition of that "bond" and that "common spiritual patrimony" that exists between Jews and Christians.

This is the hope expressed in the fourth paragraph of the Council's declaration *Nostra Aetate*, which I have just mentioned, on the relationship of the Church to non-Christian religions. The decisive turning-point in relations between the Catholic Church and Judaism, and with individual Jews, was occasioned by this brief but incisive paragraph.

We are all aware that, among the riches of this paragraph number four of *Nostra Aetate, three points* are especially relevant. I would like to underline them here, before you today, in this truly unique circumstance.

The *first* is that the Church of Christ discovers her "bond" with Judaism by "searching into her own mystery" [cf. *Nostra Aetate*, ibid.] The Jewish religion is not "extrinsic" to us, but in a certain way is "intrinsic" to our own religion. With Judaism, therefore, we have a relationship which we do not have with any other religion. You are our dearly beloved brothers and, in a certain way, it could be said that you are our elder brothers.

The *second* point noted by the Council is that no ancestral or collective blame can be imputed to the Jews as a people for "what happened in Christ's passion" [cf. *Nostra Aetate*, ibid.]—not indiscriminately to the Jews of that time, nor to those who came afterwards, nor to those of today. So any alleged theological justification for discriminatory measures or, worse still, for acts of persecution, is unfounded. The Lord will judge each one "according to his own works," Jews and Christians alike [cf. Rom. 2:6].

The *third* point that I would like to emphasize in the Council's declaration is a consequence of the second. Notwithstanding the

Church's awareness of her own identity, it is not lawful to say that the Jews are "repudiated or cursed," as if this were taught or could be deduced from the sacred Scriptures of the Old or the New Testament [cf. *Nostra Aetate*, ibid.] Indeed, the Council had already said in this same text of *Nostra Aetate*, and also in the dogmatic constitution *Lumen Gentium* [16], referring to St. Paul in the Letter to the Romans [11:28–29], that the Jews are beloved of God, who has called them with an irrevocable calling.

5. On these convictions rest our present relations. On the occasion of this visit to your synagogue, I wish to reaffirm them and to proclaim them in their perennial value.

For this is the meaning which is to be attributed to my visit to you, to the Jews of Rome.

It is not of course because the differences between us have now been overcome that I have come among you. We know well that this is not so.

First of all, each of our religions, in the full awareness of the many bonds which unite them to each other, and in the first place that "bond" which the Council spoke of, wishes to be recognized and respected in its own identity, beyond any syncretism and any ambiguous appropriation.

Furthermore, it is necessary to say that the path undertaken is still at the beginning, and therefore a considerable amount of time will still be needed, notwithstanding the great efforts already made on both sides, to remove all forms of prejudice, even subtle ones, to readjust every manner of self-expression, and therefore to present always and everywhere, to ourselves and to others, the true face of the Jews and of Judaism, as likewise of Christians and of Christianity, and this at every level of outlook, teaching, and communication.

In this regard, I would like to remind my brothers and sisters of the Catholic Church, also those living in Rome, of the fact that the guidelines for implementing the Council in this precise field are already available to everyone in the two documents published respectively in 1974 and in 1985 by the Holy See's Commission for Religious Relations with the Jews. It is only a question of studying them carefully, of immersing oneself in their teachings, and of putting them into practice.

Perhaps there still remain between us difficulties of the practical order waiting to be overcome on the level of fraternal relations; these are the result of centuries of mutual misunderstanding, and also of different positions and attitudes, not easily settled, in complex and important matters.

No one is unaware that the fundamental difference from the very beginning has been the attachment of us Catholics to the person and teaching of Jesus of Nazareth, a son of your people . . . from which were also born the Virgin Mary, the apostles who were the "foundations and pillars of the Church," and the greater part of the first Christian community. But this attachment is located in the order of faith, that is to say, in the free assent of the mind and heart guided by the Spirit, and it can never be the object of exterior pressure, in one sense or the other. This is the reason why we wish to deepen dialogue in loyalty and friendship, in respect for one another's intimate convictions, taking as a fundamental basis the elements of the revelation which we have in common, as a "great spiritual patrimony" [cf. *Nostra Aetate*, 4].

6. It must be said, then, that the ways opened for our collaboration, in the light of our common heritage drawn from the Law and the Prophets, are various and important. We wish to recall first of all a collaboration in favor of man, his life from conception until natural death, his dignity, his freedom, his rights, his self-development in a society which is not hostile but friendly and favorable, where justice reigns and where, in this nation, on the various continents and throughout the world, it is peace that rules, the *shalom* hoped for by the lawmakers, Prophets, and wise men of Israel.

More in general, there is the problem of morality, the great field of individual and social ethics. We are all aware of how acute the crisis is on this point in the age in which we are living. In a society which is often lost in agnosticism and individualism and which is suffering the bitter consequences of selfishness and violence, Jews and Christians are the trustees and witnesses of an ethic marked by the Ten Commandments, in the observance of which man finds his truth and freedom. To promote a common reflection and collaboration on this point is one of the great duties of the hour.

And finally I wish to address a thought to this city in which there live side by side the Catholic community with its bishop, and the Jewish community with its authorities and its chief rabbi.

Let this not be a mere "coexistence," a kind of juxtaposition, interspersed with limited and occasional meetings, but let it be animated by fraternal love.

7. The problems of Rome are many. You know this well. Each one of us, in the light of that blessed heritage to which I alluded earlier, is conscious of an obligation to work together, at least to some degree, for their solution. Let us seek, as far as possible, to do so together. From this visit of mine and from the harmony and serenity which we have attained may there flow forth a fresh and health-giving spring like the river that Ezekiel saw gushing from the eastern gate of the Temple of Jerusalem [cf. Ezek. 47:1 ff.], which will help to heal the wounds from which Rome is suffering.

In doing this, I venture to say, we shall each be faithful to our most sacred commitments, and also to that which most profoundly unites and gathers us together: faith in the One God who "loves strangers" and "renders justice to the orphan and the widow" [cf. Deut. 10:18], commanding us, too, to love and help them [cf. ibid, and Lev. 19:18, 34]. Christians have learned this desire of the Lord from the Torah, which you here venerate, and from Jesus, who took to its extreme consequences the love demanded by the Torah.

8. All that remains for me now, as at the beginning of my address, is to turn my eyes and my mind to the Lord, to thank him and praise him for this joyful meeting and for the good things which are already flowing from it, for the rediscovered brotherhood and for the new and more profound understanding between us here in Rome, and between the Church and Judaism everywhere, in every country, for the benefit of all.

Therefore I would like to say with the Psalmist, in his original language which is also your own inheritance:

hodû la Adonai ki tob
ki le olam hasdô
yomar-na Yisrael
ki le olam hasdô
yomerû-na jir'è Adonai
ki le olam hasdô [Ps. 118:1–2, 4].

O give thanks to the Lord for he is good,
his steadfast love endures for ever!
Let Israel say,
"His steadfast love endures for ever."
Let those who fear the Lord say,
"His steadfast love endures for ever."
Amen.

Address by Chief Rabbi Elio Toaff

Your Holiness:

As the chief rabbi of this community, whose history goes back thousands of years, I wish to express to you my intense satisfaction at the gesture you have wished to carry out today, visiting a synagogue for the first time in the history of the Church. This gesture is destined to be remembered throughout history. It shows itself linked with the enlightened teaching of your illustrious predecessor, John XXIII, who, one Sabbath morning, became the first pope to stop and bless the Jews of Rome who were leaving this temple after prayer, and it follows the path marked out by the Second Vatican Council, which, with the declaration *Nostra Aetate*, produced that revolution in relations between the Church and Judaism that has made today's visit possible.

We thus find ourselves before a true turning point in Church policy. The Church now looks upon the Jews with sentiments of esteem and appreciation, abandoning that teaching of disdain whose inadmissibility Jules Isaac—may he be remembered here in blessing—brought to the attention of Pope John.

At this historic moment, my thoughts turn with admiration, gratitude, and mourning to the infinite number of Jewish martyrs who serenely faced death for the sanctification of God's name. Theirs is the merit if our faith has never wavered and if fidelity to the Lord and his Law has not failed in the long course of the centuries. Thanks to them, the Jewish people lives still, the only surviving people from antiquity.

Thus, we cannot forget the past, but today we wish to begin, with faith and hope, this new historical phase, which fruitfully points the way to common undertakings finally carried out on a plane of equality and mutual esteem in the interest of all humanity.

We propose to spread the idea of the spiritual and moral monotheism of Israel in order to bring together mankind and the universe in the love, the power and the justice of God, who is the God of all, and to bring light to the minds and hearts of all men, so as to cause order, morality, goodness, harmony, and peace to flourish in the world.

At the same time, we reaffirm God's universal fatherhood over all men, taking our inspiration from the Prophets, who taught it as that filial love which joins all living beings to the maternal womb of the infinite as to their natural matrix. It is therefore man who must be taken into consideration; man, who was created by God in his image and likeness, with the aim of conferring upon him a dignity and nobility that he can maintain only if he wills to follow the Father's teaching. It is written in Deuteronomy, "You are children of the Lord your God," in order to indicate the relationship that must join men to their Creator, a relationship of Father and child, of love and benevolent indulgence, but also a relationship of brotherhood which must reign among all human beings. If this truly existed, we would not today have to struggle against the terrorism and twisted acts of violence that reap so many innocent victims— men, women, the elderly, and children—as happened not long ago even at the threshold of this temple.

Our common task in society should therefore be that of teaching our fellow man the duty of mutual respect, showing the iniquity of the evils afflicting the world; such as terrorism, which is the exaltation of blind and inhuman violence, and which strikes out against defenseless people, including Jews in every country, simply because they are Jews; likewise, anti-Semitism and racism, which we vainly felt to be forever vanquished after the last world war.

The condemnation that the Council pronounced against every form of anti-Semitism should be rigorously applied, as well as the condemnation of all violence, in order to keep all mankind from drowning in corruption, immorality, and injustice.

The invitation that we read in the book of Leviticus—"I am the Lord your God; sanctify yourselves, be holy, because I am Holy"—is meant to be an exhortation to imitate the holiness of the Lord in our lives.

In this way, the image of God in potency in man from the first moment of his creation becomes the image of God in act. The *Kedoshim Tiiyu* is the imitation on the part of man of what are called the "Ways of the Lord."

In this way, by seeking to subject all their actions to the spirit, man gives the spirit dominion over material reality.

The reward for this kind of conduct is great, and God already revealed this to Abraham when he brought him out to gaze at the sky on a starry night: "I am the Lord who brought you out of Ur Casdim in order to give you possession of this land." The possession of the promised land is obtained as a reward for having followed the ways of the Lord, and the end of days will come when the people have returned there.

This return is being realized: Those who escaped from the Nazi death camps have found in the land of Israel a refuge and a new life in regained liberty and dignity. It is for this reason that their return has been called by our teachers "the beginning of the coming of final redemption—*Reshit tzemihat geulatenu.*"

The return of the Jewish people to its land must be recognized as a good and an inalienable gain for the world, because it constitutes the prelude—according to the teachings of the Prophets—to that epoch of universal brotherhood to which we all aspire, and to that redemptive peace that finds its sure promise in the Bible. The recognition of Israel's irreplaceable role in the final plan of redemption that God has promised us cannot be denied.

We will thus be able to strive together to affirm man's right to freedom, a complete freedom that encounters an inviolable boundary only when it infringes upon or limits the freedom of others. Man is born free, is free by nature; thus all men, no matter to what people they belong, must be equally free, because all have the same dignity and participate in the same rights. There are no men who can consider themselves superior and others inferior, because there is in everyone that divine spark that makes them equal.

Yet even in our own day, there are still countries in the world where freedom is limited and discrimination and alienation are practiced without any hesitation. I am referring in particular to blacks in South Africa, and, as far as freedom of religion is concerned, to Jews and Catholics in the Soviet Union. Our common task ought to be that of proclaiming the fact that from man's fundamental freedom there arise inalienable human rights: like the right to life, to freedom of thought, conscience, and religion.

The right to life must be understood not only as the right to exist, but to see one's life guaranteed, from its birth, to see one's existence assured against every threat, every violence; it means a guarantee of the means of subsistence through a more equitable distribution of wealth, so that there are no longer people dying of hunger in the world. It means the right of each person to see his honor, his good name, safeguarded against calumny and prejudice, including that of a religious nature. It means the condemnation of every attack on a person's self-respect, considered by Judaism to be equivalent to bloodshed. It means to fight against falsehood because of the disastrous consequences it can have on society, and against hate, which provokes violence and is considered by Judaism the same as hate of the Lord, of whom man is the image.

Freedom of thought also includes freedom of conscience and religious freedom. We have to strive with all our power in order to prevent man even today from being persecuted or condemned for the ideas he professes or for his religious convictions.

The concept of freedom—as we see—is a composite one, and if one of its components is suppressed, it is inevitable that sooner or later the whole complex reality of freedom will be lost, because it is a unity that has an absolute and indivisible value. It is an ideal in and of itself, one of the objects of that reign of universal justice preached in the Bible, by virtue of which men and peoples have the inalienable right to be their own masters.

Your Holiness, at this very important moment in the history of relations between our two religions, as our hearts open to the hope that the misfortunes of the past might be replaced by a fruitful dialogue that—even while respecting our existing differences—might give us the possibility of a concordant activity, of sincere and honest cooperation toward the realization of those universal ends that are found in our common roots, allow me to conclude my reflections with the words of the Prophet Isaiah: "I will greatly rejoice in the Lord, my soul shall exult in my God; for he has clothed me with the garments of salvation, he has covered me with the robe of righteousness, as a bridegroom decks himself with a garland, and as a bride adorns herself with her jewels. For as the earth brings forth its shoots, and as a garden causes what is sown in it to spring up, so the Lord God will cause righteousness and praise to spring forth before all the nations" [Isa. 61:10–11].

Address by Prof. Giacomo Saban

The president of the Jewish Community of Rome greeted the Holy Father with the following words:

Your Holiness:

I have the honor of being the first to welcome you to this major temple on the banks of the Tiber. I greet you on behalf of the most ancient Jewish community of the Diaspora, a community that I have been given the privilege of serving. In expressing our satisfaction at seeing a Roman pontiff for the first time cross the threshold of a synagogue, I feel it my duty to recount briefly the history of the Jewish community of this city, a history which goes back several thousand years.

Having settled on the banks of the Tiber almost two centuries prior to the destruction of the Second Temple, the fathers of the Jews who lived in Rome for centuries lived here as free Roman citizens. They wept, together with the multitude, over the mortal remains of Caesar; they applauded, together with the delirious populace, the triumph of Augustus. They were not spared, however, during the reigns of less glorious emperors, suffering, together with the rest of the inhabitants of Rome, from their wickedness and tyranny.

Their number grew with the arrival of the prisoners of the Jewish wars, and—at first slaves, but then quickly freed—they enjoyed a relatively tranquil life. Witness to this fact is a stone tablet between the fourth and the fifth mile of the ancient Appian Way. . . . But I am here speaking of the majority, because there were also those who came to Rome to ascend the glorious stairway of martyrdom, and the names of some of these are inscribed in the lists of the Mamertine Prison, from Aristobulus, son of Herod the Great, the victim of dark political designs, to Simon bar Ghiora, who fought relentlessly for our people's freedom.

Contrary to the legislation of Augustus Caesar, which, inscribed in bronze tablets and hung in the forums of the principal cities of the Empire, safeguarded the rights of our ancestors, the Theodosian Code limited their freedom, activity, and development. Nonetheless, they remained—faithful to the city—perhaps the only constant component in the mosaic of populations that converged on Rome from throughout the Empire. Nor did their life consist only of trade and commerce; our commentators speak of flourishing rabbinical academies, and many inscriptions in the catacombs witness to the fact that they constituted an inviting center of spirituality and a source of pure monotheistic faith in the midst of a world in which paganism was moving toward its extinction.

The dark centuries which followed and which saw, together with the end of the Western Empire, the decline of the city, were borne by this community with serene courage. Shortly after the end of the first millennium, when the temporal power of the popes was being consolidated, a son of this community, Nathan ben Jechiel Anav, whose house is found in Travestevere, not far from here, wrote in Rome the *Arukh*, the first normative compendium of the Judaism of the Diaspora.

This community escaped the massacres that were inflicted upon Judaism on the other side of the Alps by croziers and crusades; it did not, however, remain indifferent to the lot of those brothers in the faith, as is documented by the ancient funerary liturgy still in use among the Jews of Rome.

The first centuries after the year 1000 were difficult and painful for both the Jews and the rest of the population of Rome. Relations with the ruling power went through alternating phases, and violent acts were inflicted upon this community in the persons of its teachers. But those were the years in which Dante showed his appreciation of Immanuel Romano, who entered the world of Italian literature, bringing his meter, style, and same poetic structures into Jewish literature.

The year 1492 saw the community grow with the arrival of refugees from Spain, and the liberal attitude of the pope assured them a haven in this city.

In the following half-century, the situation was to change radically. In September of 1553, hundreds of copies of the Talmud were burned not far from here, in Campo di Fiori, and this blaze, which was not the first, would be reignited more than once in subsequent centuries. After the accession of Paul IV, with the bull *Cum nimis absurdum* . . . of July 14, 1555, the ghetto of Rome was established precisely where we find ourselves today. The measures introduced, harshly restrictive with regard to study and worship, as well as normal everyday activities, reduced the inhabitants of the ghetto to economic and cultural misery, depriving them of some of their most fundamental rights.

Limitations of every sort and lack of freedom were thus the lot reserved to Roman Jews for a period of more than three centuries. It was only 115 years ago that this complex of restrictions, enslavement, and humiliations came to cease, and not without some very sad last eruptions, such as the *Caso Mortara*. . . .

It took more than sixty years for the community of Rome to begin to refashion a normal existence worthy of the position that it occupies in the framework of Italian Judaism, both in terms of number and historical tradition. This process was cruelly cut short by the events immediately preceding the Second World War, with persecutions which were much more horrible in that they aimed at the complete annihilation of Judaism worldwide.

It does not fall to us to judge what took place in Rome during those years, as we are too near in time to those days. What was taking place on one of the banks of the Tiber could not have been unknown on the other side of the river, nor could what was happening elsewhere on the European continent. Nonetheless, many of our brethren found help and refuge through courageous initiatives precisely within those convents and monasteries that they had learned to fear for so many centuries.

An apostolic nuncio who would be called to the papacy fifteen years later was not ignorant of the misdeeds that were being carried out in those days in the heart of our continent.

That pope, John XXIII, wished to see the development of a spirituality suited to the tormented world that was finally experiencing the healing of the atrocious wounds of the war. With the Second Vatican Council he wished to give the Church an opportunity to begin anew to mediate upon fundamental values. *Nostra Aetate*, that Council document which most relates to us, introduces a different relationship between the faith of Israel and that of the surrounding world, restoring to us not only what for centuries we had been denied, but also the dignity that it had always been our right to see recognized.

The work of that "just man" has always had our praise and total appreciation; that work has been eminently carried on by his successors. That work must continue. The efforts of men of goodwill must in fact tend toward greater understanding of peoples, fully respecting their diversity. It is in this context that I feel I must manifest the aspiration to see abandoned certain reticence regarding the State of Israel. The land of Israel has a role that is central, emotionally and spiritually, in the heart of every Jew, and a change of attitude in its regard would gratify not only those present here, but Judaism worldwide. It would also, in my opinion, make a real contribution to the pacification of a region of the world that today presents threats and perils to the entire Western world.

This would be a further step, then, in the "fraternal dialogue" of which *Nostra Aetate* speaks. I do not hesitate to believe that this step will be taken. Today's visit, Your Holiness, that you have held to be opportune—I would even say necessary—is a lively testimony to the spirit of the Council. It fills us all with joy, inasmuch as it is a sign which foreshadows better days, days in which all those who believe in the One God—may His Holy Name be blessed—will be able, united, to contribute to the creation of a better world.

"Relations with Non-Christian Religions" at General Audience

June 5, 1986

At the general audience in St. Peter's Square on Wednesday, June 5, the Holy Father resumed his series of talks on faith and revelation after a reading from the Book of Revelation [21:23–26]. While speaking of non-Christian religions in general, the pope singled out the Church's "special relationship" with the Jewish people. The pertinent section, 6, follows:

6. A special relationship—with non-Christian religions—is the one that the Church has with those who profess faith in the Old Testament, the heirs of the patriarchs and Prophets of Israel. The Council in fact recalls "the spiritual bond linking the people of the New Covenant with Abraham's stock" [*Nostra Aetate*, 4].

This bond, to which we have already referred in the catechesis dedicated to the Old Testament, and which brings us close to the Jews, is again emphasized by the declaration *Nostra Aetate* when it refers to those common beginnings of faith, which are found in the patriarchs, Moses, and the Prophets. The Church "professes that all who believe in Christ, Abraham's sons according to faith, are included in the same patriarch's call . . . the Church cannot forget that she received the revelation of the Old Testament through the people with whom God in his inexpressible mercy designed to establish the ancient Covenant" [*Nostra Aetate*, 4], From this same people comes "Christ in his human origins" [Rom. 9:5], son of the Virgin Mary, as also his apostles are its sons.

All this spiritual heritage, common to Christians and Jews, constitutes an organic foundation for a mutual relationship, even though a great part of the children of Israel "did not accept the Gospel." Nevertheless the Church [together with the Prophets and the apostle Paul] "awaits the day, known to God alone, on which all peoples will address the Lord in a single voice and 'serve him with one accord" [Zeph. 3:9; *Nostra Aetate*, 4].

Pastoral Visit to France

October 7, 1986

Address to the Jewish Community of Lyons

After the discourse of the chief rabbi of Lyons, the Holy Father responded in this way:

Mr. Chief Rabbi, Friends:

It is a joy to meet with you on the day following the feast of *Rosh ha-Shanah* and to extend to you, as well as to the whole Jewish community of Lyons and of this region, my best wishes. May God, the Father of all humankind, fill you with his abundant blessings.

During these days in which I am visiting the Catholic community of this region, our brief meeting is intended to be a sign of the esteem and respect that we have for one another. The sincere and fraternal dialogue between us, as well as our collaboration on behalf of humankind and of society, have as their fundamental basis a certain number of elements of revelation that we have in common and which the conciliar decree *Nostra Aetate* recognizes as a "great spiritual patrimony." In recent years, the relations between our two religions have clearly improved. We owe this change in great part to gestures of generosity and of friendship on the part of those who have known how to overcome prejudices or ignorance, pledging themselves to the way of fraternal love. I know that the history of the relations between Jews and Christians in Lyons and in this region does not lack examples of this kind. And I know that today, in this place, such relationships will deepen in regard to the deepest convictions of both communities, and in looking to do God's will. I therefore give thanks to the Lord.

"Not to us, Lord, not to us, but to your name be the glory, for your faithfulness and for your love" [Ps. 115:1].

"Give thanks to the Lord for he is good, and his mercy endures forever" [Ps. 107:1].

Assisi: World Day of Prayer for Peace with Representatives of Churches and Ecclesial Communities and of World Religions, at the Invitation of Pope John Paul II

October 27, 1986

The Jewish Prayer for Peace: Rabbi Elio Toaff, Chief Rabbi of Rome

Our God in heaven, the Lord of Peace will have compassion and mercy upon us and upon the peoples of the earth who implore his mercy and his compassion, asking for peace, seeking peace.

Our God in Heaven gives us the strength to act, to work, and to live until the spirit from above manifests itself upon us, and the desert becomes a vineyard, and the vineyard is seen as a forest.

Justice will have a home in the desert, and charity will have a dwelling in the vineyard. The action of justice will produce peace, and the work of justice will yield tranquility and security forever. And my people will be surrounded by peace, in safe dwellings, and in places of repose undisturbed.

And so, O Lord our God and God of our fathers, bring to fulfillment for us and for all the world the promise you made through the prophet Micah: "It shall come to pass in the latter days that the mountain of the house of the Lord shall be established as the highest of the mountains, and shall be raised up above the hills; and peoples shall flow to it, and many nations shall come, and say:

'Come, let us go up to the mountain of the Lord, to the house of the God of Jacob, that he may teach us his ways and we may walk in his paths.' For out of Zion shall go forth the Law, and the word of the Lord from Jerusalem. He shall judge between many peoples, and shall decide for strong nations afar off, and they shall beat their swords into ploughshares, and their spears into pruning hooks; nation shall not lift up sword against nation, neither shall they learn war any more; but they shall sit every man under his vine and under his fig tree, and none shall make them afraid; for the mouth of the Lord of hosts has spoken."

O Lord in heaven, give peace to the earth, give well-being to the world, establish tranquility in our dwellings.

And let us say Amen!

Final Allocution by Pope John Paul II

My Brothers and Sisters,
Heads and Representatives of the Christian Churches and Ecclesial
Communities and of the World Religions.
Dear Friends:

1. In concluding this World Day of Prayer for Peace, to which you have come from many parts of the world, kindly accepting my invitation, I would like now to express my feelings, as a brother and friend, but also as a believer in Jesus Christ, and, in the Catholic Church, the first witness of faith in him.

2. It is, in fact, my faith conviction which has made me turn to you, representatives of the Christian churches and ecclesial communities and world religions, in deep love and respect.

With the other Christians we share many convictions and, particularly, in what concerns peace.

With the world religions we share a common respect of and obedience to conscience, which teaches all of us to seek the truth, to love and serve all individuals and peoples, and therefore to make peace among individuals and among nations.

Yes, we all hold conscience and obedience to the voice of conscience to be an essential element in the road toward a better and peaceful world.

Could it be otherwise, since all men and women in this world have a common nature, a common origin, and a common destiny?

If there are many and important differences among us, there is also a common ground, whence to operate together in the solution of this dramatic challenge of our age; true peace or catastrophic war.

3. Yes, there is the dimension of prayer, which in the very real diversity of religions tries to express communication with a power above all our human forces.

Peace depends basically on this power, which we call God, and as Christians believe, has revealed himself in Christ.

This is the meaning of this World Day of Prayer.

For the first time in history, we have come together from everywhere, Christian churches and ecclesial communities, and world religions, in this sacred placed dedicated to Saint Francis, to witness before the world, each according to his own conviction, about the transcendent quality of peace.

The form and content of our prayers are very different, as we have seen, and there can be no question of reducing them to a kind of common denominator.

4. Yet, in this very difference we have perhaps discovered anew that, regarding the problem of peace and its relation to religious commitment, there is something which binds us together.

The challenge of peace, as it is presently posed to every human conscience, is the problem of a reasonable quality of life for all, the problem of survival for humanity, the problem of life and death.

In the face of such a problem, two things seem to have supreme importance and both of them are common to us all.

The first is the inner imperative of the moral conscience, which enjoins us to respect, protect, and promote human life, from the womb to the deathbed, for individuals and peoples, but especially for the weak, the destitute, the derelict: the imperative to overcome selfishness, greed, and the spirit of vengeance.

The second common thing is the conviction that peace goes much beyond human efforts, particularly in the present plight of the world, and therefore that its source and realization is to be sought in that reality beyond all of us.

This is why each of us prays for peace. Even if we think, as we do, that the relation between that reality and the gift of peace is a different one, according to our respective religious convictions, we all affirm that such a relation exists.

This is what we express by praying for it.

I humbly repeat here my own conviction: Peace bears the name of Jesus Christ.

5. But, at the same time and in the same breath, I am ready to acknowledge that Catholics have not always been faithful to this affirmation of faith. We have not been always "peace-makers."

For ourselves, therefore, but also perhaps, in a sense, for all, this encounter at Assisi is an act of *penance*. We have prayed, each in his own way, we have fasted, we have marched together.

In this way we have tried to open our hearts to the divine reality beyond us and to our fellow men and women.

Yes, while we have *fasted*, we have kept in mind the sufferings which senseless wars have brought about and are still bringing about on humanity. Thereby we have tried to be spiritually close to the millions who are the victims of hunger throughout the world.

While we *have walked* in silence, we have reflected on the past our human family treads: either in hostility, if we fail to accept one another in love; or as a common journey to our lofty destiny, if we realize that other people are our brothers and sisters. The very fact that we have come to Assisi from various quarters of the world is in itself a sign of this common path which humanity is called to tread. Either we learn to walk together in peace and harmony, or we drift apart and ruin ourselves and others. We hope that this pilgrimage to Assisi has taught us anew to be aware of the common origin and common destiny of humanity. Let us see in it an anticipation of what God would like the developing history of humanity to be: a fraternal journey in which we accompany one another toward the transcendent goal which he sets for us.

Prayer, fasting, pilgrimage.

6. This day at Assisi has helped us become more aware of our religious commitments. But it has also made the world, looking at us through the media, more aware of the responsibility of each religion regarding problems of war and peace.

More perhaps than ever before in history, the intrinsic link between an authentic religious attitude and the great good of peace has become evident to all.

What a tremendous weight for human shoulders to carry! But at the same time what a marvelous, exhilarating call to follow.

Although prayer is in itself action, this does not excuse us from working for peace. Here we are acting as the heralds of the moral awareness of humanity as such, humanity that wants peace, needs peace.

Second Angelicum Colloquium

November 6, 1986

The second international Catholic-Jewish scholars' colloquium, like the first, was held at the Pontifical University of St. Thomas Aquinas (the Angelicum). The pope's statement lists the sponsors of both colloquia. There follows here the statement of Nathan Perlmutter, director of the Anti-Defamation League, and then the response and welcoming statement of the pope during his audience with the participants.

Statement of Nathan Perlmutter

Your Holiness:

We are deeply honored to again visit with you as we did when the Anti-Defamation League joined with institutions of the Church in the commemoration of the twentieth anniversary of *Nostra Aetate*.

As you know so well, modernity brings its complex challenges to individuals and to their institutions. And the Church and its children, the Synagogue and its children strive to meet these challenges. We strive to retain what has served our ancestors so well and to fashion continuity for our future generations.

The Church stands tall and proud on the foundation of faith and tradition. And you, Your Holiness, have served as its loving and inspired leader.

So, too, have Jews cherished faith and tradition. Central to Judaism is God, Torah, and Israel, the land and its people. It has been central to our past, inextricably interwoven with our future.

To profess caring concern for Catholicism without respect for its faith and tradition is to love it less. So, too, Jews look to their neighbors' approbation for the bedrock of their faith, Jerusalem as the spiritual and recognized capital of Israel.

Your Holiness, we in ADL were deeply honored to be represented in your Day of Prayer, and Day of Peace in Assisi. How appropriate Assisi, rich in the tradition of St. Francis. Where armies have failed to bring about peace, perhaps in your example, prayer and love will facilitate peace.

The world continues to be beset by acts of terrorism, and Your Holiness knows the ravages only too well. Perhaps what is needed in addition to a Day of Prayer for Peace, is a day in which we contemplate the evil of terrorism, and as the site for such prayers against the scourge of terrorism and war, where more appropriate than in the City of Peace, Jerusalem? And personally led by whom, more appropriately, than by your prophetic voice of peace.

Response of the Pope

Dear Friends:

1. I am very happy to welcome you on the occasion of your Second International Catholic-Jewish Theological Colloquium. In 1985, the theological faculty of the Pontifical University of St. Thomas Aquinas, the Anti-Defamation League, the *Centra Pro Unione*, and the *Service de Documentation Judéo-Chrétienne* [SIDIC], in cooperation with the Holy See's Commission for Religious Relations with

the Jews, opened this series of theological research in commemoration of the twentieth anniversary of the conciliar declaration *Nostra Aetate*. According to the spirit and the perspectives of the Council, the topic chosen for your second colloquium, which has now come to an end, is: *Salvation and Redemption in the Jewish and Christian Theological Traditions and in Contemporary Theology.*

2. Contemplation of the mystery of universal redemption inspired the Prophet Isaiah to wonder: "Who has directed the Spirit of the Lord, or as his counsellor has instructed him? Whom did he consult for his enlightenment, and who taught him the path of justice, and taught him knowledge, and showed him the way of understanding?" [Isa. 40:13–14; cf. Rom. 11:34]. We are hereby invited to receive with humble docility the mystery of the love of God, Father and Redeemer, and to contemplate it in our heart [cf. Luke 2:51] in order to express it in our works and in our praise.

Theological reflection is part of the proper response of human intelligence and so gives witness to our conscious acceptance of God's gift. At the same time, the other human sciences, such as history, philosophy, and art, also offer their own contribution to an organic deepening of our faith. This is why both the Jewish and Christian traditions have always had such high appreciation for religious study. Honoring our respective traditions, theological dialogue based on sincere esteem can contribute greatly to mutual knowledge of our respective patrimonies of faith and can help us to be more aware of our links with one another in terms of our understanding of salvation.

3. Your colloquium can help to avoid the misunderstanding of syncretism, the confusion of one another's identities as believers, the shadow and suspicion of proselytism. You are effectively carrying out the insights of the Second Vatican Council, which have also been the theme of subsequent documents of the Holy See's Commission for Religious Relations with the Jews.

This mutual effort will certainly deepen common commitment to the building of justice and peace among all people, children of the one heavenly Father. Let us, in this common hope for peace, confidently express our praise with the words of the psalm, inviting all people to pray: "Praise the Lord, all nations! Extol him, all peoples! For great is his steadfast love toward us, and the faithfulness of the Lord endures forever. *Hallelû-Yah* [Psalm 117].

4. As I said recently in Assisi, Christians are convinced that in Jesus Christ, as Savior of all, true peace is to be found, "peace to those who are far off and peace to those who are near" [Eph. 2:17; cf. Isa. 57:19; 52:7; Zech. 9:10]. This universal gift has its origins in the call directed to Abraham, Isaac, and Jacob, and it finds its fulfillment in Jesus Christ, who was obedient to the Father even unto death on the cross [cf. Matt. 5:17; Phil. 2:8]. Whereas faith in Jesus Christ distinguishes and separates us from our Jewish brothers and sisters, we can at the same time affirm with profound conviction "the spiritual bond linking the people of the New Covenant with Abraham's stock" [*Nostra Aetate*, 4]. Thus, we have here a bond which, notwithstanding our differences, makes us brethren; it is an unfathomable mystery of grace which we dare to scrutinize in confidence, grateful to a God who grants us to contemplate together his plan of salvation.

Grateful for every initiative promoting dialogue between Christians and Jews, and especially for this International Catholic—Jewish Theological Colloquium, I implore the blessing of Almighty God upon all of you and pray that your work will bear fruit for better understanding and increasing relations between Jews and Christians.

Pastoral Visit to Australia

November 26, 1986

Address to the Jewish Community

The attitude of Catholics toward the Jewish religion "should be one of the greatest respect," Pope John Paul II told Australia's Jewish leaders on November 26 in Sydney. For the Jewish people, "Catholics should have not only respect but also great fraternal love, for it is the teaching of both the Hebrew and the Christian Scriptures that the Jews are beloved of God, who has called them with an irrevocable calling." The pope said, "no valid theological justification could ever be found for acts of discrimination or persecution against Jews. In fact, such acts must be held to be sinful." The text of the pope's talk follows.

1. Earlier this year, I had the pleasure and privilege of visiting the Synagogue in Rome and of speaking with the rabbis and the assembled congregation. At that time, I gave "thanks and praise to the Lord, who stretched out the heavens and laid the foundation of the earth [cf. Isa. 51:16] and who chose Abraham in order to make him the father of a multitude of children, as numerous 'as the stars of heaven and as the sand which is on the seashore'" [Gen. 22:17; cf. Isa. 15:5].

I gave thanks and praise to Him because it had been His good pleasure, in the mystery of His providence, that the meeting was taking place. Today, I praise and thank Him again because He has brought me, in this great southern land, into the company of another group of Abraham's descendants, a group which is representative of many Jewish people in Australia. May he bless you and make you strong for his service!

2. It is my understanding that although the experience of Jews in Australia—an experience going right back to the beginning of white settlement in 1788—has not been without its measure of

sorrow, prejudice, and discrimination, it has included more civil and religious freedom than was to be found in many of the countries of the Old World. At the same time, this is still the century of the *Shoah*, the inhuman and ruthless attempt to exterminate European Jewry, and I know that Australia has given asylum and a new home to thousands of refugees and survivors from that ghastly series of events. To them in particular I say, as I said to your brothers and sisters, the Jews of Rome, "the Church, in the words of the well-known declaration *Nostra Aetate*, 'deplores the hatred, persecutions, and displays of anti-Semitism directed against the Jews at any time and by anyone.'"

3. My hope for this meeting is that it will help to consolidate and extend the improved relations you already have with members of the Catholic community in this country. I know that there are men and women throughout Australia, Jews and Catholics alike, who are working, as I stated at the synagogue in Rome, "to overcome old prejudices and to secure ever wider and fuller recognition of that 'bond' and that 'common spiritual patrimony' that exists between Jews and Christians." I give thanks to God for this.

4. Where Catholics are concerned, it will continue to be an explicit and very important part of my mission to repeat and emphasize that our attitude to the Jewish religion should be one of the greatest respect, since the Catholic faith is rooted in the eternal truths contained in the Hebrew Scriptures, and in the irrevocable covenant made with Abraham. We, too, gratefully hold these same truths of our Jewish heritage and look upon you as our brothers and sisters in the Lord.

For the Jewish people themselves, Catholics should have not only respect but also great fraternal love for it is the teaching of both the Hebrew and Christian Scriptures that the Jews are beloved of God, who has called them with an irrevocable calling. No valid theological justification could ever be found for acts of discrimination or persecution against Jews. In fact, such acts must be held to be sinful.

5. In order to be frank and sincere we must recognize the fact that there are still obvious differences between us in religious belief and practice. The most fundamental difference is in our respective

views on the person and work of Jesus of Nazareth. Nothing, however, prevents us from true and fraternal cooperation in many worthy enterprises, such as biblical studies and numerous works of justice and charity. Such combined undertakings can bring us ever closer together in friendship and trust.

Through the Law and the Prophets, we, like you, have been taught to put a high value on human life and on fundamental and inalienable human rights. Today, human life, which should be held sacred from the moment of conception, is being threatened in many different ways. Violations of human rights are widespread. This makes it all the more important for all people of goodwill to stand together to defend life, to defend the freedom of religious belief and practice, and to defend all other fundamental human freedoms.

6. Finally, I am sure we agree that in a secularized society there are many widely held values which we cannot accept. In particular, consumerism and materialism are often presented, especially to the young, as the answers to human problems. I express my admiration for your children in order to help them evaluate the world around them from the perspective of faith in God. As you know, Australian Catholics have done the same. In secularized society, such institutions are always likely to be attacked for one reason or another. Since Catholics and Jews value them for the same reasons, let us work together whenever possible in order to protect and promote the religious instruction of our children. In this way we can bear common witness to the Lord of all.

7. Mr. President and members of the Executive Council of Australian Jewry, I thank you once again for this meeting, and I give praise and thanks to the Lord in the words of the psalmist:

> *Praise the Lord, all nations!*
> *Extol him, all peoples!*
> *For great is his steadfast*
> *love toward us;*
> *And the faithfulness of the*
> *Lord endures forever.*
> *Praise the Lord! [Psalm 116]*

Looking Back: Assisi in Perspective

December 22, 1986

Christmas Address to Roman Curia

On Monday, December 22, the Holy Father received in audience the cardinals and members of the Roman Curia. The Christmas greetings of those present were conveyed by Cardinal Agnelo Rossi, dean of the College of Cardinals, to the pope, who then gave the following address.

1. It is with particular joy that I greet you in this traditional meeting which sees us gathered together to exchange with one another greetings for Christmas and for the New Year. I thank the new dean of the Sacred College of Cardinals for the noble words with which he has expressed the sentiments that are suggested by this occasion of family closeness.

In these days immediately preceding the great feast of Christmas, in which we both celebrate and recall the Word of God, life and light of men [cf. John 1:4], who for our sake "became flesh and came to dwell in our midst" [John 1:14], my spirit spontaneously relives with you, revered and dear brothers of the Roman Curia, what seems to have been the *religious event* that attracted the greatest attention in the world in this year which is drawing to its close: the World Day of Prayer for Peace at Assisi on October 27 last.

Indeed, on that day, and in the prayer which was its motivation and its entire content, there seemed for a moment to be even a visible expression of the hidden but radical unity which the divine Word, "in whom everything was created, and in whom everything exists" [Col.1:16; John 1:3], has established among the men and women of this world, both those who now share together the anxieties and the joys of this portion of the twentieth century, and those who have gone before us in history, and also those who will take up our places "until the Lord comes" [cf. 1 Cor. 11:26]. The fact that we came together in Assisi to pray, to fast, and to walk in silence—and this, in support of the peace which is always fragile and threatened, perhaps today more than ever—has been, as it were, a clear sign of the profound unity of those who seek in religion spiritual and transcendent values that respond to the great questions of the human heart, despite the concrete divisions [cf. *Nostra Aetate*, 1]. . . .

8. The source of inspiration, and the fundamental orientation, for such a commitment is always the mystery of unity, both the unity *already* attained in Christ through faith and baptism and the unity which is expressed in the condition of being "orientated" towards the people of God and hence is *still* to be attained perfectly.

Thus, as the first unity finds its adequate expression in the decree *Unitatis Redintegratio* on ecumenism, which continues to be valid, the second unity is formulated on the level of interreligious relationships and dialogue in the declaration *Nostra Aetate*. Both of these are to be read in the context of the constitution *Lumen Gentium*.

And it is within this second dimension—still somewhat novel, when compared with the first—that the Day of Assisi offers us precious elements for our reflection, elements that are illuminated by an attentive reading of this declaration on the non-Christian religions.

Here too, the Council speaks of the "one community" formed by people in this world [1] and explains this as the fruit of the "one origin" held in common, "because God made the entire human race dwell on all the face of the earth" [ibid.] so that the race might make toward "one single ultimate goal, God, whose providence, testimony of goodness, and plan of salvation include all persons, so that the elect may come together in the Holy City which will be lit up by the glory of God, and where the peoples will walk in his light" [ibid.]; in this endeavor, the Council wishes to see "a ray of truth that enlightens all men" [2]. And thus "the Catholic Church rejects nothing in these religions that is true and holy," and indeed "exhorts her children with prudence and charity . . . while always bearing witness to the Christian faith and life, to recognize, conserve, and promote the spiritual, moral, and social values that are found in them" [ibid.].

In doing this, the Church intends above all to recognize and respect that "orientation" to the people of God of which the constitution *Lumen Gentium* speaks [16], to which I have referred earlier. When the Church behaves in this way, she is aware that she follows a divine indication, because it is the Creator and Redeemer who, in his plan of love, has ordained this mysterious relationship between religious men and women and the unity of the people of God.

There is above all a relationship with the Hebrew people: "that people to whom we were given the covenants and the promises, and of whom Christ was born according to the flesh" [*Lumen Gentium*, 16], and who is united to us by a spiritual "bond" [cf. *Nostra Aetate*, 2]. There is also a relationship to "those who recognize the Creator, and among these in the first place are the Muslims who, professing to maintain the faith of Abraham, adore together with us a God who is unique and mysterious, and who will judge men on the last day" [*Lumen Gentium*, 16]. Furthermore, there is a relationship to those "who seek an unknown God in shadows and images," and from whom "God himself is not far off" [cf. *Lumen Gentium.*, 19].

9. The Day of Assisi, showing the Catholic Church holding the hands of brother Christians, and showing up all these joining hands with the brothers of the other religions, was a visible expression of these statements of the Second Vatican Council. With this day, and by means of it, we have succeeded, by the grace of God, in realizing this conviction of ours inculcated by the Council, about the unity of the origin and goal of the human family, and about the meaning and the value of the non-Christian religions—without the least shadow of confusion or syncretism.

Homily at Mass Marking the Close of the Year

December 31, 1986

During the homily the pope recalled his visit to the synagogue:

There is one other event which transcends the limits of the year, since it is measured in centuries and millennia in the history of this city and of this Church. *I thank Divine Providence* that I was able to visit our "elder brothers" in the faith of Abraham in their Roman synagogue! Blessed be the God of our fathers! The God of peace!

1987

Address to Diplomatic Corps Related to the Holy See

January 1, 1987

... During my visit to the Synagogue of Rome, I stressed that "Jews and Christians are the trustees and witnesses of an ethic marked by the Ten Commandments, in the observance of which man finds his truth and freedom" and also that "Jesus took to its extreme consequences the love demanded by the Torah."

Pastoral Visit to Argentina

April 9, 1987

Address to Jewish Representatives at Buenos Aires

Dear Representatives of the Jewish Community of Argentina:

First of all, I thank you for your presence here and for your desire to meet the pope on the occasion of his visit to this country, where your community is so active and numerous.

Meeting representatives of the Jewish community has been a frequent occurrence during my visits to different countries from the beginning of my pontificate. This is not just a casual meeting, nor is it a mere expression of an obligation of courtesy.

You know well that, since the Second Vatican Council and its declaration *Nostra Aetate* [4], the relations between the Catholic Church and Judaism have been built on a new foundation, which is in fact very old, since it refers to the closeness of our respective religions, united by what the Council precisely calls a spiritual "bond."

The years that followed, and the constant progress of the dialogue on both sides, have deepened even more the awareness of that "bond" and the need to strengthen it always through mutual knowledge, esteem, and the overcoming of the prejudices which succeeded in separating us in the past.

The universal Church, as well as the Church in Argentina, is committed to this great task of bringing us closer in fraternal friendship and collaboration in all the areas where this is possible.

From your part, I ask you to contribute, as you already do, to this openness and convergence, which will undoubtedly redound to the good of our respective religious communities, as well as the entire Argentinean society and of the men and women who compose it.

Peace be with you: *Shalom alehem.*

Thank you very much: *Todah rabab.*

Pastoral Visit to Germany

April 30, 1987

Address to the Central Committee of German Catholics

. . . As you are aware, my second pastoral visit to your country is connected with the beatifications of Sister Edith Stein and Father Rupert Mayer. We honor the courageous testimony for Christ and for selfless love of their fellow men manifested in the lives of these two saints. Edith Stein saw her being transported to Auschwitz as an expression of solidarity with the Jewish people, of which she was a member and with whom she felt connected right up to the moment of her agonizing death. She said to her sister: "Come, we will go for our people." Testimony for Christ and helping our fellow men are part and parcel of Christian life and closely connected with the Church's doctrine for salvation and all the elements of the Church.

May 1, 1987

Address to Members of the Jewish Central Council at Cologne

Gentlemen, dear Brothers:

1. I am filled with joy and gratitude for the chance to meet you again during my second pastoral visit to the Federal Republic of Germany. This meeting provides me with an opportunity to make special reference to the fact that today there are still Jewish communities in this country. The Vatican guidelines for a correct depiction of Jews and Jewry in the sermons and catechism of the Catholic Church [1985], which I highly recommend to all Catholics, call to mind Jewish history, the Diaspora, a phenomenon that has allowed

Israel to bear what has often been heroic testimony out into the entire world of its faithfulness to the One God [see VI, 25]. As early as antiquity, the Jews brought this witness of their faithfulness up to the Rhineland and established a strong and fertile culture.

2. My dear brothers, you are preserving a valuable historical and spiritual legacy in your communities today, and you continue to develop it. Furthermore, your communities are particularly significant in view of the attempt of the National Socialists in this country to exterminate the Jews and their culture. The existence of your communities is evidence of the fact that God, who is "the fountain of life" [Ps. 36:9], and whom the psalmist praises as "Lord, Father and Master of my life" [Sir. 23:1], does not allow the power of death to speak the last word. May the one benevolent and merciful Father of life watch over your communities and bless them, especially during the times you are assembled together to hear his holy word.

3. Today the Church is honoring a daughter of Israel who remained faithful, as a Jew, to the Jewish people, and, as a Catholic, to our crucified Lord Jesus Christ. Together with millions of fellow believers she endured humiliation and suffering culminating in the final brutal drama of extermination, the *Shoah*. In an act of heroic faith Edith Stein placed her life in the hands of a holy and just God, whose mysteries she had sought to understand better and to love throughout her entire life.

May the day of her beatification be a day for all of us to join together in praising God, who has done marvelous works through his saints and exalted himself through the people of Israel. Let us pause in reverent silence to reflect on the terrible consequences which can arise from a denial of God and from collective racial hatred. In this connection we recall the suffering of many peoples in Europe in recent times, and we declare our commitment to a common effort on the part of all people of goodwill to establish a new "civilization of love" here in Europe, inspired by the highest Jewish and Christian ideals. At the same time we must speak out when necessary, not lose sight of our examples, and remain alert for all new forms of anti-Semitism, racism, and neo-pagan religious persecution. Such a joint effort would be the most precious gift

Europe could give the world in its arduous effort to develop and attain justice.

4. By virtue of the life she lived, the blessed Edith Stein reminds us all, Jews and Christians alike, of the call of the Holy Scriptures: "You shall be holy because I am holy" [Lev. 11:45]. This summons to all of us also embraces a common responsibility to help build the "City of God," the city of God s peace. We spontaneously think of Jerusalem, the "City of Peace," of which the prophet Isaiah wrote: "Yes, the Lord shall comfort Zion and have pity on all her ruins; her deserts he shall make like Eden, her wasteland like the garden of the Lord; joy and gladness shall be found in her, thanksgiving and the sound of song" [Isa. 51:3]. With this hope for peace we entreat the Lord to show us the fullness of his merciful peace.

May 1, 1987

Homily at the Beatification of Edith Stein, Cologne

"There are the ones who have survived the great period of trial; they have washed their robes and made them white in the blood of the lamb." [Rev. 7:14].

1. Today we greet in profound honor and holy joy a daughter of the Jewish people, rich in wisdom and courage, among these blessed men and women. Having grown up in the strict traditions of Israel, and having lived a life of virtue and self-denial in a religious order, she demonstrated her heroic character on the way to the extermination camp. Unified with our crucified Lord, she gave her life "for genuine peace" and "for the people" [see *Edith Stein, Golden, Philosophin, Ordensfrau, Märtyrin*].

Cardinal, dear Brothers and Sisters:

Today's beatification marks the realization of a long-outstanding wish on the part of the Archdiocese of Cologne as well as on the part of many individuals and groups within the Church. Seven years ago, the members of the German Bishops' Conference sent a unanimous request for this beatification to the Holy See. Numerous bishops from other countries joined them in making this request.

As such, we are all greatly gratified that I am able to fulfil this wish today and can present Sister Teresa Benedicta of the Cross to the faithful on behalf of the Church as blessed in the glory of God. From this moment on we can honor her as a martyr and ask for her intercession at the throne of God. In this I would like to express congratulations to all, most of all to her fellow sisters in the order of Our Lady of Mount Carmel here in Cologne and in Echt, as well as in the entire order. The fact that Jewish brothers and sisters, relatives of Edith Stein's in particular, are present at this liturgical ceremony today fills us with great joy and gratitude.

2. "O Lord, manifest yourself in the time of our distress and give us courage." [Esther 4:17r]

The words of this call for help from the first reading of today's liturgy were spoken by Esther, a daughter of Israel, at the time of the Babylonian captivity. Her prayer, which she directs to the Lord God at a time when her people were exposed to a deadly threat, are profoundly moving:

"My Lord, our King, you alone are God. Help me, who am alone and have no help but you, for I am taking my life in my hand . . . you, O Lord, chose Israel from among all peoples . . . and our fathers from among all their ancestors as a lasting heritage . . . be mindful of us, O Lord. . . . Save us by your power." [Esther 4:17 1–t]

Esther's deathly fear arose when, under the influence of the mighty Haman, an archenemy of the Jews, the order for their destruction was given out in all of the Persian empire. With God's help and by sacrificing her own life, Esther rendered a key contribution towards saving her people.

3. Today's liturgy places this more than two-thousand-year-old prayer for help in the mouth of Edith Stein, a servant of God and a daughter of Israel in our century. This prayer became relevant again when here, in the heart of Europe, a new plan for the destruction of the Jews was laid out. An insane ideology decided on this plan in the name of a wretched form of racism and carried it out mercilessly.

Extermination camps and crematoriums were rapidly built, parallel to the dramatic events of the Second World War. Several million sons and daughters of Israel were killed at these places of horror—from children to the elderly. The enormously powerful machinery of the totalitarian state spared no one and undertook extremely cruel measures against those who had the courage to defend the Jews.

4. Edith Stein died at the Auschwitz extermination camp, the daughter of a martyred people. Despite the fact that she moved from Cologne to the Dutch Carmelite community in Echt, her protection against the growing persecution of the Jews was only temporary. The Nazi policy of exterminating the Jews was rapidly implemented in Holland, too, after the country had been occupied. Jews who had converted to Christianity were initially left alone. However, when the Catholic bishops in the Netherlands issued a pastoral letter in which they sharply protested against the deportation of the Jews, the Nazi rulers reacted by ordering the extermination of the Catholic Jews as well. This was the cause of the martyrdom suffered by Sister Teresa Benedicta of the Cross together with her sister, Rosa, who had also sought refuge with the Carmelites in Echt.

On leaving their convent Edith took her sister by the hand and said: "Come, we will go for our people." On the strength of Christ's willingness to sacrifice himself for others she saw in her seeming impotence a way to render a final service to her people. A few years previously she had compared herself with Queen Esther in exile at the Persian court. In one of her letters we read: "I am confident that the Lord has taken my life for all [Jews]. I always have to think of Queen Esther who was taken from her people for the express purpose of standing before the king for her people. I am the very poor, weak, and small Esther, but the King who selected me is infinitely great and merciful."

5. Dear brothers and sisters, Saint Paul, in his letter to the Galatians, wrote: "May I never boast of anything but the cross of our Lord, Jesus Christ. Through it, the world has been crucified to me and I to the world" [Gal. 6:14].

During her lifetime, Edith Stein, too, encountered the secret of the cross that Saint Paul announces to the Christians in this letter.

Edith encountered Christ and this encounter led her step by step into the Carmelite community. In the extermination camp she died as a daughter of Israel "for the glory of the Most Holy Name" and, at the same time, as Sister Teresa Benedicta of the Cross, literally, "blessed by the Cross."

Edith Stein's entire life is characterized by an incessant search for truth and is illuminated by the blessing of the cross of Christ. She encountered the cross for the first time in the strongly religious widow of a university friend. Instead of despairing, this woman took strength and hope from the cross of Christ. Later she wrote about this: "It was my first encounter with the cross and the divine strength it gives to those who bear it . . . It was the moment in which my atheism collapsed . . . and Christ shone brightly: Christ in the mystery of the cross." Her own life and the cross she had to bear were intimately connected with the destiny of the Jewish people. In a prayer she confessed to the Savior that she knew that it was his cross that was now being laid on the Jewish people and that those who realized this would have to accept it willingly on behalf of all the others. "I wanted to do it—all he has to do is show me how." At the same time she attains the inner certainty that God has heard her prayer. The more often swastikas were seen on the streets, the higher the cross of Jesus Christ rose up in her life. When she entered the Carmelite order of nuns in Cologne as Sister Teresa Benedicta a Cruce in order to experience the cross of Christ ever more profoundly, she knew that she was "married to the Lord in the sign of the cross." On the day of her first vows she felt, in her own words, "like the bride of the lamb." She was convinced that her heavenly Groom would introduce her to the profound mysteries of the cross.

6. *Teresa, Blessed by the Cross* was the name given in a religious order to a woman who began her spiritual life with the conviction that God does not exist. At that time, in her schoolgirl years and when she was at university, her life was not yet filled with the redeeming cross of Christ. However, it was already the object of constant searching on the part of her sharp intellect. As a fifteen-year-old schoolgirl in her home town of Breslau, Edith, who had been raised in a Jewish household, suddenly decided, as she herself put it, "not to pray anymore." Despite the fact that she was deeply impressed by the strict devotion of her mother, during her school and university years Edith slipped into the intellectual world

of atheism. She considered the existence of a personal God to be unworthy of belief.

In the years when she studied psychology, philosophy, history, and German at the Universities of Breslau, Göttingen, and Freiburg, God didn't play an important role, at least initially. Her thinking was based on a demanding ethical idealism. In keeping with her intellectual abilities, she did not want to accept anything without careful examination, not even the faith of her fathers. She wanted to get to the bottom of things herself. As such, she was engaged in a constant search for the truth. Looking back on this period of intellectual unrest in her life, she saw in it an important phase in a process of spiritual maturation. She said: "My search for the truth was a constant prayer." This is a comforting bit of testimony for those who have a hard time believing in God. The search for truth is, itself, in a very profound sense a search for God.

Under the influence of Edmund Husserl and his phenomenological school of thought, the student Edith Stein became increasingly dedicated to the study of philosophy. She gradually learned to "view things free of prejudice and to throw off 'blinkers.'" She came into contact for the first time with Catholic ideas through a meeting with Max Scheler in Göttingen. She described her reaction to this meeting as follows: "The barriers of rationalistic prejudice, something I grew up with without being aware of it, fell and suddenly I was confronted with the world of faith. People I dealt with on a daily basis, people I looked up to in admiration, lived in that world."

Her long struggle for a personal decision to believe in Jesus Christ was not to come to an end until 1921, when she began to read the autobiographical *Life of Saint Teresa of Avila*. She was immediately taken with the book and could not put it down until she had finished. Edith Stein commented: "When I closed the book I said to myself: 'That is the truth.'" She had read through the night until sunrise. In that night she found truth—not the truth of philosophy, but rather the truth in person, the loving person of God. Edith Stein had sought the truth and found God. She was baptized soon after that and entered the Catholic Church.

7. For Edith Stein, baptism as a Christian was by no means a break with her Jewish heritage. Quite on the contrary she said: "I had given up my practice of the Jewish religion as a girl of fourteen. My return to God made me feel Jewish again." She was always mindful of the fact that she was related to Christ "not only in a spiritual sense, but also in blood terms." She suffered profoundly from the pain she caused her mother through her conversion to Catholicism. She continued to accompany her to services in the synagogue and to pray the psalms with her. In reaction to her mother's observation that it was possible for her to be pious in a Jewish sense as well, she answered: "Of course, seeing as it is something I grew up with."

Although becoming a member of the Carmelite order was Edith Stein's objective from the time of her encounter with the writings of Saint Teresa of Avila, she had to wait more than a decade before Christ showed her the way. In her activity as a teacher and lecturer at schools and in adult education mostly in Speyer, but also in Münster, she made a continuous effort to combine science and religion and to convey them together. In this she only wanted to be a "tool of the Lord." "Those who come to me I would like to lead to him," she said. During this period of her life she already lived like a nun. She took the vows privately and became a great and gifted woman of prayer. From her intensive study of the writings of Saint Thomas Aquinas she learned that it is possible "to approach science from a religious standpoint." She said that it was only thus that she was able to decide to return seriously [after her conversion] to academic work. Despite her respect for scholarship, Edith Stein became increasingly aware that the essence of being a Christian is not scholarship, but rather love.

When Edith Stein finally entered the Carmelite order in Cologne in 1933, this step did not represent an escape from the world or from responsibility for her, but rather a resolved commitment to the heritage of Christ on the cross. She said in her first conversation with the prioress there: "It is not human activity that helps us—it is the suffering of Christ. To share in this is my desire." On being registered in the order she expressed the wish to be named "Blessed by the Cross." She had the words of Saint John of the Cross printed on the devotional picture presented to her on taking her final vows: *My only vocation is that of living more.*

8. Dear brothers and sisters. We bow today with the entire Church before this great woman whom we from now on may call upon as one of the blessed in God's glory, before this great daughter of Israel, who found the fulfillment of her faith and her vocation for the people of God in Christ the Savior. In her conviction, those who enter the Carmelite order are not lost to their own—on the contrary, they are won for them. It is our vocation to stand before God for everyone. After she began seeing the destiny of Israel from the standpoint of the cross, our newly beatified sister let Christ lead her more and more deeply into the mystery of his salvation to be able to bear the multiple pains of mankind in spiritual union with him and to help atone for the outrageous injustices in the world. As "Benedicta a Cruce"—Blessed by the Cross—she wanted to bear the cross with Christ for the salvation of her people, her Church, and the world as a whole. She offered herself to God as a "sacrifice for genuine peace" and above all for her threatened and humiliated Jewish people. After she recognized that God had once again laid a heavy hand on his people, she was convinced "that the destiny of this people was also my destiny."

When Sister Teresa Benedicta a Cruce began her last theological work, "The Science of the Cross," at the Carmelite convent in Echt (the work remained incomplete since it was interrupted by her own encounter with the cross) she noted: "When we speak of the science of the cross this is not . . . mere theory . . . but rather vibrant, genuine and effective truth." When the deadly threat to the Jewish people gathered like a dark cloud over her as well as she was willing to realize with her own life what she had recognized earlier: "There is a vocation for suffering with Christ and by that means for involvement in his salvation. . . . Christ continues to live and to suffer in his members. The suffering gone through in union with the Lord is his suffering, and is a fruitful part of the great plan of salvation."

With her people and "for" her people, Sister Teresa Benedicta a Cruce traveled the road to death with her sister Rosa. She did not accept suffering and death passively, but instead combined these consciously with the atoning sacrifice of our Savior Jesus Christ. A few years earlier she had written in her will: "I will gladly accept the death God chooses for me, in full submission to his holy will. I ask the Lord to accept my suffering and death for his honor and glory, and for all interests . . . of the holy Church." The Lord heard her prayer.

The Church now presents Sister Teresa Benedicta a Cruce to us as a blessed martyr, as an example of a heroic follower of Christ, for us to honor and to emulate. Let us open ourselves up for her message to us as a woman of the spirit and of the mind, who saw in the science of the cross the acme of all wisdom, as a great daughter of the Jewish people, and as a believing Christian in the midst of millions of innocent fellow men made martyrs. She saw the inexorable approach of the cross. She did not flee in fear. Instead, she embraced it in Christian hope with final love and sacrifice, and in the mystery of Easter even welcomed it with the salutation *ave crux spes unica*. As Cardinal Höffner said in his recent pastoral letter, "Edith Stein is a gift, an invocation, and a promise for our time. May she be an intercessor with God for us and for our people and for all people."

9. Dear brothers and sisters, today the Church of the twentieth century is experiencing a great day. We bow in profound respect before the testimony of the life and death of Edith Stein, an outstanding daughter of Israel and, at the same time, a daughter of Carmel, Sister Teresa Benedicta a Cruce, a person who embodied a dramatic synthesis of our century in her rich life. Hers was a synthesis of a history full of deep wounds, wounds that still hurt, and for the healing of which responsible men and women have continued to work up to the present day. At the same time, it was a synthesis of the full truth on man, in a heart that remained restless and unsatisfied "until it finally found peace in God."

When we pay a spiritual visit to the place where this great Jewish woman and Christian experienced martyrdom, the place of horrible events today referred to as "Shoah," we hear the voice of Christ the Messiah and Son of Man, our Lord and Savior.

As the bearer of the message of God's unfathomable mystery of salvation, he said to the women from Samaria at Jacob's well:

"After all, salvation is from the Jews. Yet an hour is coming, and is already here when authentic worshipers will worship the Father in spirit and truth. Indeed, it is just such worshipers the Father seeks. God is Spirit, and those who worship him must worship in spirit and truth" [John 4:22–24].

Blessed be Edith Stein, Sister Teresa Benedicta a Cruce, a true worshiper of God—in spirit and in truth.

She is among the blessed. Amen.

Pastoral Visit to Poland

June 14, 1987

Address to Jewish Leaders in Warsaw

I should like above all to thank you for this meeting which has found its place in my program. It recalls much to my memory, many experiences of my youth—and certainly not of my youth alone. Memories and experiences were good, and then terrible, terrible. Be sure, dear brothers, that the Poles, this Polish Church, is in a spirit of profound solidarity with you when she looks closely at the terrible reality of the extermination—the unconditional extermination—of your nation, an extermination carried out with premeditation. The threat against you was also a threat against us; this latter was not realized to the same extent, because it did not have the time to be realized to the same extent. It was you who suffered this terrible sacrifice of extermination: One might say that you suffered it also on behalf of those who were in the purifying power of suffering. The more atrocious the suffering, the greater the purification. The more painful the experiences, the greater the hope.

I think that today the nation of Israel, perhaps more than ever before, finds itself at the center of the attention of the nations of the world, above all because of this terrible experience, through which you have become a loud warning voice for all humanity, for all nations, all the powers of this world, all systems and every person. More than anyone else, it is precisely you who have become this saving warning. I think that in this sense you continue your particular vocation, showing yourselves to be still the heirs of that election to which God is faithful. This is your mission in the contemporary world before the peoples, the nations, all of humanity, the Church. And in this Church all peoples and nations feel united to you in this mission. Certainly they give great prominence to your nation and its sufferings, its Holocaust, when they wish to speak a warning to individuals and to nations; in your name, the pope, too, lifts up his voice in this warning. The Polish pope has a particular relationship with all this, because, along with you, he has in a certain sense lived all this here, in this land.

This is just one thought that I wished to put before you, thanking you for coming here, thanking you for this meeting. There have been many meetings with your brothers in various countries of the world. I cannot forget the visit last year, the first visit after very many centuries, to the Synagogue of Rome. I value this meeting in Poland in a particular way; it is especially meaningful for me, and I think that it will also be particularly fruitful. It helps me and all the Church to become even more aware of what unites us in the disposition of the Divine Covenant, as your spokesman has just said. This is what unites us in today's world, in face of the great tasks which this world sets you and the Church in the field of justice and of peace among the nations, in accordance with your biblical word *shalom*. I thank you for the words spoken in the spirit of faith, of the faith in the same God who is your God and our God: the God of Abraham. I extend the greeting of peace and my respectful sentiments to the few heirs of the great Israelite community which existed in Poland, perhaps the largest community in the world. *Shalom!*

Letter to Archbishop John L. May

August 8, 1987

To my dear Brother
John L. May
Archbishop of St. Louis
President of the National Conference of Catholic Bishops

As my second Pastoral Visit to the United States approaches, I wish to express to you my profound gratitude for your kindness in sending me the volume[1] containing the texts of my statements on the subject of the Jews and Judaism. This significant undertaking is the result of cooperation between Catholics and Jews in America, which is a further source of satisfaction.

In my pastoral concerns, journeys, and meetings and in my teachings during the years of my pontificate, I have constantly sought to develop and deepen our relationships with the Jews, "our elder brothers in the faith of Abraham," and I therefore encourage and bless not only this initiative but the initiatives of all those who, in fidelity to the directives of the Second Vatican Council and animated by goodwill and religious hope, foster relationships of mutual esteem and friendship and promote the Jewish—Christian dialogue in the appropriate places and with due theological competence and historical objectivity. The more we try to be faithful in loving obedience to the God of the Covenant, the Creator and Savior, contemplating in prayer his wonderful plan of Redemption and loving our neighbor as ourselves, the deeper will be the roots of our dialogue and the more abundant its results.

With our hearts filled with this unyielding hope, we Christians approach with immense respect the terrifying experience of the

---

1. Eugene J. Fisher and Leon Klenicki, eds., *Pope John Paul II on Jews and Judaism* (Washington D.C.: U.S. Catholic Conference and Anti-Defamation League, 1987).

extermination, the *Shoah*, suffered by the Jews during World War II, and we seek to grasp its most authentic, specific, and universal meaning.

As I said recently in Warsaw, it is precisely by reason of this terrible experience that the nation of Israel, her sufferings, and her Holocaust are today before the eyes of the Church, of all peoples and of all nations, as a warning, a witness, and a silent cry. Before the vivid memory of the extermination, as recounted to us by the survivors and by all Jews now living, and as it is continually offered for our meditation within the narration of the Pesah *Haggadah*—as Jewish families are accustomed to do today—it is not permissible for anyone to pass by with indifference. Reflection upon the *Shoah* shows us to what terrible consequences the lack of faith in God and a contempt for man created in his image can lead. It also impels us to promote the necessary historical and religious studies on this event which concerns the whole of humanity today. In this regard I look forward to positive results from the work of the forthcoming Thirteenth Plenary Session of the International Catholic-Jewish Liaison Committee, to be held in Washington precisely on the subject, "The *Shoah*, Its Significance and Implications Seen From a Historical and Religious Perspective."

There is no doubt that the sufferings endured by the Jews are also for the Catholic Church a motive of sincere sorrow, especially when one thinks of the indifference and sometimes resentment which, in particular historical circumstances, have divided Jews and Christians. Indeed, this evokes in us still firmer resolutions to cooperate for justice and true peace.

As I said at Assisi, I wish we could create ever newer opportunities for showing "what God would like the developing history of humanity to be: a fraternal journey in which we accompany one another towards the transcendent goal which he sets for us."

In this spirit of peace and universal fraternal solidarity I am preparing to renew to you and to the beloved Jewish community in the United States the joyful proclamation of peace, the *shalom* announced by the Prophets and awaited by the whole world. I express the hope that his peace will well up like a stream of living water from the bosom of Jerusalem and that there may be accomplished that which was foretold by Zechariah: "The Lord shall become king over the whole earth; on that day the Lord shall be the only one, and his name the only one" [Zech. 14:9].

And as I look forward to our meeting in your beloved country, I impart to you and to your brother Bishops my Apostolic Blessing.

From the Vatican, August 8, 1987.
Joannes Paulus II PP.

Meeting in Rome and Castel Gandolfo

September 1, 1987

Joint Press Communique

I

Representatives of the Holy See's Commission for Religious Relations with the Jews and of the International Jewish Committee on Inter-religious Consultations[1] met in Rome on Monday, August 31, 1987. The meeting was joined by a representative of the Council for Public Affairs of the Church. The meeting was described by its cosponsors as part of an ongoing process in response to difficulties which have risen in the relationship in recent months. The agenda for the meeting included the *Shoah* [Holocaust], contemporary anti-Semitism, Catholic teaching on Jews and Judaism, and relations between the Holy See and the State of Israel. The discussion was open and free and all issues were discussed in candor and friendship.

In the discussion of the *Shoah*, the Catholic delegation recalled the importance of Pope John Paul II's moving statement in Warsaw on June 14, 1987, his letter to Archbishop John May, president of the National Conference of Catholic Bishops [U.S.] of August 8, 1987,

---

1. IJCIC is composed of: World Jewish Congress, Synagogue Council of America, American Jewish Committee, B'nai B'rith International, Israel Jewish Committee on Interreligious Consultations.

and the decision to discuss the *Shoah* "in its religious and historical perspectives" at the next meeting of the International Catholic-
Jewish Liaison Committee in Washington, D.C. in December 1987.

In the context of the discussion on the moral implications of
the *Shoah*, the delegations explained their different perception of
the papal audience with [Austrian] President Kurt Waldheim. The
Jewish delegation expressed its dismay and concern over the moral
problems raised for the Jewish people by the audience. The Catholic delegation acknowledged the seriousness of and the Church's
sensitivity to those Jewish concerns, and set forth the serious reasons behind the judgment of the Holy See.

Cardinal John Willebrands, president of the Commission for Religious Relations with the Jews, announced the intention of the commission to prepare an official Catholic document on the *Shoah*, the historical background of anti-Semitism and its contemporary manifestations.

The Jewish delegation warmly welcomed this initiative and
expressed the conviction that such a document will contribute significantly to combatting attempts to revise and to deny the reality
of the *Shoah* and to trivialize its religious significance for Christians, Jews, and humanity.

It was also noted that Nazi ideology was not only anti-Semitic
but also profoundly demonic and anti-Christian.

The delegation received reports on the current state of anti-
Semitism in various countries and expressed concern over recent
manifestations of anti-Semitism and also of anti-Catholicism. The
group called for an intensification of existing efforts to counter religious and cultural prejudice.

The Jewish delegation expressed the concern of world Jewry at
the absence of full diplomatic relations between the Holy See and
the State of Israel. Representatives of the Holy See declared that
there exist no theological reasons in Catholic doctrine that would
inhibit such relations, but noted that there do exist some serious
and unresolved problems in the area.

In view of recent controversies and to avoid future misunderstandings, Cardinal Willebrands envisaged the development of a
special mechanism that would more closely follow the trends and
concerns within the world Jewish community and improve contacts

and collaboration where the need arises, including contacts with the Secretariat of State. The Jewish delegation in turn committed itself to adapt its own structures as appropriate.

On the issue of the presentation of Judaism in Catholic teaching and preaching, the Jewish group expressed gratification for progress made over the years. The Catholic side acknowledged that much further work still needs to be done to implement the Second Vatican Council and subsequent official statements within the life of the Church.

The Jewish delegation declared its strong opposition to any and all anti-Catholic manifestations and pledged itself to join with Catholics in opposing them.

II

On Tuesday morning, the Jewish delegation met with Cardinal Agostino Casaroli, Secretary of State. In this cordial meeting various concerns were discussed.

It was agreed that, as occasions require, in areas which are of concern to the world Jewish community and where religious and political issues intertwine, future exchanges between IJCIC and the Secretariat of State will be possible from time to time.

Regarding the State of Israel, the Cardinal stated that, while diplomatic relations have not been "Perfected," there do exist good relations on many levels, including official visits to the Holy See by Israeli leaders.

III

At noon on Tuesday, September 1, 1987, the participants were received at Castel Gandolfo by His Holiness John Paul II. The meeting took the form of a free and open conversation among those present. The participants expressed themselves fully on all the issues that had been discussed on the previous day.

The Jewish delegates expressed their appreciation for this unusual meeting, and also their concerns and hopes for the future.

The pope welcomed the Jewish delegation as representatives of the Jewish people, to whom the existence of Israel is central.

The pope affirmed the importance of the proposed document on the *Shoah* and anti-Semitism for the Church and for the world. The pope spoke of his personal experience in Poland and his memories of living close to a Jewish community now destroyed. He recalled his recent spontaneous address to the Jewish community in Warsaw, in which he spoke of the Jewish people as a force of conscience in the world today and of Jewish memory of the *Shoah* as a "warning, a witness, and a silent cry" to all humanity.

Citing the Exodus of the Jewish people from Egypt as a paradigm and a continuing source of hope, the pope movingly expressed his deep conviction that, with God's help, evil can be overcome in history, even the awesome evil of the *Shoah*.

Pastoral Visit to the United States

September 11, 1987

Address to Jewish Leaders in Miami

Dear Friends, Representatives of so many Jewish organizations assembled here from across the United States, my dear Jewish Brothers and Sisters:

1. I am grateful to you for your kind words of greeting. I am indeed pleased to be with you, especially at this time when the U.S. tour of the Vatican Judaica Collections begins. The wonderful material, including illuminated Bibles and prayerbooks, demonstrates but a small part of the immense spiritual resources often used in fruitful cooperation with Christian artists.

It is fitting at the beginning of our meeting to emphasize our faith in the one God, who chose Abraham, Isaac, and Jacob, and made with them a covenant of eternal love which was never revoked [cf. Gen. 27:13; Rom. 11:29]. It was rather confirmed by the gift of the Torah to Moses, opened by the Prophets to the hope of eternal redemption and to the universal commitment for justice and peace. The Jewish people, the Church, and all believers in the merciful God—who is invoked in the Jewish prayers as "*Av Ha-Rakhamim*"—can find in this fundamental covenant with the patriarchs a very substantial starting point for our dialogue and our common witness in the world.

It is also fitting to recall God's promise to Abraham and the spiritual fraternity which it established: "In your descendants all the nations shall find blessing—all this because you obeyed my command" [Gen. 22:18]. This spiritual fraternity, linked to obedience to God, requires a great mutual respect in humility and confidence. An objective consideration of our relations during the centuries must take into account this great need.

2. It is indeed worthy of note that the United States was founded by people who came to these shores, often as religious refugees. They aspired to being treated justly and to being accorded hospitality according to the word of God, as we read in Leviticus: "You shall treat the alien who resides with you not differently than the natives born among you; have the same love for him as for yourself; for you too were once aliens in the land of Egypt. I, the Lord, am your God" [Lev. 19:34].

Among these millions of immigrants there was a large number of Catholics and Jews. The same basic religious principles of freedom and justice, of equality and moral solidarity, affirmed in the Torah as well as in the Gospel, were in fact reflected in the high human ideals and in the protection of universal rights found in the United States. These in turn exercised a strong positive influence on the history of Europe and other parts of the world.

But the paths of the immigrants in their new land were not always easy. Sadly enough, prejudice and discrimination were also known in the New World as well as in the Old. Nevertheless, together, Jews and Catholics have contributed to the success of the American experiment in religious freedom, and, in this unique context, have given to the world a vigorous form of interreligious dialogue between our two ancient traditions. For those engaged in this dialogue, so important to the Church and to the Jewish people, I pray: May God bless you and make you strong for his service.

3. At the same time, our common heritage, task, and hope do not eliminate our distinctive identities. Because of her specific Christian wit nesses, "the Church must preach Jesus Christ to the world." In so doing we proclaim that "Christ is our peace" [Eph. 2:14], As the apostle Paul said: "All this is from God, who through Christ reconciled us to himself and gave us the ministry of reconciliation" [2 Cor. 5:18]. At the same time, we recognize and appreciate the spiritual treasures of the Jewish people and their religious witness to God. A fraternal theological dialogue will try to understand, in the light of the mystery of redemption, how differences in faith should not cause enmity but open the way of "reconciliation," so that in the end "God may be all in all" [1 Cor. 15:28].

In this regard I am pleased that the National Conference of Catholic Bishops and the Synagogue Council of America are initiating a consultation between Jewish leaders and bishops which should carry forward a dialogue on issues of the greatest interest to the faith communities.

4. Considering history in light of the principles of faith in God, we must also reflect on the catastrophic event of the *Shoah*, that ruthless and inhuman attempt to exterminate the Jewish people in Europe, an attempt that resulted in millions of victims—including women and children, the elderly and the sick—exterminated only because they were Jews.

Considering this mystery of the suffering of Israel's children, their witness of hope, of faith, and of humanity under dehumanizing outrages, the Church experiences ever more deeply her common bond with the Jewish people and with their treasure of spiritual riches in the past and in the present.

It is also fitting to recall the strong, unequivocal efforts of the popes against anti-Semitism and Nazism at the height of the persecution against the Jews. Back in 1938, Pius XI declared that "anti-Semitism cannot be admitted" [September 6, 1938], and he declared the total opposition between Christianity and Nazism by stating that the Nazi cross is an "enemy of the cross of Christ"

[Christmas Allocution, 1938]. And I am convinced that history will reveal ever more clearly and convincingly how deeply Pius XII felt the tragedy of the Jewish people, and how hard and effectively he worked to assist them during the Second World War.

Speaking in the name of humanity and Christian principles, the Bishops' Conference of the United States denounced the atrocities with a clear statement: "Since the murderous assault on Poland, utterly devoid of every semblance of humanity, there has been a premeditated and systematic extermination of the people of this nation. The same satanic technique is being applied to many other peoples. We feel a deep sense of revulsion against the cruel indignities heaped upon the Jews in conquered countries and upon defenseless peoples not of our faith" [November 14, 1942].

We also remember many others who, at risk to their own lives, helped persecuted Jews, and are honored by the Jews with the title of *Tzaddique 'ummot ha-'olam* [righteous of the nations].

5. The terrible tragedy of your people has led many Jewish thinkers to reflect on the human condition with acute insights. Their vision of man and the roots of this vision in the teachings of the Bible, which we share in our common heritage of the Hebrew Scriptures, offer Jewish and Catholic scholars much useful material for reflection and dialogue. And I am thinking here above all of the contribution of Martin Buber and also of Emmanuel Levinas.

In order to understand even more deeply the meaning of the *Shoah* and the historical roots of anti-Semitism that are related to it, joint collaboration and studies by Catholics and Jews on the *Shoah* should be continued. Such studies have already taken place through many conferences in your country, such as the national workshops on Christian-Jewish relations. The religious and historical implications of the *Shoah* for Christians and Jews will now be taken up formally by the International Catholic—Jewish Liaison Committee, meeting later this year in the United States for the first time. And as we affirmed in the important and very cordial meeting I had with Jewish leaders in Castel Gandolfo on September 1, a Catholic document on the *Shoah* and anti-Semitism will be forthcoming, resulting from such serious studies.

Similarly, it is to be hoped that common educational programs on our historical and religious relations, which are well developed in your country, will truly promote mutual respect and teach future generations about the Holocaust so that never again will such a horror be possible. Never again!

When meeting the leaders of the Polish Jewish community in Warsaw in June of this year, I underscored the fact that through the terrible experience of the *Shoah*, your people have become "a loud warning voice for all of humanity, for all nations, for all the powers of this world, for every system and every individual. . . . A saving warning" [*Address*, June 14, 1987].

6. It is also desirable that in every diocese Catholics should implement, under the direction of the bishops, the statement of the Second Vatican Council and the subsequent instructions issued by the Holy See regarding the correct way to preach and teach about Jews and Judaism. I know that a great many efforts in this direction have already been made by Catholics, and I wish to express my gratitude to all those who have worked so diligently for this aim.

7. Necessary for any sincere dialogue is the intention of each partner to allow others to define themselves "in the light of their own religious experience" [1974 *Guidelines*, Introduction]. In fidelity to this affirmation, Catholics recognize among the elements of the Jewish experience that Jews have a religious attachment to the land, which finds its roots in biblical tradition.

After the tragic extermination of the *Shoah*, the Jews began a new period in their history. They have a right to a homeland, as does any civil nation, according to international law. "For the Jewish people who live in the State of Israel and who preserve in that land such precious testimonies to their history and their faith, we must ask for the desired security and the due tranquility that is the prerogative of every nation and condition of life and of progress for every society" [Apostolic Letter on Jerusalem, *Redemptionis Anno*, April 20, 1984].

What has been said about the right to a homeland also applies to the Palestinian people, so many of whom remain homeless and refugees. While all concerned must honestly reflect on the past—Moslems no less than Jews and Christians—it is time to forge those solutions which will lead to a just, complete, and lasting peace in that area. For this peace I earnestly pray.

8. Finally, as I thank you once again for the warmth of your greeting to me, I give praise and thanks to the Lord for this fraternal meeting, for the gift of dialogue between our peoples and for the new and deeper understanding between us. As our long relationship moves toward its third millennium, it is our great privilege in this generation to be witnesses to this progress.

It is my sincere hope that, as partners in dialogue, as fellow believers in the God who revealed himself, as children of Abraham, we will strive to render a common service to humanity, which is so much needed in this our day. We are called to collaborate in service and to unite in a common cause wherever a brother or sister is unattended, forgotten, neglected, or suffering in any way; wherever human rights are endangered or human dignity offended; wherever the rights of God are violated or ignored.

With the psalmist, I now repeat: "I will hear what God proclaims; the Lord—for he proclaims peace to his people, and to his faithful ones, and to those who put in him their hope" [Ps. 85:9].

To all of you, dear friends, dear brothers and sisters; to all of you dear Jewish people of America: With great hope I wish you the peace of the Lord: *Shalom! Shalom!* God bless you on this Sabbat and in this year: *Shabbat Shalom! Shanah Tovah we-Hatimah Tovah!*

Rabbi Mordecai Waxman's Address to the Pope

It is our honor and pleasure to welcome you to the United States. We do so in behalf of the Jewish organizations who are represented here today, organizations that have been in fruitful conversations with the Roman Catholic Church through the years. They include representatives of the American Jewish Committee, the American Jewish Congress, the Anti-Defamation League, and the Synagogue Council of America, which is here representing the Union of American Hebrew Congregations, United Synagogues of America, Central Conference of American Rabbis, and Rabbinical Assembly. Also present with us this morning are the leaders of other major organizations in American life, as well as members of the Greater Miami Jewish community.

The men and women assembled here reflect the rich diversity of American Jewish life; we constitute a variety of religious and communal affiliations: American-born and immigrant; some are survivors of the *Shoah*, the Nazi Holocaust, while others have never experienced the dark shadow of anti-Semitism in their own lives. We come from all sections of the United States, and we come as full participants in the pluralistic and democratic society that has encouraged us to be proudly American and fully Jewish at the same time. Your visit to this country happily coincides with the two hundredth anniversary of the U.S. Constitution, a document that guarantees religious liberty for all American citizens which has enabled all faith communities to flourish in an atmosphere of religious pluralism. This has made possible a free and flourishing religious life for all.

It has been twenty-two years since the conclusion of the Second Vatican Council, and the promulgation of *Nostra Aetate*. The broad teachings that emerged in 1965 have been further enriched and strengthened by a series of formal Catholic documents and pronouncements, some of them your own. These statements have transformed Catholic-Jewish relationships throughout the world, and this positive change is especially evident here in the United States.

As the largest Jewish community in the world, we have developed close and respectful ties with many Roman Catholics, both lay and clergy, and we value these warm relationships and treasure these friendships. We particularly cherish our relationship with the National Conference of Catholic Bishops and its Secretariat for Catholic-Jewish Relations. In almost every place where Catholics and Jews live in the United States, we relate to each other in some organized fashion. We constantly exchange views and opinions and, as Jews and Catholics, we often share our positions, sometimes agreeing, sometimes disagreeing, but always striving for a spirit of mutual respect and understanding.

Throughout the United States, American Jews and Catholics work in concert with one another on a wide range of social justice issues and fight for global human rights and against all forms of racism and bigotry. Our common agenda has always embraced, and our future agenda will continue to embrace, the many crucial problems of the human family as a whole.

One of the major achievements of our joint encounters is the shared recognition that each community must be understood in its own terms, as it understands itself. It is particularly gratifying that our Catholic—Jewish meetings are conducted in a spirit of candor and mutual respect.

Such meetings took place last week at the Vatican and at Castel Gandolfo. These conversations, although quickly arranged, were highly significant. You and high Church leaders listened to the deeply felt concerns of the Jewish community that were raised following last June's state visit to the Vatican by Austrian President Kurt Waldheim, who has never expressed regrets for his Nazi past.

Obviously, the differences expressed at last week's meetings have not been resolved. However, this opportunity for us to express the pain and anger of the Jewish community in face-to-face meetings, and for you and leaders of your Church to listen with respect and openness, represents an important confirmation of the progress our communities have made in recent decades. One of the results of those meetings will be an instrumentality to develop closer communication and contact between our communities.

A basic belief of our Jewish faith is the need "to mend the world under the sovereignty of God" . . . *L'takken olam b'malkut Shaddai.* To mend the world means to do God's work in the world. It is in this spirit that Catholics and Jews should continue to address the social, moral, economic, and political problems of the world. Your presence here in the United States affords us the opportunity to reaffirm our commitment to the sacred imperative of *tikkun olam,* "the mending of the world."

But before we can mend the world, we must first mend ourselves. A meeting such as this is part of the healing process that is now visibly under way between our two communities. It is clear that the teachings proclaimed in *Nostra Aetate* are becoming major concerns of the Catholic Church and under your leadership are being implemented in the teachings of the Church and in the life of Catholics everywhere.

Catholics and Jews have begun the long overdue process of reconciliation. We still have some way to go because Catholic—Jewish relations are often filled with ambivalences, ambiguities, and a painful history which must be confronted. Yet in a world of increasing interreligious, interracial, and interethnic strife, the progress in Catholic-Jewish relations is one of this century's most positive developments.

We remain concerned with the persistence of anti-Semitism—the hatred of Jews and Judaism, which is on the rise in some parts of the world. We are encouraged by your vigorous leadership in denouncing all forms of anti-Semitism, and by the Church's recent teachings. The Church's repudiation of anti-Semitism is of critical importance in the struggle to eradicate this virulent plague from the entire human family. Anti-Semitism may affect the body of the Jew, but history has tragically shown that it assaults the soul of the Christian world and all others who succumb to this ancient, but persistent, pathology.

We hope that your strong condemnations of anti-Semitism will continue to be implemented in the schools, the parishes, teaching materials, and the liturgy, and reflected in the attitudes and behavior of Catholics throughout the world. Greater attention needs to be paid to the Christian roots of anti-Semitism. The "teaching of contempt" for the Jews and Judaism must be ended once and for all.

The "teaching of contempt" reaped a demonic harvest during the *Shoah* in which one-third of the Jewish people were murdered as a central component of a nation's policy. The Nazi Holocaust (*Shoah*) brought together two very different forms of evil: on the one hand it represented the triumph of an ideology of nationalism and racism, the suppression of human conscience, and the deification of the state—concepts that are profoundly anti-Christian as well as anti-Jewish. On the other hand, the *Shoah* was the culmination of centuries of anti-Semitism in European culture for which Christian teachings bear a heavy responsibility.

While your sensitive concerns and your noteworthy pronouncements about the *Shoah* have been heartening, we have observed recent tendencies to obscure the fact that Jews were the major target of Nazi genocidal policies. It is possible to visit Nazi death camps today and not be informed that the majority of its victims were Jews. Your letter about the *Shoah*, sent last month to Archbishop John May, the president of the National Conference of Catholic Bishops, represented a deep level of understanding of that terrible period.

We look forward to the forthcoming Vatican document on the *Shoah*, the historical background of anti-Semitism, and its contemporary manifestations.

Many Catholic schools in the U.S. are already teaching about the Holocaust and efforts are under way to develop a specific curriculum about the *Shoah* for Catholic students. These materials are being jointly developed by Catholic and Jewish educators.

Even though many of the great centers of Jewish learning were destroyed during the *Shoah*, there has been a remarkable renewal of Jewish religious life throughout the world. This renaissance of the spirit is taking place not only in the United States, in the State of Israel, and in other lands of freedom, but in the Soviet Union as well. Many Soviet Jews are discovering that the covenant between God and the people of Israel is indeed "irrevocable" as you declared last year at the Grand Synagogue in Rome. The struggle of Soviet Jews to achieve freedom is a major concern of the Jewish community, and we appreciate the support American Catholics have given to this cause.

The return to Zion and the reestablishment of Jewish sovereignty in the land of Israel play a paramount role in Jewish self-understanding today. Because of the importance that the State of Israel occupies in the mind, spirit, and heart of Jews, whenever Christians and Jews meet in a serious conversation, Israel is at the center of that encounter. The reemergence of an independent Jewish State onto the world stage in 1948 has compelled Christians and Jews to examine themselves and each other in a new light.

We must express our concern at the absence of full diplomatic relations between the Holy See and the State of Israel. We welcome the recent statements from Vatican leaders declaring that no theological reasons exist in Catholic doctrine to inhibit such relations. We strongly urge once again that full and formal diplomatic relations be established soon between the Vatican and the State of Israel. Such a step would be a positive and constructive contribution by the Vatican to the peace process, and it would send a strong signal to the international community that the Holy See recognizes Israel as a permanent and legitimate member of the family of nations.

One of the most welcome results of the recent Catholic-Jewish encounter has been the recognition by Catholics that Judaism has continued and deepened its unique spiritual development after the separation of the Christian Church from the Jewish people some nineteen hundred years ago.

A meeting such as today's is a vivid reminder that we live in a historic moment. Clearly, as two great communities of faith, repositories of moral and spiritual values, Catholics and Jews need to move together in this new moment. The last quarter-century has irreversibly changed the way we perceive and act towards each other.

In an age of great challenges and great possibilities there is a compelling need for a "vision for the times," *Chazon L'moed* [Hab. 2:3]. Our vision for Catholics and Jews is a prayer of the synagogue.

At the end of the Torah reading, the scroll is held high so the entire congregation may see the words of God, and together the congregation prays, *Hazak, Hazak, v'nithazek,* "Be strong, be very strong, and let us strengthen one another."

September 16, 1987

Meeting with Interreligious Leaders, Los Angeles

During his interreligious meeting in Los Angeles, on September 16, Pope John Paul II gave a general speech in which there was also a particular reference to the relations with the Jews.

... *To the Jewish Community*: I repeat the Second Vatican Council's conviction that the Church "cannot forget that she received the revelation of the Old Testament through the people with whom God in his mercy established the ancient Covenant. Nor can she forget that she draws sustenance from the root of that good olive tree onto which has been grafted the wild olive branches of the Gentile" [cf. Rom. 11:17–24; *Nostra Aetate*, 4]. With you, I oppose every form of anti-Semitism. May we work for the day when all peoples and nations may enjoy security, harmony and peace.

September 23, 1987

General Audience

The pope described his pastoral visit in the United States of America, including his meeting with Jewish representatives.

6. Very much alive also are the contacts with the non-Christian religions which come from Asia [Buddhism and Hinduism], especially at Los Angeles and San Francisco. There, I had a meeting with the representatives of these religions, as well as with those of Islam and Judaism.

The Jewish community in the United States is very numerous and exercises a great influence. One of the most important moments of the visit was the programmed meeting at the beginning of the pilgrimage in Miami, which constitutes a new, important step on the path of dialogue between the Church and Judaism, in the spirit of the Council's declaration *Nostra Aetate*.

1988

Excerpt from Encyclical,
Sollicitudo Rei Socialis

February 19, 1988

27. The examination which the encyclical invites us to make of the contemporary world leads us to note in the first place that development *is not* a straightforward process, *as it were automatic* and *in itself limitless*, as though, given certain conditions, the human race were able to progress rapidly towards an undefined perfection of some kind.[1]

Such an idea—linked to a notion of "progress" with philosophical connotations deriving from the Enlightenment, rather than to the notion of "development,"[2] which is used in a specifically economic and social sense—now seems to be seriously called into doubt, particularly since the tragic experience of the two world wars, the planned and partly achieved destruction of whole peoples, and the looming atomic peril. A naive *mechanistic optimism* has been replaced by a well-founded anxiety for the fate of humanity.

---

1. Cf. apostolic exhortation *Familiaris Consortio* (November 22, 1981), 6: *AAS* 74 (1982); p. 88: "history is not simply a fixed progression towards what is better, but rather an event of freedom, and even a struggle between freedoms."

2. For this reason the word "development" was used in the encyclical rather than the word "progress," but with an attempt to give the word "development" its fullest meaning.

Pastoral Visit to Austria

June 24, 1988

Lamentation at Mauthausen Concentration Camp

Pope John Paul II visited Austria June 23–27; on the second day of his visit, he went to the former World War II concentration camp at Mauthausen.

1. It is hard to find more expressive words than those which we have just heard from Lamentations, attributed to the prophet Jeremiah.

More than forty years have gone by since the time when the death camps, one of which was Mauthausen, spread fear and terror. This occurred in the middle of this century, toward the end of the second millennium after Christ.

The Lamentations of Jeremiah announce the coming of the Messiah and his sufferings. They speak of a man, a man of suffering, whose cross has been erected on Golgotha before the walls of the Holy City of Jerusalem. They speak of him and in a certain sense even bear witness to his own words. The words of the prophet and his personal fate convey this special message to us.

2. At the same time, however, these lamentations of one man are the expression of the sufferings of all, particularly of those who underwent the agonies in such concentration camps during the frightful war years in Europe.

What the prophet says could be spoken by any one of those people. Not only could it come from their lips but from their own innermost beings, which were so brutally treated here and then condemned to annihilation in the terrible living conditions of the concentration camps.

These are the words of each human soul, of the person of suffering, who will find his enduring archetype in the "man of suffering" in the Bible and Gospel.

3. "I am a man who knows affliction from the rod of his anger, one whom he has led and forced to walk in darkness, not in the light. Against me alone he brings back his hand again and again all the day" [Lam. 3:1–3]. Who is this "he"?

Likewise does the human being, the prisoner from Mauthausen, explain his own sufferings. This statement is at the same time a question, an important question regarding the suffering of humanity over the ages. Doesn't this question actually change into an accusation?

Who is accused by this man of suffering? Who is placed under accusation by this tormented person, this prisoner from the concentration camp? Or perhaps . . . is he accusing God himself?—"I am a man who knows affliction from the rod of his anger."

"He has worn away my flesh and my skin, he has broken my bones" [Lam. 3:4]. In this place there were men who cruelly mistreated other human beings . . . literally, as foretold in Lamentations.

In this place here in Mauthausen there were those who, in the name of an insane ideology, set in motion an entire system of contempt and hatred against other human beings. They performed tortures, broke their bones, and cruelly mistreated bodies and souls. They persecuted their victims with their cruelty. "He has beset me round about with poverty and weariness. He has left me to dwell in the dark like those long dead" [Lam. 3:5–6].

Here, too, prisoners were "walled up" and closed in this concentration camp. They "weighed them down with chains" and "blocked their way with fitted stones" [Lam. 3:7–9], closing off the way to the freedom, dignity, and basic rights of every human being. Here was planned the death and annihilation of any person considered an enemy. Not only this, but also perhaps simply for being "different." Or perhaps only because this was a human being?

This insane plan was one of turning Europe back from the path it had followed for thousands of years!

4. Is it true that the "way has been blocked" for populations, society and humanity? Certainly people have been crushed to pieces. They have been, as the prophet says "sated . . . with bitter food" and made to drink their "fill of wormwood" and then in the end "pressed . . . in the dust" [Lam. 3:15–16].

Here . . . and in so many other places where a totalitarian domination existed.

From this, one of the most terrifying experiences in its history, Europe emerges defeated . . . defeated in what seemed to be its inheritance and mission . . . "Its ways are blocked." The burden of doubt has come down hard on the history of people, nations, and continents.

Are the questions of our own conscience strong enough? Are the pangs of conscience that have remained in us strong enough?

5. You people who have experienced fearful tortures—how worthy you are of the Lamentations of Jeremiah!

What is your last word? Your word after so many years which separate our generation from the sufferings in the Mauthausen concentration camp and in many others?

You people of yesterday, and you people of today, if the system of extermination camps continues somewhere in the world even today, tell us, what message can our century convey to the next?

Tell us, in our great hurry, haven't we forgotten your hell? Aren't we extinguishing traces of great crimes in our memories and consciousness?

Tell us, what direction should Europe and humanity follow "after Auschwitz" . . . and "after Mauthausen"? Is the direction we are following away from those past dreadful experiences the right one?

Tell us, how should today's person be and how should this generation of humanity live in the wake of the great defeat of the human being? How must that person be? How much should he require of himself?

Tell us, how must nations and societies be? How must Europe go on living?

Speak, you have the right to do so—you who have suffered and lost your lives. We have the duty to listen to your testimony.

6. Hasn't humanity and the system established by humanity aroused the anger of God with the abuses they have created?

Hasn't humanity darkened the image of God in the consciousness of generations?

Nevertheless, the prophet calls out with the words of Lamentations: "The favors of the Lord are not exhausted, his mercies are not spent. They are renewed each morning, so great is his faithfulness" [Lam. 3:22–23].

Yes. Faithfulness. There is only one "man of suffering" who has been true to all people of suffering, here in Mauthausen and wherever in the world they endure or have endured an inhuman system of contempt.

There was such a man of suffering, and such a person continues to exist. His cross remains ever present in world history.

Should we turn away from the cross? Can we pass it by in the future?

Europe, can you pass it by?

Must you not at least stand by it, even if the generations of your sons and daughters move away from it, and the past vanishes?

7. Christ! The Christ of so many human sufferings, humiliations, and devastation. Christ, crucified and resurrected. In this place, one of so many, which cannot be erased from the history of this century.

I, the bishop of Rome and the successor to Peter the apostle, beg you fervently: Remain!

Remain and live on in our future!

Remain and live on!

Where should we go? You have the word of life that has been covered up neither by death nor by destruction. . . . You have the words of eternal life [cf. John 6:68].

Blessed Marcel Callo, martyr of Mauthausen; and Blessed Sister Teresa Benedicta of the Cross, Edith Stein; and St. Maximilian Kolbe, honored and venerated martyrs of Auschwitz: Pray for all those who were tortured and martyred in these places! Pray for all the victims of unjust power in both the present and past—pray, too, for their executioners!

Jesus Christ, the lamb of God, have mercy on them all, have mercy on us all!

June 24, 1988

Address to Jewish Community in Vienna

*In the morning of Friday, June 24, the Holy Father welcomed leaders
of the Jewish community in Austria to the apostolic nunciature. During
the meeting, the pope gave the following address.*

Mr. President of the Israelite Worship Communities,
Dear Chief Rabbi,
Dear Listeners:

1. In the Book of Jeremiah [31:15] we read: "A sound is heard in
Ramah, the sound is bitter weeping. Rachel is crying for her children; they are gone."

Such a lament is also the keynote of your words of greeting with
which you addressed me this very moment in the name of the Jewish communities in Austria. I was profoundly moved by it. I return
your greeting with love and appreciation and assure you that this
love also includes the awareness of all that afflicts you. Fifty years
ago this city's synagogue went up in flames. Thousands of people
were sent from here to death camps; multitudes were driven by
flight. Those incomprehensible sufferings, pains, and tears are
before my eyes and leave a deep impression on my soul. Indeed,
one can love only someone he knows.

I am happy that during my pastoral visit I also was able to meet
you. May this be a sign of our mutual esteem and manifest a readiness to get to know one another better, to remove deep fears and to
share with one another trust-inspiring experiences.

"*Shalom!*" "Peace!" This religious greeting is an invitation to
peace. It has a central significance at our encounter this morning before the *Shabbat*; it also has a central Christian significance
from the greetings of peace of the Risen Lord to the apostles in
the upper room. Peace comprises the offer and the possibility of
forgiveness and mercy, the outstanding qualities of our God, the
God of the Covenant. You experience and celebrate in faith this
certainty, when you annually keep the great Day of Reparation, the
Yom Kippur, as a feast day. We Christians contemplate this mystery

in the heart of Christ who—pierced by our sins and those of the whole world—dies on the cross. That is the highest degree of solidarity and fraternity by the power of grace. Hatred is extinguished and erased, the Covenant of love is renewed. This is the Covenant which the Church lives in faith, in which she experiences her deep and mysterious union in love and faith with the Jewish people. No historical event, however painful it may be, can be so powerful that it could contradict this reality which belongs to God's plan for our salvation and fraternal reconciliation.

2. The relationship between Jews and Christians has essentially changed and improved since the Second Vatican Council and its solemn declaration *Nostra Aetate*. Since then there is an official dialogue whose proper and central dimension should be the "encounter between the present Christian Churches and today's people of the Covenant made with Moses," as I expressed on another occasion [Address to the representatives of the Jews at Mainz, November 17, 1980].

Meanwhile, further steps have been made towards reconciliation; my visit to the Roman Synagogue also testifies to this.

Yet you and we are still burdened by the memory of the *Shoah*, the murder of millions of Jews in the concentration camps. It would be, of course, unjust and untrue to put the blame for those unspeakable crimes on Christianity. Rather, here is revealed the dreadful face of a world without, and even against, God, whose intentions to kill were clearly directed against the Jewish people, but also against the faith of those who revere in the Jew, Jesus of Nazareth, the Redeemer of the world. Individual solemn protests and appeals caused their intentions to become still more fanatical.

An appropriate meditation on the suffering and martyrdom of the Jewish people cannot be made without a profound reference to the faith experience which marks its history, beginning with the faith of Abraham, to the Exodus from slavery in Egypt, to the sealing of the Covenant on Sinai. It is a journey in faith and obedience in response to the loving call of God. As I said last year to the representatives of the Jewish community in Warsaw, out of those cruel sufferings can grow a much deeper hope, can rise a saving cry of warning for the whole human race. To remember the *Shoah* means to hope and to see to it that there will never be a repetition of it.

We cannot remain insensitive in the face of such immeasurable suffering; yet faith tells us that God does not desert the persecuted, but rather reveals himself to them and by it enlightens that people on the way to salvation. This is the teaching of Holy Scripture, this is revealed to us in the Prophets, in Isaiah and Jeremiah. In this faith, the common heritage of both Jews and Christians, are the roots of Europe's history. For us Christians, every human suffering finds its ultimate meaning in the Cross of Jesus Christ. However, this does not hinder us, but urges us to sympathize much more in solidarity with the deep wounds which were inflicted on the Jewish people in the persecutions, especially in this century, due to modern anti-Semitism.

3. The process of complete reconciliation between Jews and Christians has to be carried on in full force on all levels of relationships between our communities. Collaboration and common studies should help to explore in a deeper way the significance of the Shoah. The causes which are responsible for anti-Semitism or which still more universally lead to the so-called "Holy Wars" must be discovered and, if at all possible, removed. From what we see happening in the ecumenical sphere, I am confident that it will be possible to speak openly among ourselves about the rivalries, the radicalism, and the conflicts of the past. We must try to recognize them also in their historical conditions and overcome them by our common efforts for peace, for a consistent witness of faith and the promotion of the moral values which should characterize individuals and nations.

Already, in the past, there was no lack of clear and emphatic warnings against every kind of religious discrimination. I recall here especially the express condemnation of anti-Semitism through a decree of the Holy See in 1928 where it says that the Holy See rigorously condemns hatred of the Jewish people, "that hate, namely, which one usually calls today 'anti-Semitism.'" The same condemnation was also expressed by Pope Pius XI in 1938. Among the manifold modern initiatives which have arisen in the spirit of the Council for the Jewish—Christian dialogue, I would like to point to the Centre for Information, Education, Meetings, and Prayer which will be established in Poland. Its purpose is to explore the *Shoah* as well as the martyrdom of the Polish people and that of the other European nations during the time of National Socialism and also to enter into discussions about them. We hope that it will bear rich fruit and serve as an example for other nations. Initiatives of that kind will also enrich the civil life of all social groups, animating them to care in mutual respect for the weak, the needy, and marginalized, to overcome hostilities and prejudices, as well as to defend human rights, especially the right to religious freedom for each individual and community.

In this extensive program of action to which we invite Jews, Christians, and all people of goodwill, the Catholics of Austria have already taken part for many years, bishops and faithful as well as different groups. Very recently, fruitful encounters with Jewish leaders have taken place in Vienna.

4. The unity and harmony of diverse groups within a nation is also a firm prerequisite for an effective contribution towards promoting peace and understanding among nations, as the Austrian history of the last decades has shown. The matter of peace concerns all of us intimately, especially in the Holy Land, in Israel, in Lebanon, in the Middle East. These are regions with which we have deep ties on a biblical, historical, religious, and cultural level. Peace is, according to the teachings of the Prophets of Israel, a fruit of justice and law and at the same time an undeserved gift of the Messianic period. Therefore here also we have to do away with any sort of violence, which is a repetition of old mistakes and therefore causes hatred, fanaticism, and religious integralism, which are enemies of human harmony. In this connection each one should examine his own conscience according to his responsibility and competence. Above all, it is necessary that we promote a constructive dialogue between Jews, Christians, and Muslims so that the common faith in the God of Abraham, Isaac, and Jacob [Exod. 3:6] becomes effectively fruitful in the search for mutual understanding and fraternal living without violating the rights of anybody.

In this sense, every initiative of the Holy See has to be understood, when it tries to seek the recognition of equal dignity for the

Jewish people in the State of Israel and for the Palestinian people. As I pointed out to the representatives of the Jewish communities in the United States of America, the Jewish people have a right to a homeland like any other nation, according to international law. The same goes also for the Palestinian people, many of whom are homeless and refugees. By a common readiness of understanding and compromise solutions can be found which lead to a just, comprehensive, and lasting peace in this area [*Address*, September 11, 1987]. If only forgiveness and love are sown in plenty, the weeds of hate cannot grow; they will be smothered. To remember the Shoah also means to oppose every germ of violence and to protect and promote with patience and perseverance every tender shoot of freedom and peace.

In this spirit of readiness for Christian reconciliation, I return from my heart your *shalom* and implore for all of us the gift of fraternal harmony and the blessing of the almighty and bountiful God of Abraham, your Father in the faith and ours.

July 6, 1988

Looking Back: General Audience

During the general audience in the Paul VI Hall on July 6, the Holy Father gave an account of his recent apostolic journey in Austria (June 23–27, 1988).

. . . My pastoral visit began and ended with Vespers. . . . Besides meeting the state authorities, I also had a meeting at Vienna with the representatives of the Jewish community in Austria. This meeting had its thematic-historical complement in my visit to the concentration camp of Mauthausen.

As regards Austria, the year 1938—half a century ago—recalled a traumatic event which left a tragic imprint on the history of that country and—as is known—on other countries and nations of Europe. In 1938, Austria was annexed to Germany (the *Anschluss*) and subjected to the power of Hitler and Nazism. The present papal visit—after fifty years—could not fail to make reference to that period. This was expressed first of all by the commemorative cross placed in the extermination camp of Mauthausen, and, also in that same place of death, the liturgy inspired by the Lamentations of Jeremiah. Alongside the state authorities, survivors of that camp and their families also took part in the commemoration.

. . . The dreadful years of Nazi terror caused millions of victims of many nations. A special measure of extermination was reserved, unfortunately, for the Jewish nation. This fact came to the fore in the meeting with the representatives of the Israelite community living in Austria. . . .

Discourse Concerning the Death of Christ: General Audience

September 28, 1988

In this discourse concerning the death of Christ as a historical event, the pope referred to the teaching of Nostra Aetate, No. 4.

. . . Historical responsibility for Christ's crucifixion rests with those mentioned in the Gospels, at least in part, by name. Jesus himself says so when he says to Pilate during the trial: "He who delivered me to you has the greater sin" [John 19:11]. In another passage also: "The Son of man goes as it is written of him, but woe to that man by whom the Son of man is betrayed! It would have been better for that man if he had not been born" [Mark 14:21; Matt. 26:24; Luke 22:22]. Jesus alludes to various persons who, in different ways, will be responsible for his death: Judas, the representatives of the Sanhedrin, Pilate, and the others. . . . Simon Peter, also, in his discourse after Pentecost, will charge the leaders of the Sanhedrin with the killing of Jesus: "You crucified and killed him by the hands of law-less men" [Acts 2:23].

9. However, this accusation cannot be extended beyond the circle of people responsible. We read in a document of the Second Vatican Council: "Even though the Jewish authorities and those who followed their lead pressed for the death of Christ, neither all Jews indiscriminately at that time, nor Jews today, can be charged with the crimes committed during the passion" [*Nostra Aetate*, 4]. . . .

Pastoral Visit to France

October 9, 1988

Address to Leaders of the Jewish Community in Strasbourg

On Sunday, October 9, following his discourse to Christian leaders, the pope returned to the archbishop's residence at Strasbourg for a fraternal meeting with leaders of the Jewish community.

Mr. Chief Rabbi,
Mr. President of the Jewish Consistory of the Lower Rhine,
Mr. President of the Jewish Community of Strasbourg,
Gentlemen:

Your cordial greeting and the spiritual reflection on the meaning of history which you just made to me cannot but inspire me in my turn to wishes for peace and prosperity for you and for the entire Jewish community.

1. In thanking you for so many signs of attention, I would like to continue these reflections, taking as my point of departure the biblical verse of the prophet Malachi, which is so beautifully inscribed

on your "Synagogue of Peace" and which you also inscribed in the heart of your address: *Ha-'lo 'av' Ehad le-Kullanu"* [Mai. 2:10]; "Have we not all the one Father?" That is the message of faith and truth of which you are the bearers and witnesses throughout history, in the light of God's word and Covenant with Abraham, Isaac, and Jacob and all his descendants; this witness extended to martyrdom, survived the long darkness of misunderstanding, and the horrible abyss of the *Shoah.*

2. After the Second Vatican Ecumenical Council, thanks also to the work of the Commission for Religious Relations with the Jews and the International Catholic-Jewish Liaison Committee, we have continued—and still continue—to enlarge the already solid foundations of our fraternal relations and to draw conclusions in the area of cooperation on all levels. It is especially in these institutions that I encourage Jewish—Christian dialogue, and I rejoice with you in the progress made thanks to your participation in this task, with a mutual esteem nourished in an atmosphere of prayer, conversion, and readiness to hear and obey the word of God which calls us to love and pardon.

3. Yes, through my voice, the Catholic Church, faithful to that which the Second Vatican Ecumenical Council has declared, recognizes the value of the religious witness of your people, chosen by God, as Saint Paul says: "In respect to election, they are beloved because of the patriarchs. For the gifts and the call of God are irrevocable" [Rom. 11:28–29, quoted in *Lumen Gentium,* 16]. It is a matter of an election, as you have just said, for the "sanctification of his name" for the service of all of humanity. That vocation to the sanctification of his name you express in your daily prayer of the *Kaddish*: "May your great name be magnified and sanctified!" Or you proclaim it in the words of Isaiah: "Holy, Holy, Holy is the Lord God of hosts! All the earth is filled with his glory!" [Isa. 6:3]. In the prayers of joy and repentance which are characteristic of the feasts of *Rosh ha-Shanah, Yom Kippur,* and *Sukkot,* which you celebrated several days ago, you ask and acclaim the Eternal One: "Our Father, our King, pardon us our sins! *Hosh 'na,* Save us!"

4. All the sacred Scriptures, which you venerate with a deep devotion as the source of life, celebrate the beautiful name of

God, the Father, the rock who begot *Yesbouroun*, "The God who gave you birth," as Moses says in his canticle [cf. Deut. 32:18]. "Yes, I am a Father to Israel," the Lord says through the oracle of Jeremiah, who says further, "Ephraim is my first-born" [Jer. 31:9]; Isaiah returns towards him, saying: "Lord, our Father, it is you!" [Isa. 64:7]. The psalms celebrate his name: "My Father! My God! the rock who saves me!" [Ps. 89:27]. In his mercy he also revealed his name which recalls his motherly love, his labour as a mother who gives birth to a child: "Thus the Lord passed before Moses and proclaimed: the Lord, the Lord, a merciful and gracious God!" [Exod. 34:6].

5. It is then through your prayer, your history, and your experience of faith, that you continue to affirm the fundamental unity of God, his fatherhood and mercy towards every man and woman, the mystery of his plan of universal salvation, and the consequences which come from it according to the principles expressed by the Prophets, in the commitment for justice, peace, and other ethical values.

6. With the greatest respect for the Jewish religious identity, I would also like to emphasize that for us Christians, the Church, the people of God and Mystical Body of Christ, is called throughout her journey in history to proclaim to all the Good News of salvation in the consolation of the Holy Spirit. According to the teaching of the Second Vatican Council, she could better understand her bond with you, certainly thanks to fraternal dialogue, but also by meditating upon her own mystery [*Nostra Aetate*, 4]. Now that mystery is rooted in the mystery of the person of Jesus Christ, a Jew, crucified and glorified. In his Letter to the Ephesians, Saint Paul wrote: [That mystery,] "God did not make known to human beings in other generations as it has now been revealed to his holy apostles and prophets by the Spirit, that the Gentiles are co-heirs, members of the same body, and co-partners in the promise of Christ Jesus through the Gospel" [Eph. 3:5–6]. Previously the apostle, in addressing "all the beloved of God in Rome" [Rom. 1:7], had affirmed: "For those who are led by the Spirit of God are children of God. For you did not receive a spirit of slavery to fall back into fear, but you received a spirit of adoption, through which

we cry, '*Abba*,' 'Father'!" [Rom. 8:15]. Therefore we also recognize and celebrate the glory of God, the Father, Lord of those who adore him "in spirit and in truth" [John 4:24].

7. European civilization thus keeps its profound roots near that source of living water which are the Holy Scriptures: the one God reveals himself as our father and, through his commandments, asks us to respond to him through love in freedom. At the dawn of a new millennium, the Church, in announcing to Europe the Gospel of Jesus Christ, discovers even better, with joy, the common values, both Christian and Jews, through which we recognize one another as brothers and sisters and to which the history, language, art, and culture of the peoples and nations of this continent refer.

8. Where should we place our hope, to share with all those who thirst for fraternal consolation, for a message of life, for a lasting and sincere solidarity? What should we preach together to offer a spiritual service to Europe, so rich in so many resources, yet at the same time being questioned about what meaning to give to these resources in the context of international development? Permit me to propose three considerations here:

- that the European peoples do not forget that we draw our origin from a common Father, and from that source there comes, for us, the duty of a mutual and fraternal responsibility which must extend with the same depth of concern for each person, the image of God, and each people of the world;
- that we Christians become ever more aware of the particular task that we have to fulfill in cooperation with the Jews, by reason of our common heritage which impels us to promote justice and peace, to live according to the demands of the Commandments, faithful to the voice of God, in respect for every creature. I also wish that true collaboration on the social level may develop, in many areas, according to the principles which I expressed in my encyclical *Sollicitudo Rei Socialis*;
- it is in deep fidelity to the vocation to which the God of peace and justice calls us, and with us, all European peoples, that I repeat again with you the strongest condemnation of all anti-Semitism and racism, which is opposed to the principles of Christianity, and for which there exists no justification in the cultures to which we

refer. For the same reasons, we must set aside all religious prejudice which history has shown us to be inspired by anti-Jewish attitudes, or to contradict the dignity of each person.

May God confirm us in these intentions and in the faith, and give us his consolation, as the psalm says:
"The Lord himself will give his benefits, our land shall yield its increase. Justice shall walk before him, and salvation, along the way of his steps" [Ps. 85:13–14].

Pope's Letter to the Director of the Vatican Observatory

October 26, 1988

A study week sponsored by the Holy See marked the three hundredth anniversary of the publication of Sir Isaac Newton's Philosophiae Naturalia Principia Mathematica. As preparations were under way to publish the papers presented at the study week, the pope wrote a letter to the director of the Vatican Observatory, which included this excerpt.

. . . As never before in her history, the Church has entered into the movement for the union of all Christians, fostering common study, prayer, and discussion that "all may be one" [John 17:20]. She [the Church] has attempted to rid herself of every vestige of anti-Semitism and to emphasize her origins in and her religious debt to Judaism. In reflection and prayer, she has reached out to the great world religions, recognizing the values we all hold in common and our universal and utter dependence upon God. . . .

1989

Letter to Classmate Jerzy Kluger

March 30, 1989

Dear Jurek,

On the ninth day of May of this year, 1989, on the site of the synagogue which was destroyed during the last world war, a plate will be unveiled commemorating the Jews from Wadowice and nearby, who were victims of persecution and were exterminated by the Nazis.

I thank you very much for the letter in which you advise me of this event. Many of those who perished, your coreligionists and our fellow-countrymen, were our colleagues in our elementary school and, later, in the high school where we graduated together, fifty years ago. All were citizens of Wadowice, the town to which both you and I are bound together by our memories of childhood and youth.

I remember very clearly the Wadowice Synagogue, which was near to our high school. I have in front of my eyes the numerous worshipers, who during their holidays passed on their way to pray there.

If you are able to be there, in Wadowice, on the ninth of May, tell all who are gathered there, that, together with them, how I venerate the memory of their cruelly killed coreligionists and compatriots and also this place of worship, which the invaders destroyed.

I embrace with deep reverence all those whom you are remembering this day—the ninth of May 1989 in Wadowice.

Allow me to quote the words, which I have pronounced to the representatives of the Jewish community of Warsaw during my third pilgrimage to the Fatherland:

The Church and all peoples and nations within this Church are united with you. . . . Indeed, when they speak with warning to people, nations, and even to the whole humanity, they place in the forefront your nation, its suffering, its persecutions, its extermination. Also the pope raises his voice of warning in your name. This has a special significance to the pope from Poland, because together with you, he survived all that happened in this land [June 14, 1987].

Should you consider it proper, you can read this letter in public. I greet you from my heart.

Joannes Paulus II PP.

On the Occasion of the Fiftieth Anniversary of the Outbreak of World War II

August 26, 1989

Message to the Polish Episcopal Conference

. . . In this message the pope called attention to the crime of the extermination of the Jews:

. . . It is truly difficult to calculate the magnitude of the losses suffered, and even more, of the sufferings which were inflicted upon individuals, families, and communities. Many facts are already known; many more must yet be brought to light. The war was waged not only on the front, but as a total war, a war which struck entire societies. Whole groups were deported. Thousands became victims of prison, torture, and execution. Quite apart from strict combat, people died as victims of bombing and of systematic terror.

The organized instruments of the latter were the concentration camps, ostensibly established for labor, yet transformed in reality into death camps. One particular crime of World War II remains the massive extermination of the Jews, who were doomed to the gas chambers because of racial hatred. . . .

August 27, 1989

Apostolic Letter on the Fiftieth Anniversary of the Outbreak of World War II

In one section of this apostolic letter, the pope called attention to the persecution of the Jews.

. . . Among all these antihuman measures, however, there is one which will forever remain a shame for humanity: the planned barbarism which was unleashed against the Jewish people.

As the object of the "Final Solution" devised by an erroneous ideology, the Jews were subjected to deprivations and brutalities that are almost indescribable. Persecuted at first through measures designed to harass and discriminate, they were ultimately to die by the millions in extermination camps.

The Jews of Poland, more than others, lived this immense suffering: The images of the Warsaw Ghetto under siege, as well as what we have come to learn about the camps at Auschwitz, Majdanek, and Treblinka, surpass in horror anything that can be humanly imagined.

One must also remember that this murderous madness was directed against many other groups whose crime was to be "different" or to have rebelled against the tyranny of the occupier.

On the occasion of this sorrowful anniversary, once again I issue an appeal to all people, inviting them to overcome their prejudices and to combat every form of racism by agreeing to recognize the fundamental dignity and the goodness that dwell within every human being, and to be ever more conscious that they belong to a single human family, willed and gathered together by God.

I wish to repeat here in the strongest possible way that hostility and hatred against Judaism are in complete contradiction to the Christian vision of human dignity.

The new paganism and the systems related to it were certainly directed against the Jews, but they were likewise aimed at Christianity, whose teaching had shaped the soul of Europe. In the people of whose race "according to the flesh, is the Christ" [Rom. 9:5], the Gospel message of the equal dignity of all God's children was being held up to ridicule.

In his encyclical *Mit brennender Sorge* (1937), my predecessor, Pope Pius XI, clearly stated: "He who takes race, or the people or the State, or the form of government, the bearers of the power of the state, or other fundamental elements of human society . . . and makes them the ultimate norm of all, even of religious values, and deifies them with an idolatrous worship, perverts and falsifies the order of things created and commanded by God" [March 14, 1937: AAS 29 (1937) pp. 149 and 171].

This pretension on the part of the ideology of the National Socialist system did not spare the Churches, in particular the Catholic Church, which before and during the conflict experienced her own "passion." Her fate was certainly no better in the lands where the Marxist ideology of dialectical materialism was imposed.

We must give thanks to God, however, for the many witnesses, known and unknown, who in those hours of tribulation had the courage to profess their faith steadfastly, who knew how to rise above the atheist's arbitrariness, and who did not give in to force.

Address to Representatives of United Bible Societies

October 26, 1989

The following passage was included in the pope's address:

. . . Holy Scripture nourishes faith, strengthens ecclesial unity, and is an important element of our common spiritual patrimony with Abraham's stock, our Jewish brothers and sisters. . . .

1990

Address to Representatives of the American Jewish Committee

March 16, 1990

The Holy Father received in audience on March 16 representatives of the American Jewish Committee. They included President and Mrs. Shalom D. Camay; Mr. Alfred Moses, chairman of the Board of Governors; Mrs. Mimi Alperin, chairperson of the National Executive Council, and her daughter, Ms. Juli Alperin; Elmer L. Winter, honorary president; Jerome Goldstein, vice president; Mr. Morton Lowenthal, member of the Board of Governors, and Mrs. Eleanor Lowenthal; and Rabbi A. James Rudin, National Interreligious Affairs Director.

The Pope's Address

Mr. President,
Distinguished Members of the American Jewish Committee:

1. *Shalom!* This is my greeting to each of you as I welcome you to the Vatican. Our meeting today reminds me of a similar visit of the American Jewish Committee in 1985 for the purpose of commemorating the twentieth anniversary of *Nostra Aetate*, the Second Vatican Council's *Declaration on the Relationship of the Church to Non-Christian Religions.* That declaration does not cease to impart an important and timely message, inspiring us with hope and promise for the future.

Although the Catholic teaching concerning Jews and Judaism is summarized in article four of the declaration, many of its fundamental elements are also present in other documents of the

Council. References to the same topic can be found in *Dogmatic Constitution on the Church* and *on Divine Revelation in the Declaration on Religious Freedom,* in the *Pastoral Constitution on the Church in the Modern World,* and in the *Constitution on the Sacred Liturgy.* Perhaps the time has come, after twenty-five years, to make a systematic study of the Council's teaching on this matter. We would do well to pursue this as part of our dialogue. Today, I would like to limit myself to some general observations.

2. *Nostra Aetate* speaks of "the spiritual bond linking the people of the New Covenant with Abraham's stock" [4].

This reference is complemented by another text found in the *Dogmatic Constitution on the Church.* There we read: "Those who have not yet received the Gospel are related in various ways to the people of God. In the first place there is the people to whom the covenants and the promises were given and from whom Christ was born according to the flesh [cf. Rom. 9:4–5]. On account of their fathers, this people remains most dear to God, for God does not repent of the gifts he makes nor of the calls he issues [cf. Rom. 11:28–29]" [§ 16].

The origin of our "common spiritual heritage" [cf. *Nostra Aetate,* 4] therefore is to be found in the faith of Abraham, Isaac, and Jacob. Within this common heritage we may include veneration of the Holy Scriptures, confession of the One Living God [cf. Exod. 20:3, 23; Deut. 6:4], love of neighbor [cf. Lev. 19:18], and a prophetic witness to justice and peace. We likewise live in confident expectation of the coming of God's Kingdom, and we pray that God's will be done on earth as it is in heaven.

As a result, we can effectively work together in promoting the dignity of every human person and in safeguarding human rights, especially religious freedom. We must also be united in combating all forms of racial, ethnic, or religious discrimination and hatred, including anti-Semitism. I am pleased to note the significant level of cooperation that has been achieved in these areas over the past quarter-century, and it is my fervent hope that these efforts will continue and increase.

3. In the new and positive atmosphere that has developed since the Council, among Catholics, it is the task of every local church to

promote cooperation between Christians and Jews. As the successor of Saint Peter, I have a special concern for all the Churches, and am therefore committed to furthering such a policy throughout the world. At the same time, I gratefully acknowledge the initiatives taken by yourselves in this area. I hope that your forthcoming meeting in Poland with the Episcopal Commission for Dialogue with the Jews will be a very fruitful one. May it be a hopeful sign of genuine brotherhood between Christians and Jews in Central and Eastern Europe and thus contribute to the process of peaceful and democratic development taking place there.

This initiative and the continuing exchange of information between your committee and the Holy See's Commission for Religious Relations with the Jews reflect our common desire for better understanding and greater harmony. May this serve to benefit both of our communities and to foster justice and peace in the world, especially in the land of the Fathers and in Jerusalem—the land and the city considered holy by millions of believers: Jews, Christians, and Muslims.

May that day come when all nations "shall beat their swords into ploughshares and their spears into pruning hooks," when "nation shall not lift up sword against nation, neither shall they learn war any more" [Isa. 2:4]. Upon all of you I invoke an abundance of divine blessings.

Pastoral Visit to Mexico

May 9, 1990

Address to the Representatives of the Jewish Community

During his pastoral visit to Mexico in May, the Holy Father met in Mexico City with representatives of the Jewish community and addressed them with these words.

Ladies and Gentlemen:

I am very grateful for your presence at this moment during my second visit to Mexico. The world in which we live suffers because of its many divisions. But at the same time, our world is characterized by a search for unity, unification, and reconciliation. The Second Vatican Council, in its document *Nostra Aetate*, addressed one of the central themes of this reconciliation. We can, and indeed we must, affirm that the Jewish people is "our elder brother," as I stated again when visiting the Synagogue of Rome. Humanity's search for unity touches upon many areas: ecumenism, international relations, the relationship between the powers of the world. It touches upon ideology and religion, and particularly the relationship between the various children of the religious mosaic of Moses, descendants of Abraham, our common father in the faith, as well as the followers of Islam, all of them. I want, therefore, to thank you all for your presence, for having expressed the desire to move forward, in spite of all the difficulties, along this path of reconciliation and unity. I want also to offer to all those present and to the entire Mexican Jewish community, in your nation, in their homeland, and in the various countries of the world, my good wishes, and my prayer that the Lord will bless you, one and all.

Thank you very much.

Discourse to Preparatory Consultation for the Special Assembly for Europe of the Synod of Bishops

June 5, 1990

One aspect of the speech referred to the plight of the Jews during World War II.

. . . The tragic series of events that have followed one after another during this century, particularly since the outbreak of World War II, have contributed perhaps in some measure to opening the human heart to the freedom which comes from the Spirit, that freedom by which Christ has set us free [cf. Gal. 5:1].

The war itself with its immense cruelty, a cruelty that reached its most brutal expression in the organized extermination of the Jews, as well as of the Gypsies and of other categories of people, revealed to the European the other side of a civilization that he was inclined to consider superior to all. . . .

Letter to the President of the World Catholic Federation for the Biblical Apostolate

June 14, 1990

On the occasion of the Fourth Assembly of the World Catholic Federation for the Biblical Apostolate, held in Bogotà, Colombia, June 27– July 6, 1990, the pope sent a greeting to the participants. It included the following passage:

The Bible is also a treasure which in large part is revered in common with the Hebrew people, to whom the Church is united by a special spiritual bond since its beginnings. Lastly, this holy book, to which in a certain way, the peoples of Islam relate, can inspire all interreligious dialogue between peoples that believe in God; and in this way it contributes towards bringing about a universal prayer, acceptable to God, for peace, in the hearts of all.

Jasna Gora Meditation

September 26, 1990

This is the twenty-eighth Jasna Gora meditation. The pope delivered it during the General Audience on September 26.

We began our Jasna Gora Cycle on the feast of Saints Cyril and Methodius [February 14]. We come to you every week, O Mother, in the wide wake that leads through the history of peoples and nations, especially our neighboring countries and kindred nations.

Behold, our time in the midst of Europe is beginning anew. In this new historic beginning we also have our part and our place. There is a great bond with the distant past, and with many recent events in the history of this century. In this century. . . . In this dramatic twentieth century, which brings to a close the second millennium after Christ.

There is yet another nation, a particular people: the people of the patriarchs, of Moses and the Prophets, the heirs of the faith of Abraham.

"The Church keeps ever before her mind the words of the Apostle Paul about his kinsmen: 'to them belong the sonship, the glory, the covenants, the giving of the Law, the worship and the promises; to them belong the patriarchs, and of their race according to the flesh, is the Christ'" [Rom. 9:4–5] [Vatican II, Declaration *Nostra Aetate*, 4].

Christ and the Apostles. And you yourself, O Virgin Mother, Daughter of Sion.

This people lived arm in arm with us for generations on that same land which became a kind of new homeland during the Diaspora.

This people was afflicted by the terrible deaths of millions of its sons and daughters. First they were marked with special signs, then they were shoved into ghettos, into isolated quarters. Then they were carried off to the gas chambers, put to death—simply because they were the sons and daughters of this people.

The assassins did all this on our land, perhaps to cloak it in infamy. However, one cannot cloak a land in infamy by the death of innocent victims. By such deaths the land becomes a sacred relic.

The people who lived with us for many generations has remained with us after the terrible death of millions of its sons and daughters. Together we await the Day of Judgment and Resurrection.

Address to the New Ambassador of the Federal Republic of Germany to the Holy See

November 8, 1990

On November 8, the Holy Father received H. E. Hans-Joachim Hallier, the new ambassador of the Federal Republic of Germany to the Holy See, This is a translation of a passage of the pope's address in German.

... Our first meeting today, as you yourself mentioned, takes place under the influence of the political events of recent months and the completion of German unity on October 3 of this year; it was achieved not least of all through the collaboration of the Churches in your country. ...

... It was really the Second World War which came to an end on October 3 and made many people aware of what fate and guilt mean to all peoples and individuals. We think of the millions of people, most of them totally innocent, who died in that war: soldiers, civilians, women, the elderly and children, people of different nationalities and religions.

In this context we should also mention the tragedy of the Jews. For Christians the heavy burden of guilt for the murder of the Jewish people must be an enduring call to repentance; thereby we can overcome every form of anti-Semitism and establish a new relationship with our kindred nation of the Old Covenant. The Church, "mindful of her common patrimony with the Jews, and motivated by the Gospels' spiritual love and by no political considerations, ... deplores the hatred, persecutions, and displays of anti-Semitism directed against the Jews at any time and from any source" [Second Vatican Council, declaration *Nostra Aetate*, 4]. Guilt should not oppress and lead to self-agonizing thoughts, but must always be the point of departure for conversion.

Address to the British Council for Christians and Jews

November 16, 1990

On Friday, November 16, the Holy Father met with a delegation from the British Council of Christians and Jews. They included the Very Rev. Edward Carpenter, KCVO, chairman (Anglican); Dr. Sidney Corob, joint vice-chairman (Jewish); Right Rev. Gerald Mahon, MHM, joint vice-chairman (Catholic); Sir Sigmund Sternberg, KCSG, O. St., J., treasurer (Jewish); and Rev. Canon Jim Richardson, director (Anglican). The pope gave the following address:

Your Excellency,
Distinguished Visitors:

I am pleased to welcome to the Vatican the members of the British Council for Christians and Jews, and I greet you with a joyful word that has profound significance for us all: *Shalom!*

Peace is, before all else, a gift of God: the fullness of redemption for humanity and for the whole of creation. That peace, which is so seriously threatened today, is at the same time something which is integral to the rational and moral nature of men and women, created as they are in the image and likeness of God. In the human order, peace requires and implies justice and mercy, and culminates in the love of God and of neighbor which is the highest point of the teaching of the Torah and of the Prophets.

On this matter Jesus Christ himself affirms: "Think not that I have come to abolish the Law and the Prophets. I have come not to abolish them but to fulfill them" [Matt. 5:17]. Truly great is the spiritual patrimony shared by Christians and the Jewish people [cf. *Nostra Aetate*, 4]! For this reason, in the period after the Second Vatican Council, cooperation between Christians and Jews has become ever more intense, and I am very pleased that important contacts continue, such as the recent meetings which took place in Prague.

At the thirteenth meeting of the International Catholic-Jewish Liaison Committee, the themes of anti-Semitism and of the *Shoah* were addressed, as well as the wider question of human rights. It was rightly acknowledged that anti-Semitism as well as all forms of racism are "a sin against God and humanity," and as such must be rejected and condemned. In a renewed spirit of collaboration, Catholic and Jewish delegates set out new orientation for joint efforts aimed at defending human rights, safeguarding freedom and dignity where they are lacking or imperiled, and promoting responsible stewardship of the environment. I offer my heartfelt encouragement to the British Council of Christians and Jews to continue actively to foster friendly dialogue, brotherly understanding, and the exchange of spiritual values at the national level, as well as at the level of the International Council of Christians and Jews of which you form part.

Finally, I take this occasion to express once again the sorrow— but also the hope—that I share with the peoples of the Holy Land, the land of our fathers in faith. With you and with all who are heirs to the faith of Abraham—and I am thinking also of our Islamic brothers and sisters—I raise up the prayer of the psalmist:

> For the peace of Jerusalem pray,
> "Peace be to your homes,
> May peace reign in your walls,
> In your palaces, peace." [Ps. 121:6–7].

May God grant that progress towards peace in the Holy Land will not be long in coming!

Address to the International Liaison Committee between the Catholic Church and IJCIC in Rome

December 6, 1990

Your Eminences,
Distinguished Visitors:

1. As delegates of the International Jewish Committee on Interreligious Consultations and members of the Commission for Religious Relations with the Jews, you have come together to commemorate the twenty-fifth anniversary of the Second Vatican Council's declaration *Nostra Aetate*. In effect, what you are celebrating is nothing other than the divine mercy which is guiding Christians and Jews to mutual awareness, respect, cooperation, and solidarity. Conscious of our sharing in the same hope and promises made to Abraham and to his de scendants, I am indeed pleased to welcome you in this house! "*Baruch ha-ba be-Shem Adonai!* Blessed is he who comes in the name of the Lord!" [Ps. 119, Vg. 118:26].

2. The brief but significant document *Nostra Aetate* occupied an important place in the work of the Council. After a quarter of a century it has lost none of its vigor. The strength of the document and its abiding interest derive from the fact that it speaks to all peoples and about all peoples from a religious perspective, a perspective which is the deepest and most mysterious of the many dimensions of the human person, the image of the Creator [cf. Gen. 1:26].

The universal openness of *Nostra Aetate*, however, is anchored in and takes its orientation from a high sense of the absolute singularity of God's choice of a particular people, "His own" people, Israel according to the flesh, already called "God's Church" [*Lumen*

Gentium, 9; cf. Neh. 13:1; Num. 20:4; Deut. 23:1ff]. Thus, the Church's reflection on her mission and on her very nature is intrinsically linked with her reflection on the stock of Abraham and on the nature of the Jewish people [cf. Nostra Aetate, 4]. The Church is fully aware that sacred Scriptures bears witness that the Jewish people, this community of faith and custodian of a tradition thousands of years old, is an intimate part of the "mystery" of revelation and of salvation. In our own times, many Catholic writers have spoken of that "mystery" which is the Jewish people: among them Geremia Bonomelli, Jacques Maritain, and Thomas Merton.

The Church therefore, particularly through her biblical scholars and theologians, but also through the work of other writers, artists, and catechists, continues to reflect upon and express more thoroughly her own thinking on the mystery of this people. I am happy that the Commission for Religious Relations with the Jews is intensely promoting study on this theme in a theological and exegetical context.

3. When we consider Jewish tradition we see how profoundly you venerate sacred Scripture, the Miqra, and in particular the Torah. You live in a special relationship with the Torah, the living teaching of the living God. You study it with love in the Talmud Torah, so as to put it into practice with joy. Its teaching on love, on justice, and on the Law is reiterated in the Prophets—*Nevi'im*—and in the *Ketuvim*. God, His holy Torah, the synagogal liturgy and family traditions, the land of holiness, are surely what characterize your people from the religious point of view. And these are things that constitute the foundation of our dialogue and of our cooperation.

At the center of the Holy Land, almost as its hallowed heart, lies Jerusalem. It is a city holy to three great religions, to Jews, Christians, and Muslims. Its very name evokes peace. I should like you to join in praying daily for peace, justice, and respect for the fundamental human and religious rights of the three peoples, the three communities of faith who inhabit that beloved land.

4. No dialogue between Christians and Jews can overlook the painful and terrible experience of the *Shoah*. During the meeting at Prague in September of this year, the Jewish—Catholic International Liaison Committee considered at length the religious and

historical dimensions of the Shoah and of anti-Semitism, and came to conclusions that are of great importance for the continuation of our dialogue and cooperation. It is my hope that these may be widely recognized and that the recommendations then formulated will be implemented wherever human and religious rights are violated.

May God grant that the commemoration of the twenty-fifth anniversary of *Nostra Aetate* will bring fresh results of spiritual and moral renewal for us and for the world. May it bring above all the fruit of cooperation in promoting justice and peace. In the Babylonian Talmud we read: "The world stands upon the single column that is the just man" [Hagigah, 12b]. In the Gospel, Jesus Christ tells us that blessed are the peacemakers [cf. Matt. 5:9]. May justice and peace fill our hearts and guide our steps towards the fullness of redemption for all peoples and for the whole universe. May God hear our prayers!

1991

For Peace in the Middle East: General Audience

March 6, 1991

During the general audience on March 6, the Holy Father interrupted his continuing series of catecheses in order to celebrate a special prayer for peace with the patriarchs of the Catholic Churches of the Middle East, the presidents of the bishops' conferences of the countries most directly involved in the recent war, and the pilgrims who had come to Rome from many parts of the world. This is a translation of his address.

... The reference to the land where Christ was born directed our thoughts to the city where he preached, died, and rose: Jerusalem, with its holy places which are also dear to the Muslims and their communities. Jerusalem, called to be a crossroads of peace, cannot continue to be the cause of discord and dispute. I fervently hope that some day circumstances will allow me to go as a pilgrim to that city which is unique in all the world, in order to issue again from there, together with Jewish, Christian, and Muslim believers, that message and plea for peace which was already addressed to the entire human family on October 27, 1986 from Assisi ...

What can the communities of East and West do?

The Christians of the East are often called to bear witness to their faith in societies in which they are a minority; it is their desire to do so with courage, feeling that they are builders and participants in every sense of the word in the societies to which they belong. This demands first of all a genuine and constant dialogue with their Jewish and Muslim brothers and sisters, and an authentic religious freedom based on mutual respect and reciprocity.

In this regard on January 1, I already dedicated this year's celebration of the World Day of Peace to the theme, "If you want peace, respect every person's conscience". . . .

At the end of the general audience, the pope invited all those present to join him in praying for peace. The seven intercessions were prayed in various languages; at the conclusion all joined in singing the Lord's Prayer in Latin. We include one of the intercessions:

Brothers and Sisters:

At the end of this audience, let us join our voices and pray for peace and harmony in the Middle East and the whole world, so that all the people whom God loves may work untiringly to promote that justice which alone can guarantee a true and lasting peace.

For a just and lasting peace in the Holy Land and Jerusalem; that, in the land which saw the rising of the star of hope and love, the star which changed the fate of all of humanity, the disciples of one, eternal and merciful God, may seek together, in a spirit of harmony and mutual respect, to overcome all difficulties and set in motion a joint project of pacification and development, let us pray to the Lord.

Address to Christians and Muslims from Jerusalem

March 14, 1991

On Thursday, March 14, the pope received a delegation of Christians and Muslims from Jerusalem, headed by the city's Latin patriarch, Michel Sabbah. The pope addressed the group in Italian.

Your Beatitude,

Dear Brothers:

With joy I greet this group headed by the beloved Latin patriarch of Jerusalem. Your group is numerically small but very significant.

The greater part of you come from Jerusalem, a city which is holy for Jews, Christians, and Muslims and the spiritual homeland dear to millions of the faithful of the three religions who look to it as a symbol of encounter, union and peace for the whole human family. . . .

Letter to the United Nations Secretary General

March 21, 1991

The pope wrote a letter to the United Nations secretary general, Mr. Javier Pérez de Cuellar, informing him of the concerns and conclusions which emerged during the meeting (March 4–5) of the patriarchs of the Middle East and the representatives of the bishops' conferences of some Western countries.

In the name of the bishops who participated in the talks and the Catholic communities represented by them, the pope entrusted to Mr. Pérez de Cuellar the hope that a serious commitment of those in government and of religious leaders may soon bring to the Middle East peace, justice, the desire for dialogue, freedom of conscience, and solidarity. The following is a translation of some of the Holy Fathers letter.

To His Excellency
Mr. Javier Pérez de Cuellar
Secretary General of the United Nations

As you know, on March 4–5, I met with the patriarchs of the Catholic Churches of the Middle East and representatives of the bishops' conferences of the countries that were most involved in the recent Gulf War. This meeting was convoked in order to promote an exchange of information and an evaluation of the various negative consequences of the conflict, as well as to seek together the most opportune initiatives that would allow their solution.

It was primarily a meeting of pastors, united by their common concern for the situation and the future of the Christian communities of the Middle East who, as you know, are minorities within societies which have a Muslim or Jewish majority.

The first intention which appeared was that of pursuing and developing dialogue between Christians and Muslims and between Christians and Jews, in the firm hope that it will lead to better mutual understanding, to mutual trust, and a concrete collaboration permitting all the communities to express their faith freely and to have the full rights to participate in the construction of the societies in which they live.

Furthermore, they manifested their conviction that a sincere inter-religious dialogue, developing in an atmosphere of authentic freedom of religion, could contribute notably to the pursuit of justice and the guarantee of peace, which the region of the Middle East needs so much. . . .

Address to Participants in Sant'Egidio Interreligious Meeting

April 30, 1991

On Tuesday, April 30, the Holy Father received the participants in an interreligious meeting sponsored by the Rome-based Sant'Egidio community. The pope addressed the group in Italian.

Distinguished Ladies and Gentlemen:

1. I am happy to welcome and greet you, the representatives of the Jewish, Christian, and Muslim world, who participated yesterday in the colloquium on *Peace Among Religions, Peace in Society*, held at the Campidoglio.

I extend a special greeting to the Honorable Franco Carraro, Mayor of Rome, who has also participated in this interreligious gathering.

It is significant that a meeting of this sort should take place in Rome, whose cosmopolitan and universal character offers a favorable climate for mutual understanding. The colloquium was arranged by the Community of Sant'Egidio, which is committed to interreligious dialogue and the search for peace.

Yesterday you were able to hear speeches from qualified representatives of the three monotheistic religions on such a decisive problem of our times. Above all, after the recent war, the question of peace represents a fundamental meeting point for everyone, particularly for those who do not put their trust in their own strength, but place it above all in God, who is almighty and merciful.

2. Jews, Christians, and Muslims, as we know, come from different religious traditions, but have many ties to each other. In fact, all the believers of these three religions refer back to Abraham, *pater omnium credentium* [cf. Rom. 4:11], for whom they have a profound respect, although in different ways. Peace among these religions constitutes such a great good and such an important contribution to all of human society. If there is not an amiable peace among these religions, how can harmony in society be found?

From believers, from the representatives of religion, from persons who have spent so many years of their life in meditation on the sacred books, the world is waiting for a world of peace. And this is what the Council asks of us Catholics when it "pleads with all to forget the past, and urges that a sincere effort be made to achieve mutual understanding; for the benefits of all men, let them together preserve and promote peace, liberty, social justice, and moral values" [*Nostra Aetate*, 3].

3. We sincerely feel that we are involved in this program of dialogue and mutual commitment. Therefore, I would like to thank all of you who have participated in this meeting and its organizers, who by this initiative are trying to foster an ever more fraternal and practical understanding, above all in the field of assistance to brothers and sisters who are suffering from disease, disasters, or marginalization.

With these thoughts I express my best wishes, asking abundant heavenly blessings on you and your loved ones.

Excerpt from Encyclical Letter *Centesimus Annus*[1]

May 1, 1991

. . . Reading the encyclical within the context of Pope Leo's whole magisterium, we see how it points essentially to the socioeconomic consequences of an error which has even greater implications. As has been mentioned, this error consists in an understanding of human freedom which detaches it from obedience to the truth, and consequently from the duty to respect the rights of others. The essence of freedom then becomes self-love carried to the point of contempt for God and neighbor, a self-love which leads to an unbridled affirmation of self-interest and which refuses to be limited by any demand of justice.

This very error had extreme consequences in the tragic series of wars which ravaged Europe and the world between 1914 and 1945. Some of these resulted from militarism and exaggerated nationalism, and from related forms of totalitarianism; some derived from the class struggle; still others were civil wars or wars of an ideological nature. Without the terrible burden of hatred and resentment which had built up as a result of so many injustices both on the international level and within individual states, such cruel wars would not have been possible, in which great nations invested their energies and in which there was no hesitation to violate the most sacred human rights, with the extermination of entire peoples and social groups being planned and carried out. Here we recall the Jewish people in particular, whose terrible fate has become a symbol of the aberration of which man is capable when, he turns against God.

---

1. Libreria Editrice Vaticana, Vatican City, no. 17.

However, it is only when hatred and injustice are sanctioned and organized by the ideologies based on them, rather than on the truth about man, that they take possession of entire nations and drive them to act. *Rerum Novarum* opposed ideologies of hatred and showed how violence and resentment could be overcome by justice. May the memory of those terrible events guide the actions of everyone, particularly the leaders of nations in our own time, when other forms of injustice are fueling new hatreds and when new ideologies which exalt violence are appearing on the horizon. . . .

Pastoral Visit to Poland

June 4, 1991

Homily at Mass in Radom

During his visit to Poland, the pope celebrated Mass on June 4 in Radom. During the Mass he preached the homily which included these words:

. . . Along the path of my Polish pilgrimage, I have been accompanied by the Ten Commandments, the ten words which God pronounced forcefully atop Mount Sinai, and confirmed by Christ in his Sermon on the Mount, within the context of the eight Beatitudes. . . .

In the very center of that order is the commandment, "Thou shalt not kill," a strict and absolute prohibition which is at the same time the affirmation of every person's right to life, from the moment of conception to natural death. . . .

Man's legal codes defend life and punish murderers. At the same time, it would be hard to deny that ours is a century weighed down by the death of millions of innocent people. That death was caused by a new way of waging war, which amounts to mass attrition and annihilation of noncombatant portions of the populace. . . .

Among the nations of Europe, the Polish people had an exceptionally large share of suffering in this slaughter. On Polish soil the commandment, "Thou shalt not kill," has been violated by millions of outrages and crimes.

Among these outrages was the particularly appalling systematic killing of entire national groups—the Jews first of all—but also of other ethnic groups, such as the Gypsies, motivated solely by membership in a certain nation or race.

June 7, 1991

Homily at Mass in Wloclawek

During his homily the pope made this observation:

. . . And certainly, Europe's history is one of great crises. This history of European crises has many roots. It remains and develops, and in our time has its continuation in our repeatedly tragic century. In fact, it was in this century that the philosophy was created in whose name a man could kill another man because he is different, because he is of a certain ethnic group, because he is Jewish, because he is a Gypsy, because he is Polish. A discrimination of masters against slaves. And then again the myth of the classes—all this is European, but we must liberate ourselves! Europe needs redemption. . . .

June 9, 1991

Address to Jewish Community

On Sunday morning, June 9, the Holy Father met with members of the Jewish community who reside in Poland. They were presented by Bishop Henryk Muszynski of Wloclawek, president of the Episcopal Commission for Dialogue with Jews. The Holy Father then gave the following address:

1. Meetings with the representatives of the Jewish communities constitute a constant element of my apostolic journeys. This fact possesses its own meaning. It emphasizes a unique common faith,

which connects the children of Abraham, who confess the religion of Moses and the Prophets to those who also acknowledge Abraham as their "father in faith" [John 8:39] and accept in Christ, "son of Abraham and son of David" [cf. Matt. 1:1], the entire rich heritage of Moses and the Prophets as well.

A meeting with the Jews on Polish soil is particularly meaningful every time it occurs. Today, I would like to refer to all that I have said during previous meetings on this subject and which my faith and heart dictate. This magnificent, and at the same time, tragic past of almost one thousand years of common history on Polish soil comes together, as does the responsibility for today's world of those who believe in the one God, as well as hope for the future, as we aspire to change the world through the rebirth and renewal of people who are, to an equal degree, open to the voice of God and to the needs of their neighbor.

2. During my last meeting with the representatives of the Jewish community in Poland, at the residence of the Polish primates on June 4, 1987, which I recall with gratitude and with emotion, I expressed the thoughts and feelings with which I and, I think, the overwhelming majority of Poles powerlessly watched the terrible crime perpetuated against the entire Jewish people, sometimes without knowledge of what was taking place, because those who were doing it tried to hide it. I said then that we experienced it "in the spirit of profound solidarity with you. That which threatened you also threatened us. The threat to us was not fulfilled to the same extent as the threat to you; it did not have enough time to be fulfilled to the same degree. You bore the terrible sacrifice of destruction. It can be said that you bore this sacrifice for others, who were also supposed to be destroyed."

I heartily echo the words that I found in the pastoral letter of the Polish bishops dated November 30, 1990: "The same land was a common homeland for Poles and Jews for ages; the mutual loss of life, a sea of terrible suffering and of the wrongs endured should not divide, but unite us. The places of execution, and in many cases, the common graves, call for this unity."

The human past does not disappear completely. The history of the Poles and Jews, even though there are so few Jews currently living on Polish soil, is still very much present in the lives of Jews, as well as in the lives of Poles. I brought this to the attention of those of my countrymen who visited me in Rome on September 29, 1990. "The nation which lived with us for many generations has remained with us even after the horrible death of millions of its sons and daughters," I said. "Together, we await the day of judgment and resurrection" [Jasna Góra Cycle].

3. Today it seems to be a thing of great importance that, on both sides, we try to perceive, salvage, and renew the good things that occurred in our mutual relations (and, after all, a lot of good things happened over the centuries). We should also try to find unity and friendship despite the evil, because there was also much evil in our mutual history.

Unfortunately, both the good and the evil that occurred between us was crushed by the genocide, inconceivable in its severity, to which the Jewish nation fell prey. One can at least say the unprecedented crime of killing an entire nation shocked Christian Europe and mobilized it to righting the wrongs that were perpetuated against the Jews and which were often written into the customs and way of thinking. After an interval of two thousand years, the Jews finally acquired their own state. The nations with a Christian civilization undertook the arduous task of rooting out from their mentalities all unjust prejudices against the Jews, as well as any manifestations of anti-Semitism. Christian churches, including the Catholic Church, actively participated in this task.

Last year, the universal Church as well as the local Polish Church celebrated the twenty-fifth anniversary of the declaration of the Second Vatican Council, *Nostra Aetate*. This declaration marks a significant breakthrough in the relations of Christians and Jews. The Council's teachings were developed in later documents of the Apostolic See, for example, *Guidelines and Suggestions for Implementing the Conciliar Declaration* Nostra Aetate, No. 4 [1974], as well as *Notes on the Correct Presentation of the Jews and Judaism in Catholic Preaching and Teaching* [1985]. I can happily state that all these Church documents, as well as all the papal teachings, were translated and published in Polish due to the efforts of the Polish Episcopate. I am happy that the previously mentioned pastoral letter of the Polish bishops of November 30, 1990 was recently added to this collection of documents.

Today, more than twenty-five years after the Second Vatican Council, the time has come to make a special effort to fulfill and introduce the teachings of the Church into everyday life. May the content of these documents be an inspiration to all local churches, including the Polish Church, to overcome the damaging stereotypes, established patterns, and prejudices still lingering here and there. May they come to show, in the face of the contemporary world, in which faith faces difficult trials, the beauty and deep truths of the one God and Father, who longs to be known as such and loved by all his children.

One of the more important tasks of the Church is the education of a young generation in a spirit of mutual respect, in the awareness of our mutual roots, and our common tasks in the contemporary world. But she must also bring up the young generation to learn about their own distinctiveness and identity. I heartily bless all the efforts which serve this very goal. In the words of the psalmist, I ask God Almighty to teach all the children of the Covenant to do his will:

"Teach me to do your will, for you are my God!" [Ps. 142/143:10].
"Shalom!"

June 17, 1991

Looking Back: General Audience

At the general audience, June 12, the pope reflected on his recent trip to Poland and his encounter there with the Jewish community.

. . . Lastly, I mention the meeting at the nunciature with the representatives of Polish Jews, with whom Poland has coexisted for many centuries in the same land, and with whom it has been joined since the time of the last war in the tragedy of the Holocaust caused by the racist program of Hitler's totalitarianism. The pope's meeting with Jews on Polish soil was always very cordial because it called to mind and renewed the personal bonds formed at the time of his youth and the difficult years of the occupation. . . .

Address to World Council of Churches' Dialogue Sub-Unit

June 21, 1991

On Friday, June 21, the Holy Father welcomed to the Apostolic Palace the staff members of the World Council of Churches' Dialogue Sub-Unit. In his address he made these remarks:

. . . Dialogue among Christians, Muslims, and Jews reminds us of a common heritage of belief in the One God who created us, who shows us his will, and who calls us to be happy with him in eternity. . . .

Visit to Poland for Celebration of World Youth Day

August 14, 1991

Reflections after Mass in Wadowice

Before the celebrations in Czestochowa, the Holy Father went to his hometown of Wadowice, where he celebrated Mass, consecrating the new parish church named in honor of St. Peter. At the end of the Mass in Wadowice, the pope added the following brief remark:

. . . Today I am meeting with my classmates. They are the ones who received priestly ordination with me, and who come from the three

seminaries of Krakow, Silesia, and Czestochowa. However, they are
first of all my high school classmates. My friendship with some of
them goes back to our very first years in elementary school. I want
to thank Wadowice for those schools from which I received such
great light, both the elementary school and the wonderful high
school in Wadowice named for Marcin Wadowita. Nor can I forget
that among our classmates in the school of Wadowice and in its
high school there were those who belonged to the Mosaic religion;
they are no longer with us, just as there is no longer the old synagogue next to the high school. When a stone was found in the place
where the synagogue used to be, I sent a special letter through one
of our classmates. In it we find the following words: "The Church,
and in her all peoples and nations, are united with you. Certainly
first of all your people feel your suffering, your destruction—here
we recall how close it is to Auschwitz—when they want to speak
to the individuals and people, and to all of mankind, to admonish
them. In your name this warning cry is also raised by the pope,
and the pope who comes from Poland has a special reason for this
because, in a certain way, he experienced all this with you in our
homeland. . . ."

Pastoral Visit to Hungary

August 18, 1991

Address to Jewish Leaders in Budapest

During his visit to Hungary, the Holy Father went to the apostolic nunciature in Budapest for a meeting with representatives of Hungary's Jewish community. The delegation of fifteen persons represented the approximately eighty thousand Jews in Hungary. The pope addressed the group in English.

Dear Friends:

1. It has been my particular wish to meet you personally in the course of this journey, and I thank the Lord for giving us today the grace and the joy of fraternally greeting one another and of witnessing to our faith in God the Creator and Father. I pray that he will bless this meeting and grant us peace: not just peace as it can be described and prepared with solely earthly means and from a "worldly" view point, but that peace which is *shalom*, the saving presence of God in human history.

2. "*Grant us peace, O Lord!*" How often this prayer was addressed to God, when you met in this place of worship in those days when the dark clouds of persecution were beginning to gather over the Hebrew community of Hungary and when hateful measures of discrimination were making life ever more difficult. In your hearts you repeated the prayers which from ancient times had so often been on the lips of your forefathers: "O God, why do you cast us off for ever? Why does your anger smoke against the sheep of your pasture?" [Ps. 74:1]. But persecution became ever more severe. At that time you were gripped by fear for your very lives. Thousand after thousand of the Hebrew community were imprisoned in concentration camps and progressively exterminated. In those terrible days the words of the prophet Jeremiah became once more a reality: "A

voice is heard in Ramah, lamentation and bitter weeping. Rachel is weeping for her children; she refuses to be comforted for her children, because they are not" [Jer. 31:15].

My thoughts go with deep respect to the great believers who even in those days of anguish and affliction, in those days of devastation— "*Yom Shoah*," the words of Zephaniah [cf. Zeph. 1:15]—did not fail to believe in the Lord's promises and to repeat: "He has torn, that he may heal us; he has stricken, and he will bind us up" [Hos. 6:1]. We are here now to adore the God of Israel, who this time too has stretched out his protecting hand over a blessed remnant of his people. How often this mysterious ransom has been repeated in your history!

3. Sustained by its faith in the Lord, even in its millenary dispersion, the Jewish people has preserved its identity, its rite, its tradition, and indeed has made an essential contribution to the spiritual and cultural life of the world, particularly in Europe. In this country, too, you have behind you a long history of generous dedication and commitment. And today, after the period of darkness when it seemed as though the Jews would be completely exterminated, you are here once more and making a significant contribution to Magyar national life. I rejoice at your active presence, which reveals the new vitality of your people. But, at the same time, I recall each and every one of the Jews—women and children, old men and young—who, though they lost their lives, kept their faith in the Lord's promises. In fact, I firmly believe that in their persons, too, is fulfilled the word of God written in the book of Daniel: "And many of those who sleep in the dust of the earth shall awake. . . . And those who are wise shall shine like the brightness of the firmament." [Dan. 12:2–3].

The sure expectation of the resurrection of the dead is a treasure which many children of Israel discovered at the very moment when their unconditional trust in God had to face the evidence of a situation which, humanly speaking, was desperate. This expectation, shot through with messianic hope, constituted a break on the darkened human horizon and revealed a decisive dimension of their existence. With profound respect, I salute the testimony of those brave and righteous people; I am certain that their convictions were not in vain, and I trust that all who share that expectation will always have the strength to obey God's commands.

I would like also to remember what the illustrious representatives of the Catholic Church here in Hungary, as well as in other countries, have done to defend the Jews; within the possibilities allowed by the circumstances, they committed themselves with courage; as for instance did the papal nuncio, Monsignor Angelo Rotta and Monsignor Apor, bishop of Györ.

4. Our gaze now turns from the past to a future of reconciliation in justice. Once again, I deplore and condemn, together with you, the wickedness which made you suffer and which brought about the death of so many others. Of course, we must try to "purge the evil from our midst" [cf. Deut. 17:7], but what concerns us now is not desire for revenge on the wicked, since it is fitting to leave the supreme judgement to God, but a commitment to ensure that never again can selfishness and hatred sow suffering and death. We must ensure that justice reigns at least in that part of the world over which we can exercise a certain influence, beginning in the first place with our own hearts, our families, and those who are close to us.

This fight against hatred and selfishness is a necessary requirement of fidelity to God's Law. The precept, "You shall love your neighbor as yourself" [Lev. 19:18], concerns in the first place the mutual relationship between the children of Israel, but it does not allow indifference to others. "The Lord your God . . . loves the sojourner, giving him food and clothing. Love the sojourner therefore; for you were sojourners in the land of Egypt" [Deut. 10:17–19]. The hard quest for justice, love, and peace must begin with ourselves. It would be a mistake to think that the dark force of selfishness and hatred remains totally outside of our lives and does not in some way tarnish our very existence. "The imagination of man's heart is evil from his youth" [Gen. 8:21], says the Lord. And this inclination finds echo in our ways of behaving. Therefore, with God's powerful help, true liberation from evil is a continuous crossing of the Red Sea, and involves a patient struggle, through which we have to progress by means of a daily conversion of heart, or *Teshuvà*, in repentance, fasting, and works of mercy.

Let us join therefore in a sincere quest for goodness and peace, within us and about us, day after day, so that, thanks also to our commitment, the wickedness which we detest may be more radically conquered, and that the kingdom of justice, love, and peace which corresponds to the Creator's intention may be spread ever more widely within us and about us. "Love for the one same God must be translated into concrete action in favour of men . . . in the quest for social justice and peace, at the local, national and international levels" [*Guidelines and Suggestions for Implementing the Conciliar Declaration* Nostra Aetate, No. 4; *Enchiridion Vaticanum*, 5, p. 513].

5. Knowing our weakness, and trusting in the strength of God who works in us and delivers us from evil, let us have recourse to the Lord who sets us free. He who rescues his people from forms of external slavery will also free us from slavery within. May the Lord's face shine upon our hearts, so that we shall not fix our gaze on the bitter memory of wrongs received, nor wait for others to become good first, but shall ourselves go forward in conversion to what is good and, forgetting the past, cooperate with the Creator in building a brighter future.

This "was precisely the great teaching of the Second Vatican Council, which exhorted the whole Church to study the vast treasure made up by the common spiritual patrimony [cf. *Nostra Aetate*, 4] which unites us with Abraham's stock, so as to draw from that patrimony a renewed impulse of faith and action. And from this conviction springs a common commitment for Christians and Jews to get to know one another better, to engage in dialogue, to cooperate intensely in the sphere of human rights, religious education, and the fight against anti-Semitism, in accordance with the program laid down in Prague in 1990 by the Jewish—Catholic Mixed Committee, in a spirit of fraternal esteem.

In the face of the risk of a resurgence and spread of anti-Semitic feelings, attitudes, and initiatives, of which certain disquieting signs are to be seen today, and of which we have experienced the most frightful results in the past, we must teach consciences to consider anti-Semitism, and all forms of racism, as sins against God and humanity. In order to ensure this education of consciences and effective cooperation in general, it is to be hoped that there can also be set up joint local committees.

And so, my friends, may this meeting of ours turn into a fervent prayer, after the manner of the prophet's moving supplication:

"Remember your power and your name. For you are our Lord, our God, and you, O Lord, will we praise" [Bar. 3:5–5].

May this prayer unite all the inhabitants of Hungary in the peace of the Lord.

Pastoral Visit to Brazil

October 15, 1991

Meeting with Jewish Leaders in Brasilia

On Tuesday, October 15, during his pastoral visit to Brazil, the Holy Father met with leaders of the Jewish community in the apostolic nunciature in Brasilia. The pope gave a brief discourse on the occasion.

1. It is a moment of special satisfaction for me to be able to greet Rabbi Henry Sobel and the representatives of Brazil's Jewish community. From my heart I thank you for your kindness in promoting this meeting and, at the same time, I am profoundly touched by your kind gesture in offering me this beautiful gift. I see this act as the symbolic expression of the ties which bind the Catholic Church in Brazil and the Jewish community.

However, even beyond this gesture, divine providence desired this historic moment, this meeting, to strengthen the spirit of fraternity and mutual esteem whose basis is not merely reciprocal respect, but rather faith in the one, true God.

Today, twenty-five years after the Second Vatican Council, the declaration *Nostra Aetate* continues to indicate a radical change in relations between Christians and Jews. My hope is, therefore, that the Jewish—Catholic dialogue may be strengthened ever more in virtue of the word of God. Welcomed into hearts with an authentic readiness to make it operative in our lives, the word opens our eyes to be able to recognize in all our brothers and sisters the face of the one Creator-God. Reading a large part of the Scripture together with common veneration, we should be united in accepting it, meditating on it, and putting it into practice at the service of all people, especially those who are most in need.

2. Interreligious dialogue invites all the local churches, and the Brazilian Church among them, to make ever new efforts to overcome certain preconceived ideas which still exist in many areas. In this way, they should show the world of today, in which the faith is exposed to so many difficulties, the beauty and profound truth of belief in the one God and Lord who must be known and loved as such through all those who believe in him. Adoring the one true God, in fact, we discover our common spiritual root, which is the consciousness of the brotherhood of all people. This awareness is truly the closest bond which unites Christians and the Jewish people. This common root also makes us love this people because, as the Bible says, "The Lord has loved Israel forever" [1 Kings 10:9], he has made a covenant with it which has never been broken, placing in it the messianic hope of the whole human race.

3. I am happy to learn that, thanks to the National Committee for Jewish—Catholic Religious Dialogue, relations and collaboration between you have grown greatly in recent years. Currently, the committee is made up of Catholic and Jewish members in all the principal capitals of the states of the federation, with the possibility of extending its presence to other cities in the future. I hope that the dialogue and mutual respect will continue to be the way for building mutual esteem for the spiritual heritage which unites Jews and Christians. With all my heart, I bless the efforts and initiatives which have been undertaken towards that end.

I express my wishes and pray to the Most High for peace in all the world and especially in the Holy Land where on every occasion this word is repeated as a greeting between friends. May our Jewish brothers and sisters, who have been led "out from among the peoples and gathered from the foreign lands" and brought back "to their own country" [Ezek. 34:13], to the land of their ancestors, be able to live there in peace and security on the "mountains of Israel," guarded by the protection of God, their true shepherd. *Shalom!*

1992

Message for the Twenty-Fifth Annual World Day of Prayer for Peace

January 1, 1992

[. . . The] longing for peace is deeply rooted in human nature and is found in the different religions. It expresses itself in the desire for order and tranquility, in an attitude of readiness to help others, in cooperation and sharing based on mutual respect. These values, which originate in the natural law and are propounded by the world's religions, require if they are to develop, the support of everyone—politicians, leaders of international organizations, businessmen and workers, associations and private citizens. What we are speaking of is a precise duty incumbent on everyone, and more so if one is a believer: Bearing witness to peace, and working and praying for peace are a normal part of good religious behavior.

This also explains why, in the sacred books of the different religions, references to peace occupy a prominent place in the context of man's life and his relationship with God. For example, we Christians believe that Jesus Christ, the son of the One who has "plans for welfare and not for evil" [Jer. 29:11] is "our peace" [Eph. 2:14]; for our Jewish brothers and sisters, the word "*shalom*" expresses both a wish and blessing in a situation in which man is in harmony with himself, with nature, and with God; and for the followers of Islam the term "*salam*" is so important that it constitutes one of the glorious divine names. It can be said that a religious life, if it is lived authentically, cannot fail to bring forth fruits of peace and brotherhood, for it is in the nature of religion to foster an ever-increasing fraternal relationship among people. . . .

Address to the Diplomatic Corps Accredited to the Holy See

January 11, 1992

If we consider the activity carried on in the diplomatic sector, there, too, we perceive some promising signs. I am thinking, for example, of last autumn's Madrid meeting, where for the first time Arabs and Israelis were seated at the same table and agreed to speak of subjects which until then had been considered prohibited. The perseverance of enlightened people who desire to work for peace resulted in a structure of dialogue and of negotiations being set in place, one which will enable the peoples of the region—in particular the most exposed, the Palestinians and the Lebanese—to face the future with greater confidence. It is the entire international community which ought to mobilize itself in order to accompany these peoples of the Middle East on the arduous paths of peace. What a blessing it would be if this Holy Land, where God spoke and Jesus walked, could become a special place of encounter and prayer for peoples, if the Holy City of Jerusalem could be a sign and instrument of peace and reconciliation!

There, too, believers have a mission of primary importance to accomplish. Forgetting the past and looking to the future, they are called to repentance, to reexamine their behavior and to realize once again that they are brothers and sisters by reason of the one God who loves them and invites them to cooperate in his plan for humanity. I consider dialogue between Jews, Christians, and Muslims to be a priority. In coming to know each other better, in growing to esteem one another and in living out, with respect for consciences, the various aspects of their religion, they will be, in that part of the world and elsewhere, "artisans of peace."

As I wrote in my message for the twenty-fifth World Day of Prayer for Peace, "a religious life, if it is lived authentically, cannot fail to bring forth fruits of peace and brotherhood, for it is in the nature of religion to foster an ever-increasing fraternal relationship among people" [2].

Address to the Ambassador of Lithuania

July 11, 1992

On Saturday, July 11, the Holy Father received H.E. Kazys Lozoraitis, Lithuania's first ambassador to the Holy See since the reestablishment of normal diplomatic relations was announced in August 1991. During the ceremonies for the presentation of the ambassador's letters of credence discourses were exchanged in French. The pope mentioned also the sufferings of the Jewish community in Lithuania's past.

. . . Down through the ages the path followed by the Lithuanian people would often be one of trial and suffering, one characterized by the struggle to safeguard an identity which was often on the verge of obliteration, marked by those who died for the homeland, who were also martyrs for the Catholic faith. We have a particularly vivid yet sad memory of recent times when Lithuania suffered the destructive assaults of two ideologies that wanted to impose by force upon Europe and the world concepts of life which are radically contrary to the human vocation to religious and civil freedom. We recall the extreme suffering of several bishops, thousands of priests and believers, intellectuals and politicians, labourers and farmers, and even of whole families, who were forcibly deported, more often than not without return. Many of them are now numbered among that great host of those who have been persecuted for the faith. History cannot pass over the same tragic fate experienced by the Jewish community, especially in Vilnius and Kaunas, because of a heinous racism which sought to obliterate them from the face of the earth. One hardly dares to mention that this terrible destiny shared by the sons and daughters of your land had been written into insidious agreements whose secrecy was intended to hide their dark nature. . . .

General Audience: Against Anti-Semitism and Xenophobia

October 28, 1992

During the general audience on October 28, the Holy Father spoke out against recent expressions of anti-Semitism and xenophobia. The pope spoke in Italian as follows:

I would now like to express a word of fraternal solidarity to the members of the Jewish people. Today, in fact, is the anniversary of the promulgation of the Second Vatican Council's declaration *Nostra Aetate* on the Church's relations with non-Christian religions, and in a special way with the descendants of "Abraham's stock." In addition, last week marked the close of the solemn festivities for the beginning of the year according to the Jewish calendar with the celebration of *Simhath Torah*, the Exultation for the [Divine] Law.

I mention these facts as I bear in my heart the sadness over reports of attacks and profanations which for some time have been offending the memory of the victims of the *Shoah* in the very places which witnessed the suffering of millions of innocent people. As the Council teaches, and as I myself repeated in the Synagogue of Rome, the Church "deplores all hatreds, persecutions, displays of anti-Semitism leveled at any time or from any source against the Jews" [*Nostra Aetate*, 4].

More generally, in the face of the recurrent episodes of xenophobia, racial tension, and extreme, fanatical nationalism, I feel it is my duty to emphasize that every form of racism is a sin against God and humanity, since every human person bears the stamp of the divine image.

Address to the German Bishops of the Berlin Region on the *Ad Limina* Visit

November 14, 1992

On Friday November 14, the Holy Father received the first group of German bishops on their visit Ad Limina Apostolorum. The bishops of the Berlin region are the pastors of the Church in the new federal states, the territory formerly included in the German Democratic Republic. This was their first visit since the "change," the word which Germans use to refer to the collapse of Communism and the unification of Germany, and the Holy Father took advantage of the occasion to look at their past and their present challenges, emphasizing especially the need for protecting Jews and other minority groups, and working with others in overcoming past divisions.

In 1989, the people of your country—and Christians were there in the front lines—placed the other, liberal Germany in the eyes of worldwide public opinion. Dear brothers, you must also commit yourselves to seeing that everything is done to prevent the spread of racist and nationalistic tendencies, especially among the young people, tendencies which threaten Germany's image. In no way can Christians succumb to indifference and apathy. This would be no less dangerous than violence itself. We would be encouraging dangerous developments if we only warn against and judge methods but not the motives behind this type of denial of human rights.

Therefore, I make this urgent plea to you to be committed to the protection of your Jewish fellow citizens. The desecration of synagogues and the profanation of the memorials that have meant so much to Jews throughout their sorrowful history can never be condoned. The fathers of the Second Vatican Council were aware of the special relationship between Christians and Jews, as they expressed it in their *Declaration on the Relationship of the Church to Non-Christian Religions*: "Since Christians and Jews have such a common spiritual heritage, this sacred Council wishes to encourage and further mutual understanding and appreciation. This can be obtained, especially, by way of biblical and theological enquiry and through friendly discussions" [*Nostra Aetate*, 4]. You should therefore make your contribution so that your Jewish fellow citizens do not become discouraged, and that they remain in your land, which is also their homeland, and continue to participate in its religious, cultural, and scientific life . . .

1993

Address to Rome's Civic Authorities

January 25, 1993

Political life is a noble form of charity, Rome's civic authorities were re-
minded during their annual meeting with the bishop of Rome on Janu-
ary 25. In reminding them of the Church's respect for their activity, the
pope recalled that everyone has the right to expect honesty and integrity
from public officials. The Holy Father's address included a reference to
anti-Semitism.

... As I said several months ago, "the Church is not only in Rome,
but, being present in Rome, she necessarily participates in the life
of Rome" [Address at St. John Lateran, May 30, 1992]. ...

Welcome, therefore, dear administrators of the city. A special
thanks to you, Mayor Carraro, for the kind words with which you
addressed me. With great attention I have followed the analysis
you made, in the context of the present situation in Europe and the
world, of the more important problems marking the life of our city:
from the moral and institutional questions to the economic crisis,
from the strongly felt demand for a more equitable power-sharing
to the affirmation of a real solidarity towards the weak which, by
promoting an effective culture of acceptance, opposes episodes of
xenophobic and anti-Semitic violence, and reaches out to the complex situation of immigrants, especially those who are here without
legal authorization.

Letter to the Carmelite Nuns at Auschwitz

April 9, 1993

"Now, according to the will of the Church, you should move to another place in the same Oswiecim," Pope John Paul II said in an April 9 letter to the Carmelite nuns in the convent at Auschwitz, Poland. The location of the convent near the former German Nazi World War II concentration camp developed into a source of controversy with some Jewish groups that considered the convent's presence inappropriate at a site where the attempted genocide of the Jews is recalled. In his letter to the nuns, the pope offered each of them the opportunity to move to the interfaith center in Oswiecim or to return to their mother convent. Oswiecim is the Polish name of the town in which the camp is located.

"My vocation is love. Ah yes, I am already finding my place in the Church. . . . The Church has a heart and . . . this heart burns with the fire of love. . . . Thus, love shows itself to me as an element of my vocation. . . . In the heart of the Church, my mother, I will become love itself" [autobiographical manuscripts, St. Therese of Lisieux, 1957, pp. 227–29].

The words of a holy Carmelite from Lisieux speak of the essential vocation of her Carmelite sisters: of each of you. To be love itself in the heart of the Church, you once came to Oswiecim. Should it be explained how much the heart of the Church should beat in the place? How much the love with which Christ loved mankind to the end is needed here? How much it is needed here, where in the years when hatred and contempt toward humanity ruled, a terrible harvest of destruction and death was gathered among people belonging to so many nations?

Now, according to the "will of the Church, you should move to another place in this same Oswiecim. It remains a matter for the free will of each of you whether you wish to continue living the Carmelite life within the existing community or whether you wish to return to the mother convent. For each of you, this is also a moment of trial. May it please the crucified and resurrected Christ to enable you to recognize his will and the particular calling to the Carmelite path of life.

Yet Oswiecim—and all that is connected with it as the tragic heritage of Europe and all humanity—remains a task for the Carmelites. It remains a task particularly through what is linked with this camp of the Holocaust, "Auschwitz-Birkenau," in the memory of nations: in the memory of the sons and daughters of Israel, and also through what is linked with the history of the Poles, the history of our homeland. How the future will grow from this most painful past largely depends on whether, on the threshold of Oswiecim, "the love which is greater than death" will stand watch. You, dear sisters, in a particular way, are entrusted with the mystery of this redeemed love—this love which saves the world. And how much our contemporary world—fifty years after the terrible war, which produced among other things Auschwitz—is still threatened by hatred!

Dear daughters of Carmel! Accept at the same time the *gaudium Paschale* with which the Church lives at the time of Easter. Accept this blessing in the name of the Father, Son and Holy Spirit—in the name of Jesus Christ who conquered the world [see John 16:33].

Reflections on the Fiftieth Anniversary of the Uprising of the Warsaw Ghetto

April 6, 1993

Jews from around the world gathered in Poland in April 1993 to com-
memorate the fiftieth anniversary of the uprising in the Warsaw Ghetto.
The Holy Father sent a message to Archbishop Józef Kowalczyk, apos-
tolic nuncio in Poland, to be transmitted to the Coordinating Commis-
sion of the Hebrew Organizations in Poland. The following is the text
of the pope's message, which was written in English:

At the fiftieth anniversary of the Warsaw Ghetto uprising
approaches, together with the whole Church, I wish to remember those terrible days of World War II, days of contempt for the
human person, manifested in the horror of the sufferings endured
at that time by so many of our Jewish brothers and sisters.

It is with profound grief that we call to mind what happened
then, and indeed all that happened then, and indeed all that happened in the long black night of the *Shoah*. We remember, and we
need to remember, but we need to remember with renewed trust in
God and in his all-healing blessing.

In their pastoral letter of November 30, 1990, the Polish bishops
wrote about what took place in Poland then, but also about the
present-day responsibility of Christians and Jews: "The mutual loss
of life, a sea of terrible suffering and of wrongs endured should not
divide but unite us. The places of execution, and in many cases, the
common graves, call for this unity."

As Christians and Jews, following the example of the faith of
Abraham, we are called to be a blessing for the world [cf. Gen.
12:2ff]. This is the common task awaiting us. It is therefore necessary for us, Christians and Jews, to be first a blessing to one another.

This will effectively occur if we are united in the face of the evils which are still threatening: indifference and prejudice, as well as displays of anti-Semitism.

For what has already been achieved by Catholics and Jews through dialogue and cooperation I give thanks with you to God; for what we are still called to do I offer my ardent prayers. May God further guide us along the paths of his sovereign and loving will for the human family.

From the Vatican
Joannes Paulus II PP.

Regina Coeli

April 18, 1993

Before imparting the final blessing during a Mass of beatification on April 18, the Holy Father led the faithful in reciting the Regina Coeli. In the brief reflection preceding the Marian prayer, the pope recalled the fiftieth anniversary of the uprising in the Jewish ghetto of Warsaw, a large crowd of Jews, Catholics, and Protestants had come to St. Peter's Square to participate in the commemoration.

. . . The joy of this day must not prevent us from turning our attention to an event, so filled with inhuman suffering, which took place fifty years ago: the uprising in the Warsaw Ghetto. I feel a great need to greet all those, Christians and Jews, who have come to this square to commemorate that fact and the crimes perpetrated against the Jewish people during the last world war.

In deep solidarity with that people, and in communion with the whole community of Catholics, I would like to commemorate those terrible events, so remote in time, but etched in the minds of many of us: the days of the *Shoah* marked a true night of history, with unimaginable crimes against God and humanity. How could we not be with you, dear Jewish brothers and sisters, to recall in prayer and meditation such a tragic anniversary? Be sure of this: You are not alone in bearing the pain of this memory; we pray and watch with you, under the gaze of God, the holy and just one, rich in mercy and pardon.

May our unanimous solidarity be a sign anticipating for all of rest less humanity that day of peace foretold by Isaiah, when "one nation shall not raise the sword against another, nor shall they train for war again" [Isa. 2:4]. . . .

Pastoral Visit to Spain

May 15, 1993

Address to the Diplomatic Corps, Madrid

In the afternoon of Tuesday, May 15, the Holy Father received the diplomatic corps accredited to Spain at the apostolic nunciature in Madrid. The pope addressed the diplomats about Spain's history and role in promoting peaceful coexistence.

. . . As for religious freedom, looking at this noble country's past we see that for a certain period in its history, Christianity, Judaism, and Islam existed together on the Iberian peninsula. This page, which so enriched Spanish culture and had its most important center in Toledo, could still represent an eloquent and instructive reference point in our day for promoting authentic religious values as elements of unity, understanding, and dialogue among the members of the human family.

Everybody knows the role Spain played in encouraging a peaceful solution to the Middle East conflict, which culminated with the meeting held in Madrid in October 1991. Spain, a member of the

European community and at the same time united by close ties to the Latin American countries, sees itself constantly questioned by its vocation as an integrating element of the cultures which have enriched its past. . . .

Before such a number of major diplomatic representatives of countries where the Muslim religion is professed by the majority of the population, I express my fervent wish that this praiseworthy initiative of the Spanish Church, faithfully inspired by the principles of the Second Vatican Council's declaration *Nostra Aetate*, will open new routes to cooperation and outreach. It is my heartfelt hope that dialogue and collaboration may prevail wherever members of the three religions that have enriched the spiritual and human melting pot of the Iberian peninsula live together, particularly where this coexistence is marked by a minority/majority relationship, and that injustice and discrimination may be carefully avoided. . . .

Address to the Young Leadership of the International Council of Christians and Jews

July 2, 1993

On Friday, July 2, the Holy Father received a group of Jewish and Christian young people who were on pilgrimage together to Rome and Jerusalem. The pope addressed them in English, congratulating them on their efforts to promote understanding among people of monotheistic faiths.

Dear Friends:

I extend a cordial welcome to the members of the Young Leadership Section of the International Council of Christians and Jews, and I thank your chairman for his kind words on your behalf. You have set yourselves a worthy aim: to contribute to the creation of a world of greater understanding, by promoting and encouraging Jewish—Christian dialogue, by bringing together young people of monotheistic faiths, and by confronting the challenges of racism, prejudice, intolerance, and all forms of xenophobia. I offer you my prayerful good wishes that your pilgrimage to Rome and Jerusalem will strengthen you for this work.

It is very fitting that young Christians and Jews should be united in such a great task. Our "common spiritual patrimony" spoken of by the fathers of the Second Vatican Council [*Nostra Aetate*, 4] includes two fundamental principles which should guide your activities. The first is the knowledge that the order according to which God created the world and its inhabitants is the sure and secure basis for peace among individuals and nations. The Law of the Lord of Hosts is the Law of peace [cf. Ps. 37:37], and it is through obedience to the Lord's will that mankind will achieve the harmony which all peoples long for. The second principle is the conviction that the ultimate source of violence is the corruption of the human heart. It follows that the way to achieve lasting victory over discord is through a change of heart [cf. Jer. 32:39], through moral conversion. These truths, preached by the Prophets of old and proclaimed in the church and the synagogue, are the heritage entrusted to you young people by your forebears. They are the wisdom which you can offer to the world through your united efforts.

Together you are going up to Jerusalem, the city of peace, a "symbol of coming together, of union and of universal peace for the human family" [*Apostolic Letter on the City of Jerusalem*, April 20, 1984]. Your pilgrimage is one more hopeful sign of the cooperation which the world of today needs so desperately from believers [cf. *Message for the Twenty-Fifth World Day of Prayer for Peace*, 1992, 1]. Through such deeds of solidarity may the power of the Lord of all righteousness triumph over the antagonisms of the past and the strife of the present, so that in the days to come, all men and women will live together in mutual concord and respect.

Excerpts from Encyclical: *Veritatis Splendor*

August 6, 1993

In the tenth encyclical of his papacy, Pope John Paul II treated the foundations of moral theology—"foundations which are being undermined by certain present-day tendencies." Titled Veritatis Splendor *[The Splendor of Truth], the encyclical was addressed to the world's bishops.*

Among points discussed in the encyclical were freedom, conscience, natural law, the unity of body and soul in the human person, mortal and venial sin; such questions as consequentialism, proportionalism, or the fundamental option in moral theology; dissent, the relationship of bishops and moral theologians, and their respective roles.

It addressed not only the Church's internal life, but expressed concern as well for helping present-day culture rediscover the bond between truth, freedom, and the good

10. What man is and what he must do becomes clear as soon as God reveals himself. The Decalogue is based on these words: "I am the Lord your God, who brought you out of the land of Egypt, out of the house of bondage" [Exod. 20:2–3]. In the "ten words" of the Covenant with Israel and in the whole Law, God makes himself known and acknowledged as the one who "alone is good"; the one who, despite man's sin, remains the "model" for moral action, in accordance with his command: "You shall be holy; for I the Lord your God am holy" [Lev. 19:2]; as the one who, faithful to his love for man, gives him his Law [cf. Exod. 19:9–24 and 20:18–21] in order to restore man's original and peaceful harmony with the Creator and with all creation, and, what is more, to draw him into his divine love: "I will walk among you and will be your God, and you shall be my people" [Lev. 26:12].

The moral life presents itself as the response due to the many gratuitous initiatives taken by God out of love for man. It is a response of love, according to the statement made in Deuteronomy about the fundamental commandment: "Hear, O Israel: The Lord our God is one Lord: and you shall love the Lord your God with all your heart, and with all your soul, and with all your might. And these words which I command you this day shall be upon your heart; and you shall teach them diligently to your children" [Deut. 6:4–7]. Thus the moral life, caught up in the gratuitousness of God's love, is called to reflect his glory: "For the one who loves God it is enough to be pleasing to the one whom he loves: for no greater reward should be sought than the love itself; charity in fact is of God in such a way that God himself is charity."

11. The statement that "there is only one who is good" thus brings us back to the "first tablet" of the Commandments, which calls us to acknowledge God as the one Lord of all and to worship him alone for his infinite holiness [cf. Exod. 20:2–11]. The good is belonging to God, obeying him, walking humbly with him in doing justice and in loving kindness [cf. Mic. 6:8]. Acknowledging the Lord as God is the very core, the heart of the Law, from which the particular precepts flow and toward which they are ordered. In the morality of the Commandments, the fact that the people of Israel belongs to the Lord is made evident, because God alone is the one who is good. Such is the witness of sacred Scripture, imbued in every one of its pages with a lively perception of God's absolute holiness: "Holy, holy, holy is the Lord of hosts" [Isa. 6:3].

But if God alone is the good, no human effort, not even the most rigorous observance of the Commandments, succeeds in "fulfilling" the Law, that is, acknowledging the Lord as God, and rendering him the worship due to him alone [cf. Matt. 4:10], This "fulfillment" can come only from a gift of God: the offer of a share in the divine goodness revealed and communicated in Jesus, the one whom the rich young man addresses with the words *good teacher* [Mark 10:17; Luke 18:18]. What the young man now perhaps only dimly perceives will in the end be fully revealed by Jesus himself in the invitation: "Come, follow me" [Matt. 19:21].

"If you wish to enter into life, keep the commandments" [Matt. 19:17]

12. Only God can answer the question about the good, because he is the good. But God has already given an answer to this question: He did so by creating man and ordering him with wisdom and love to his final end, through the law which is inscribed in his heart [cf. Rom. 2:15], the "natural law." The latter "is nothing other than the light of understanding infused in us by God, whereby we understand what must be done and what must be avoided. God gave this light to man at creation." He also did so in the history of Israel, particularly in the "ten words," the commandments of Sinai, whereby he brought into existence the people of the covenant [cf. Exod. 24] and called them to be his "own possession among all peoples," "a holy nation" [Exod. 19:5–6], which would radiate his holiness to all peoples [cf. Wis. 18:4; Ezek. 20:41], The gift of the Decalogue was a promise and sign of the new Covenant, in which the Law would be written in a new and definitive way upon the human heart [cf. Jer. 31:31–34], replacing the law of sin which had disfigured that heart [cf. Jer. 17:1]. In those days "a new heart" would be given, for in it would dwell "a new spirit," the Spirit of God [cf. Ezek. 36:24–28].

Consequently, after making the important clarification, "there is only one who is good," Jesus tells the young man, "If you wish to enter into life, keep the commandments" [Matt. 19:17]. In this way, a close connection is made between eternal life and obedience to God's commandments: God's commandments show man the path of life, and they lead to it. From the very lips of Jesus, the new Moses, man is once again given the Commandments of the Decalogue. Jesus himself definitely confirms them and proposes them to us as the way and condition of salvation.

The Commandments are linked to a promise. In the old Covenant, the object of the promise was the possession of a land where the people would be able to live in freedom and in accordance with righteousness [cf. Deut. 6:20–25]. In the new covenant, the object of the promise is the "kingdom of heaven," as Jesus declares at the beginning of the "Sermon on the Mount"—a sermon which contains the fullest and most complete formulation of the new Law [cf. Matt. 5–7], clearly linked to the Decalogue entrusted by God to Moses on Mount Sinai. . . .

14. Both the Old and the New Testaments explicitly affirm that without love of neighbor, made concrete in keeping the commandments, genuine love for God is not possible. Saint John makes the point with extraordinary forcefulness: "If anyone says, 'I love God' and hates his brother, he is a liar; for he who does not love his brother, whom he has seen, cannot love God whom he has not seen" [1 John 4:20]. The evangelist echoes the moral preaching of Christ, expressed in a wonderful and unambiguous way in the parable of the Good Samaritan [cf. Luke 10:30–37] and in his words about the final judgment [cf. Matt. 25:31–46].

15. In the Sermon on the Mount, the Magna Carta of Gospel morality, Jesus says: "Do not think that I have come to abolish the Law and the Prophets; I have come not to abolish them but to fulfill them" [Matt. 5:17]. Christ is the key to the Scriptures: "You search the Scriptures . . . and it is they that bear witness to me" [John 5:39]. Christ is the center of the economy of salvation, the recapitulation of the Old and New Testaments, of the promises of the Law and of their fulfillment in the Gospel; he is the living and eternal link between the old and the new covenants. Commenting on Paul's statement that "Christ is the end of the Law" [Rom. 10:4], Saint Ambrose writes: "End not in the sense of deficiency, but in the sense of the fullness of the Law: a fullness which is achieved in Christ [*plenitudo legis in Christo est*], since he came not to abolish the Law but to bring it to fulfillment. In the same way that there is an Old Testament, but all truth is in the New Testament, so it is for the Law: What was given through Moses is a figure of the true Law. Therefore, the Mosaic Law is an image of the truth."

Jesus brings God's Commandments to fulfillment, particularly the Commandment of love of neighbor, by interiorizing their demands and by bringing out their fullest meaning. Love of neighbor springs from a loving heart which, precisely because it loves, is ready to live out the loftiest challenges. Jesus shows that the Commandments must not be understood as a minimum limit not to be gone beyond, but rather as a path involving a moral and spiritual journey toward perfection, at the heart of which is love [cf. Col. 3:14]. Thus the Commandment, "you shall not murder," becomes a call to an attentive love which protects and promotes the life of one's neighbor. The precept prohibiting adultery becomes an invitation to a pure way of looking at others, capable of respecting the spousal meaning of the body: "You have heard that it was said to the men of old, 'You shall not kill; and whoever kills shall be liable to judgment.' But I say to you that every one who is angry with his brother shall be liable to judgment. . . . You have heard that it was said, "You shall not commit adultery.' But I say to you that everyone who looks at a woman lustfully has already committed adultery with her in his heart" [Matt. 5:21–22, 27–28]. Jesus himself is the living "fulfillment" of the Law inasmuch as he fulfills its authentic meaning by the total gift of himself: He himself becomes a living and personal law, who invites people to follow him; through the Spirit, he gives the grace to share his own life and love and provides the strength to bear witness to that love in personal choices and actions [cf. John 13:34–35].

"If you wish to be perfect" [Matt. 19:21].

16. The answer he receives about the Commandments does not satisfy the young man, who asks Jesus a further question. "I have kept all these; what do I still lack?" [Mart. 19:20]. It is not easy to say with a clear conscience, "I have kept all these," if one has any understanding of the real meaning of the demands contained in God's Law. And yet, even though he is able to make this reply, even though he has followed the moral ideal seriously and generously from childhood, the rich young man knows that he is still far from the goal: Before the person of Jesus he realizes that he is still lacking something. It is his awareness of this insufficiency that Jesus addresses in his final answer. Conscious of the young man's yearning for something greater, which would transcend a legalistic interpretation of the Commandments, the good teacher invites him to enter upon the path of perfection: "If you wish to be perfect, go, sell your possessions and give the money to the poor, and you will have treasure in heaven; then come, follow me" [Matt. 19:21].

Like the earlier part of Jesus' answer, this part too must be read and interpreted in the context of the whole moral message of the Gospel and in particular in the context of the Sermon on the Mount, the Beatitudes [cf. Matt. 5:3–12], the first of which is precisely the beatitude of the poor, the "poor in spirit" as Saint Matthew makes clear [Matt. 5:3], the humble. In this sense it can be said that the Beatitudes are also relevant to the answer given by Jesus to the young man's question: "What good must I do to have eternal life?" Indeed, each of the Beatitudes promises from a particular viewpoint that very "good" which opens man up to eternal life and indeed is eternal life.

The Beatitudes are not specifically concerned with certain particular rules of behavior. Rather, they speak of basic attitudes and dispositions in life, and therefore they do not coincide exactly with the Commandments. On the other hand, there is no separation or opposition between the Beatitudes and the Commandments: Both refer to the good, to eternal life. The Sermon on the Mount begins with the proclamation of the Beatitudes, but also refers to the Commandments [cf. Matt. 5:20–48]. At the same time, the Sermon on the Mount demonstrates the openness of the Commandments and their orientation toward the horizon of the perfection proper to the Beatitudes. These latter are above all promises, from which there also indirectly flow normative indications for the moral life. In their originality and profundity they are a sort of self-portrait of Christ and for this very reason are invitations to discipleship and to communion of life with Christ. . . .

23. "The Law of the spirit of rife in Christ Jesus has set me free from the Law of sin and death" [Rom. 8:2]. With these words the apostle Paul invites us to consider in the perspective of the history of salvation, which reaches its fulfillment in Christ, the relationship between the (old) Law and grace (the new Law). He recognizes the pedagogic function of the Law, which, by enabling sinful man to take stock of his own powerlessness and by stripping him of the presumption of his self-sufficiency, leads him to ask for and to receive "life in the Spirit." Only in this new life is it possible to carry out God's Commandments. Indeed, it is through faith in Christ that we have been made righteous [cf. Rom. 3:28]: The "righteousness"

which the Law demands, but is unable to give, is found by every believer to be revealed and granted by the Lord Jesus. Once again it is Saint Augustine who admirably sums up this Pauline dialectic of law and grace: "The Law was given that grace might be sought; and grace was given that the Law might be fulfilled. . . .

25. The moral prescriptions which God imparted in the Old Covenant and which attained their perfection in the new and eternal Covenant in the very person of the son of God made man must be faithfully kept and continually put into practice in the various different cultures throughout the course of history. . . .

26. From the Church's beginnings, the apostles, by virtue of their pastoral responsibility to preach the Gospel, were vigilant over the right conduct of Christians, just as they were vigilant for the purity of the faith and the handing down of the divine gifts in the sacraments. The first Christians, coming both from the Jewish people and from the gentiles, differed from the pagans not only in their faith and their liturgy but also in the witness of their moral conduct, which was inspired by the new Law. The Church is in fact a communion both of faith and of life; her rule of life is "faith working through love" [Gal. 5:6].

No damage must be done to the harmony between faith and life: The unity of the Church is damaged not only by Christians who reject or distort the truths of faith but also by those who disregard the moral obligations to which they are called by the Gospel [cf. 1 Cor. 5:9–13]. The apostles decisively rejected any separation between the commitment of the heart and actions which express or prove it [cf. 1 John 2:3–6]. . . .

45. The Church gratefully accepts and lovingly preserves the entire deposit of revelation, treating it with religious respect and fulfilling her mission of authentically interpreting God's Law in the light of the Gospel. In addition, the Church receives the gift of the new Law, which is the "fulfillment" of God's Law in Jesus Christ and in his Spirit. This is an "interior" Law [cf. Jer. 31:31–33], "written not with ink but with the Spirit of the living God, not on tablets of stone but on tablets of human hearts" [2 Cor. 3:3]; a Law of perfection and of freedom [cf. 2 Cor. 3:17]; "the Law of the Spirit of life in Christ Jesus" [Rom. 8:2]. Saint Thomas writes that

this Law "can be called Law in two ways. First, the Law of the spirit is the Holy Spirit . . . who, dwelling in the soul, not only teaches what is necessary to do by enlightening the intellect on the things to be done, but also inclines the affections to act with upright-ness. . . . Second, the Law of the spirit can be called the proper effect of the Holy Spirit, and thus faith working through love [cf. Gal. 5:6], which teaches inwardly about the things to be done . . . and inclines the affections to act."

Even if moral/theological reflection usually distinguishes between the positive or revealed Law of God and the natural law, and within the economy of salvation between the "old" and the "new" Law, it must not be forgotten that these and other useful distinctions always refer to that Law whose author is the one and the same God and which is always meant for man. The different ways in which God acting in history cares for the world and for mankind are not mutually exclusive; on the contrary, they support each other and intersect. They have their origin and goal in the eternal, wise, and loving counsel whereby God predestines men and women "to be conformed to the image of his Son" [Rom. 8:29]. God's plan poses no threat to man's genuine freedom; on the contrary, the accep-tance of God's plan is the only way to affirm that freedom.

80. Reason attests that there are objects of the human act which are by their nature "incapable of being ordered" to God, because they radically contradict the good of the person made in his image. These are the acts which, in the Church's normal tradition, have been termed "intrinsically evil" [*intrinsece malum*]: They are such always and per se, in other words, on account of their very object and quite apart from the ulterior instances. Consequently, without in the least denying the influence on morality exercised by circum-stances and especially by intentions, the Church teaches that "there exist acts which per se and in themselves, are always seriously wrong by reason of their object." The Second Vatican Council itself, in discussing the respect due to the human person, gives a number of examples of such acts:

> Whatever is hostile to life itself, such as any kind of homicide, geno-
> cide, abortion, euthanasia and voluntary suicide; whatever violates the

integrity of the human person, such as mutilation, physical and mental torture and attempts to coerce the spirit; whatever is offensive to human dignity such as subhuman living conditions, arbitrary imprisonment, deportation, slavery, prostitution and trafficking in women and children; degrading conditions of work which treat laborers as mere instruments of profit, and not as free, responsible persons: All these and the like are a disgrace, and so long as they infect human civilization they contaminate those who inflict them more than those who suffer injustice, and they are a negation of the honor due to the Creator. . . .

91. In the Old Testament we already find admirable witnesses of fidelity of the holy Law of God even to the point of a voluntary acceptance of death. A prime example is the story of Susanna: In reply to the two unjust judges who threatened to have her condemned to death if she refused to yield to their sinful passion, she says: "I am hemmed in on every side. For if I do this thing, it is death for me; and if I do not, I shall not escape your hands. I choose not to do it and to fall into your hands, rather than to sin in the sight of the Lord!" [Dan. 13:22–23]. Susanna, preferring to "fall innocent" into the hands of the judges, bears witness not only to her faith and trust in God but also to her obedience to the truth and to the absoluteness of the moral order. By her readiness to die a martyr, she proclaims that it is not right to do what God's Law qualifies as evil in order to draw some good from it. Susanna chose for herself the "better part": Hers was a perfectly clear witness, without any compromise, to the truth about the good and to the God of Israel. By her acts, she revealed the holiness of God. . . .

97. In this way, moral norms, and primarily the negative ones, those prohibiting evil, manifest their meaning and force, both personal and social. By protecting the inviolable personal dignity of every human being they help to preserve the human social fabric and its proper and fruitful development. The Commandments of the second table of the Decalogue in particular—those which Jesus quoted to the young man of the Gospel [cf. Matt. 19:19]—constitute the indispensable rules of all social life.

. . . The fundamental moral rules of social life thus entail specific demands to which both public authorities and citizens are required to pay heed. Even though intentions may sometimes be good, and circumstances frequently difficult, civil authorities and particular individuals never have authority to violate the fundamental and inalienable rights of the human person. In the end, only a morality which acknowledges certain norms as valid always and for everyone, with no exception, can guarantee the ethical foundation of social coexistence, both on the national and international levels.

1994

Address to the Diplomatic Corps: Rome

January 15, 1994

1. Christmas is simply the revelation of the divine love offered to all men and women. It is the light which illuminated the night of Bethlehem; it is the good news proclaimed to all the peoples on the day of the Epiphany. These recent celebrations have naturally turned our thoughts toward the Holy Land, where Jesus was born, to which we have been on a spiritual pilgrimage.

For the first time in very many years, peace seems possible, thanks to the goodwill of the people who live there today. Yesterday's enemies are talking to one another and talking together about the future. The dynamism of the Madrid Conference, begun in 1991, continues to inspire all those bravely striving to ensure that dialogue and negotiations will triumph over every sort of extremism and selfishness. Israelis and Palestinians, the children of Isaac and of Ishmael, have begun a journey: All their friends have a duty to help them continue it to the end. It is a question of imperious duty, for to perpetuate a situation of uncertainty and especially of heavy sufferings for the Palestinian population—trials which are well known to us—makes even more serious the present difficulties and risks putting once more out of reach the longed-for practical results of the dialogue which has been begun.

It is this background of hope and frailty which is the setting for the conversations which have enabled the State of Israel and the Holy See to sign an accord on a number of fundamental principles suitable for regulating their mutual relations and of guaranteeing for the Catholic Church in that country conditions for a normal existence. There is no doubt that all believers will also draw benefits from the accord. Furthermore, the Holy See is convinced that this new form of relationship with the State of Israel will enable it, while safeguarding its specific spiritual and moral nature, to help consolidate the desire for justice and peace entertained by all those who are involved in the peace process. Without renouncing any of the principles which have inspired its activity in the past, the Holy See will therefore continue to work to ensure that, in respect for the Law and the legitimate aspirations of individuals and peoples, it will be possible to find without delay solutions to other questions which so far have received only partial answers. It is impossible to overemphasize that among these questions is the status of the holy city of Jerusalem, which greatly interests believers in the religions of the book.

In fact, it is the whole region which should benefit from this happy development. I am thinking in particular of Lebanon, whose sovereignty and unity are not yet adequately ensured. Nor do I forget—not far from there—Iraq, whose inhabitants are still paying very dearly the price of war.

. . . 6. And here we are on the shores as it were of the "old continent," pulled between integration and fragmentation. On the one hand, in fact, Europe possesses a network of multistate institutions which ought to help it bring to fulfillment its noble community project. But on the other hand, this same Europe is, as it were, weakened by growing tendencies to individualism which are giving rise to reactions inspired by the most primitive forms of racism and nationalism. The conflicts which are steeping the Caucasus and Bosnia-Herzegovina in blood are proof of this.

These European contradictions seem to have left political leaders at a loss, unable to control these paradoxical tendencies in a global manner and through negotiation.

It is certain that the barbarous and unjustifiable war which for nearly two years has been staining Bosnia-Herzegovina in blood after devastating Croatia has considerably eroded the goodwill which Europe used to enjoy. The fighting goes on. The most iniquitous forms of extremism are still being seen. The peoples are still in the hands of torturers without morals. Innocent civilians are systematically being made the target of hidden snipers. Mosques and churches are being destroyed. The villages emptied of their inhabitants cannot be counted anymore.

This morning, before you, ladies and gentlemen, I would like once more to condemn in the most categorical manner the crimes against man and humanity which are being perpetrated before your very eyes. I would like once more to appeal to the conscience of everyone:

- To all those carrying a weapon, I ask that they put it down. What is taken or destroyed by force will never do honor to a person or to the cause he claims to uphold.
- To the humanitarian organizations, I express my admiration for the work they are accomplishing at great cost, and I ask them to continue without becoming discouraged.
- I ask European political leaders to redouble their efforts to persuade the warring factions so that reason will finally prevail.
- To the peoples of Europe I ask that they not forget, through weariness or selfishness, their brothers and sisters trapped in conflicts which have been imposed on them by their leaders.

I would like to make everyone share my firm conviction: War is not inevitable; peace is possible. It is possible because man has a conscience and a heart. It is possible because God loves each one of us, just as we are, so as to transform and make us grow.

Thus it is that, after so many years, peace in Northern Ireland could become a reality. Let no one reject it! It depends on the goodwill of every person and of every group that today's hope may be something more than an illusion.

It would in fact be a scandal to see Europe resign itself and accept that the law is ultimately scorned, that international order is ridiculed by the actions of armed bands, that society's objectives are conceived as a means to the supremacy of a particular nationality. The fact that the United Nations has set up a tribunal to judge war crimes and crimes against humanity in the former Yugoslav Federation is a sign that the ignominy perpetrated there is being recognized more and more. Some are even calling for the establishment of a permanent international tribunal to judge crimes against humanity. Does this not show that, far from progressing, international society is running a serious risk of regressing?

7. If we reflect on what is at the bottom of the collective behavior we have just described in Africa and Europe, we shall easily discover the presence of exaggerated forms of nationalism. And it is not a question of legitimate love of country or of esteem for its identity, but a rejection of others because they are different, in order more easily to dominate them. Every means is good: the exaltation of race which goes so far as to identify nation and ethnic group; the glorification of the state which thinks and decides for everyone; the imposition of a uniform economic model; the leveling out of cultural differences. We are faced with a new paganism: the deification of the nation. History has shown that the passage from nationalism to totalitarianism is swift, and that when states are no longer equal, people themselves end up by no longer being equal. Thus the natural solidarity between peoples is destroyed, the sense of proportion is distorted, the principle of the unity of humankind is held in contempt.

The Catholic Church cannot accept such a vision of things. Universal by nature, she is conscious of being at the service of all and never identifies with any one national community. She welcomes into her bosom all nations, races, and cultures. She is mindful of—indeed she knows that she is the depository of—God's design for humanity: to gather all people into one family. And this because God is the Creator and Father of all. That is the reason why every time that Christianity—whether according to its Western or Eastern tradition—becomes the instrument of a form of nationalism, it is as it were wounded in its very heart and made sterile.

My predecessor, Pope Pius XI, had already condemned these serious deviations in 1937 in his encyclical, *Mit brennender Sorge*, when he wrote: "Whoever exalts race, or the people, or the state, or a particular form of state, or the depositories of power, or any other fundamental value of the human community . . . and divinizes them to an idolatrous level, distorts and perverts an order of the world planned and created by God" [*Acta Apostolicae Sedis* 29, 1937, 8, p. 149].

Europe is now made up for the most part of states of small or medium size. But they all have their patrimony values, the same dignity and the same rights. No power can put limits on their fundamental rights unless they endanger the rights of other nations. If the international community cannot come to an agreement on the means to deal at the source with this problem of nationalist claims, it is foreseeable that whole continents will be as it were poisoned and that there will be a progressive return to relationships based on force in which the first to suffer will be people themselves. In fact, the rights of peoples go hand in hand with human rights.

8. In this regard, I would like to recall before you who are experienced diplomats the great responsibility incumbent on those who administer public life. They are in the first place the servants of their brothers and sisters and, in an uncertain world such as ours, people look to them as points of reference. In my latest encyclical I recalled that "openness in public administration, impartiality in the service of the body politic, respect for the rights of political adversaries, safeguarding the rights of the accused against summary trials and conviction, the just and honest use of public funds, the rejection of equivocal or illicit means in order to gain, preserve, or increase power at any cost—all these are principles which are primarily rooted in . . . the transcendent value of the person and the objective moral demands of the functioning of states" [*Veritatis Splendor*, 101].

In too many societies, including in Europe, those in positions of responsibility seem to have rejected the demands of a political ethic that takes into account man's transcendence and the relative nature of systems of social organization. It is time that they joined together and conformed to certain moral demands which concern public powers just as much as citizens. In this regard, I wrote in the same encyclical, "In the face of serious forms of social and economic injustice and political corruption affecting entire peoples and nations, there is a growing reaction of indignation on the part of very many people whose fundamental human rights have been trampled upon and held in contempt, as well as an ever more widespread and acute sense of the need for a radical personal and social renewal capable of ensuring justice, solidarity, honesty, and openness" [ibid., 98].

In this difficult but so necessary work of moral resurgence, Catholics, together with other believers, are called to accept their responsibility to bear witness. The presence of Catholics in the running of societies is part of the social doctrine, and the Church and civil authorities and citizens alike should be able to count on them. It is a question here of a form of proclaiming the Gospel and the values which it contains that is helpful, indeed necessary, for the building of a more human society. I am convinced that, just as they were once capable of doing in so many countries of the Europe of old, Christians will again be capable of a political and social involvement enabling them to state, and ever more to demonstrate by their generosity and unselfishness, that we are not the creators of the world. On the contrary, we receive the world from God, who creates it and creates us. Therefore we are just stewards who, out of respect for God's plan, are meant to increase goods in order to share them. Here I would like to quote the forceful words of Saint Paul: "You are called, as you know, to liberty. . . . Serve one another, rather, in words of love. . . . If you go snapping at each other and tearing each other to pieces, you had better watch or you will destroy one another" [Gal. 5:13, 15].

9. Having for too many years experienced a division imposed by reductive ideologies, the world should not now be experiencing a season of exclusions: On the contrary, now should be the season of coming together and of solidarity between East and West, between North and South. Glancing at the world today, we can only state with deep regret that too many human beings are still their brothers' victims. But we cannot resign ourselves to this.

Having begun the year which the United Nations has dedicated to the family, let us act in such a way that humanity will more and more resemble a genuine family in which each individual knows he is listened to, appreciated, and loved, in which each is ready to sacrifice self for the benefit of the other and no one hesitates to help the weaker one. Let us listen to the challenge of the apostle John: "If anyone has the world's good and sees his brother in need, yet closes his heart against him, how does God's love abide in him? [1 John 3:17].

In this Christmas season, the unheard-of tenderness of God is offered to all humankind; how clearly this is shown by the child in the crib! Each one of us is invited to the boldness of brotherhood. This is my heartfelt wish for each of you, for each of your fellow-citizens, for all the nations of the earth.

Palm Sunday Address to Youth on the Jewish Passover

March 27, 1994

Pope John Paul used the Palm Sunday celebration, which fell in 1994 on the same weekend as the Jewish Passover, to invite people "to pause spiritually" at the site of "the temple of God's Covenant with Jerusalem."

"Only a modest fragment of this remains," he said. "It is called the Wailing Wall because before its stones the children of Israel gather, recalling the greatness of the ancient sanctuary in which God made his dwelling and which rightly was the pride of all Israel."

The wall, he said, "is eloquent for the children of Israel. It is also eloquent for us because we know that in this temple God truly established his dwelling." *[Catholic News Service]*

Interview in *Parade* Magazine with Tad Szulc

April 3, 1994

The attitude of the Church toward the people of God's Old Testament—the Jews—can only be that they are our elder brothers in the faith.

It goes back to my youngest years, when, in the parish church of my native Wadowice, I listened to this psalm sung during evening Mass.

> *O, Jerusalem, glorify the Lord:*
> *Praise Your God, O Zion!*
> *For He made the bars of your gates strong,*
> *And blessed Your children within You. . . . [Psalm 147]*

I still have in my ears these words and this melody, which I have remembered all my life. And then came the terrible experience of World War II and the [Nazi] occupation, the Holocaust, which was the extermination of Jews only for the reason that they were Jews. It was a terrible upheaval that has remained in the memory of all the people who were close to these events.

But afterward, whenever I had the opportunity, I spoke about it everywhere—perhaps expressing it in the strongest fashion when I met the representatives of the Jewish community in Warsaw in 1987. I told them that they must bear witness to what happened to their people. . . .

It must be understood that Jews, who for two thousand years were dispersed among the nations of the world, had decided to return to the land of their ancestors. This is their right.

And this right is recognized even by those who look upon the nation of Israel with an unsympathetic eye. This right was also recognized from the outset by the Holy See, and the act of establishing diplomatic relations with Israel is simply an international affirmation of this relationship.

Because you ask how the present rapprochement has developed between the Holy See and Israel, I shall answer citing the words of the Second Vatican Council [held in Rome between 1962 and 1965]. In the *Nostra Aetate* [In Our Time] declaration, the Council states: "The Church ever keeps in mind the words of the apostle Paul about his kinsmen 'who have adopted as sons, and the glory and the Covenant and the legislation and the worship and the promise; who have the fathers, and from whom is Christ, according to the flesh'" [Rom. 9:4–5]. If we stand by the declaration of the Council, we must conclude that the Church's attitude toward Israel results from the same mystery of the Church that the Council undertook to plumb anew.

We trust that with the approach of the year 2000 Jerusalem will become the city of peace for the entire world and that all the people will be able to meet there, in particular the believers in the religions that find their birthright in the faith of Abraham.

Reflections at the Concert at the Vatican Commemorating the Holocaust

April 7, 1994

"Among those who are with us this evening are some who physically underwent a horrendous experience, crossing a dark wilderness where the very source of love seemed dried up," Pope John Paul II said in remarks at the conclusion of a concert in the Vatican's audience hall to commemorate the Shoah, or Holocaust. The concert took place on the day when Jews throughout the world remember the Holocaust victims. Earlier in the day, the pope met with a group of Jewish leaders and others who helped organize the concert.

1. The melodies and songs that reechoed in this auditorium were the expression of a common meditation and a shared prayer. Different voices blended in a unison of sounds and harmonies which moved and involved us intimately. We prayed in the knowledge that the Lord, if invoked, responds, cheering those who despair, breaking the chains of the oppressed, dispelling the shadows that linger in life's dark valleys.

Among those who are with us this evening are some who physically underwent a horrendous experience, crossing a dark wilderness where the very source of love seemed dried up.

Many wept at that time, and we still hear echoes of their lament. We hear it here too; their plea did not die with them but rises powerful, agonizing, heartrending, saying, "Do not forget us!" It is addressed to one and all.

2. Thus we are gathered this evening to commemorate the Holocaust of millions of Jews. The candles lit by some of the survivors are intended to show symbolically that this hall does not have narrow limits. It contains all the victims: fathers, mothers, sons,

daughters, brothers, sisters, and friends. In our memory they are all present, they are with you, they are with us.

We have a commitment, the only one, perhaps, that can give meaning to every tear shed by man because of man and to justify it.

We have seen with our eyes, we were and are witnesses of violence and hatred, which are kindled in the world all too often and consume it.

We have seen and we see peace derided, brotherhood mocked, harmony ignored, mercy scorned.

3. Nevertheless, man is inclined to justice. He is the only created being capable of conceiving it. To save man does not only mean not to kill him, not to mutilate him, not to torture him. It also means satisfying the hunger and thirst of justice that is within him.

This is our commitment. We would risk causing the victims of the most atrocious deaths to die again if we do not have an ardent desire for justice, if we do not commit ourselves, each according to his own capacities, to ensure that evil does not prevail over good as it did for millions of the children of the Jewish nation.

We must therefore redouble our efforts to free man from the specter of racism, exclusion, alienation, slavery, and xenophobia; to uproot these evils which are creeping into society and undermining the foundations of peaceful human coexistence. Evil always appears in new forms; it has many facets and its flattery is multiple. It is our task to unmask its dangerous power and neutralize it with God's help.

4. I would have liked to mention by name, as far as possible, all who have promoted this initiative and encouraged it: those who have supported it and are here with us now; the many representatives of Jewish communities and organizations throughout the world; the survivors of the *Shoah*, distinguished personages and representatives from both the religious and civil sphere; all those who have performed under the skilled direction of maestro Gilbert Levine. I thank them most cordially, for they have helped to give weight and distinction to this commemorative event. Their presence strengthens our common commitment.

5. The evocative melodies which we have listened to echo the anguished plea to the Lord, the expression of hope in him who

hearkens to those who seek him, to welcome and console them. This profound impression remains in our hearts, calling up memories and inviting us to prayer.

Before bringing this meeting to a close, I wish to invite all of you to observe a moment of silence in order to praise the Lord with the words which he will suggest to our hearts, and to hear once more the plea, "Do not forget us."

This is indeed a significant meeting, and I am especially pleased to welcome this distinguished group of Jewish leaders and persons responsible for the organization of the concert in commemoration of the *Shoah* to be held this evening in the Paul VI Hall in the Vatican. In particular, I welcome the survivors of the terrible experience of the concentration camps who honor us with their presence. A word of greeting also goes to maestro Gilbert Levine, who has done so much to make this event possible.

Your visit inevitably brings to mind the times I have gone on pilgrimage to Auschwitz and Dachau. During the first year of my pontification I again went to Auschwitz and, before the memorial stone with its Hebrew inscription, I sought to express the profound emotion evoked in me by "the memory of the people whose sons and daughters were destined for total extermination." As I said on that occasion:

"This people has its origin in Abraham, who is our father in faith [cf. Rom. 4:12], as Paul of Tarsus expressed it. It is precisely this people, which had received from God the Commandment, 'Thou shalt not kill,' which has experienced in itself to a particular degree what killing means. No one may pass by this inscription with indifference" [Speech at Brzezinka, June 7, 1979, 2].

I used these same words in 1986 when I visited the Rome Synagogue. In this city, too, the Jewish community paid a high price in blood for the simple reason of being Jewish. As on that occasion, so once again today I express "a word of abhorrence for the genocide decreed against the Jewish people during the Second World War, which led to the Holocaust of millions of innocent people" [Speech at the Rome Synagogue, April 13, 1986, 3].

The concert this evening is a commemoration of those horrifying events. The candles which will burn as we listen to the music will keep before us the long history of anti-Semitism which culminated in the *Shoah*. But it is not enough that we remember; for in our own day, regrettably, there are many new manifestations of the anti-Semitism, xenophobia, and racial hatred which were the seeds of those unspeakable crimes. Humanity cannot permit all that to happen again. Our shared hope is that the music which we shall listen to together will confirm our resolve to consolidate the good relations between our two communities, so that with the help of almighty God we can work together to prevent the repetition of such heinous evil.

We must be deeply grateful to all who work to secure ever wider and fuller recognition of the "bond" and "common spiritual patrimony" which exist between Jews and Christians [*Dignitatis Humanae*, 4]. In the past, these links have inspired deeds of courageous solidarity. In this regard, as a matter of historical fact, one cannot forget that in my own homeland, as in other countries and also here in Rome, in the terrible days of the *Shoah*, many Christians together with their pastors strove to help their brothers and sisters of the Jewish community, even at the cost of their own lives. In the face of the perils which threaten the sons and daughters of this generation, Christians and Jews together have a great deal to offer to a world struggling to distinguish good from evil, a world called by the Creator to defend and protect life but so vulnerable to voices which propagate values that only bring death and destruction.

As we listen together this evening to the music that will be performed for us, may we all be moved to repeat in our hearts David's song of ascents: "How good and how pleasant it is when brothers live in unity!" [Ps. 133:1].

This is the hope I express for Jews and Christians everywhere. This hope enlivens my prayer for peace in the Holy Land, which is so close to all our hearts.

Address to the First Ambassador of Israel to the Holy See

September 29, 1994

On Thursday, September 29, H. E. Shmuel Hadas, the first ambassador of the State of Israel to the Holy See, presented his credentials to the Holy Father. The following is a translation of the pope's French-language discourse to the new ambassador.

Mr. Ambassador:

1. I welcome you with great pleasure for the presentation of the letters accrediting you as the first ambassador extraordinary and plenipotentiary of the State of Israel to the Holy See. The importance of this ceremony will be recognized by all, since our recently established diplomatic relations become effective by the presence of a head of mission of the highest rank, in accordance with the Fundamental Agreement signed on December 30, 1993 in Jerusalem.

It is a pleasure for me to recall today that in the past, like my predecessors, I have had the opportunity to receive several important figures from the State of Israel. While taking into account the differing viewpoints on certain subjects, these contacts have made it possible to progress towards the systematic dialogue that was entrusted over two years ago to the Permanent Bilateral Working Commission. I would like to express my gratitude to the members of this commission; on both sides, they have ably devoted themselves to the deeper exchange of views that led to the signing of the Fundamental Agreement, opening up a new era in our relations.

2. Mr. Ambassador, I thank you for the words you have just addressed to me which deeply touch me. As you emphasize, it is true that diplomatic relations are not an end in themselves but represent a starting point for specific collaboration, bearing in mind the distinctive nature of the Holy See and the State of Israel. The

study of various bilateral issues is continuing, as specified in the Agreement of December 30 last, with the establishment of two subcommittees which should enable us to progress together on the path of a collaboration founded on a solid basis.

Furthermore, this collaboration does not only concern the Holy See and the State of Israel; it also involves a trusting relationship between the Israeli authorities and the different institutions of the Catholic Church present in the territory of the Holy Land.

The Middle East Peace Process Must Be Encouraged

3. As you have said, over and above bilateral negotiations, the Holy See and the State of Israel, each in its own sphere and with its own means of action, must promote the essential principles mentioned in their Fundamental Agreement. In the first place, they are linked to respect for the right to freedom of religion and conscience, an indispensable condition for the respect of every human being's dignity. They have joined forces to oppose every form of intolerance, in whatever way it is expressed. Most particularly, they are vigilantly working together to oppose all anti-Semitism, aware that we have recently been forced to observe some deplorable manifestations of it.

4. In many parts of the world, violent conflicts are unfortunately continuing to harm many peoples. The Holy See spares no effort, within the limits of its specific mission, to overcome opposition or resentment, which often originated in the distant past, and to open up the paths to peace. Without peace, integral human development is hindered, the survival of entire groups jeopardized, the culture and very identity of more than one nation are threatened with extinction.

Therefore, the Middle East peace process, which the Holy See has long desired, can only be encouraged. There is still a long and arduous way to go, but now it seems no longer Utopian to say that mutual trust between the peoples of the Middle East can be established. Noting with satisfaction what has already been achieved by the leaders of Israel and of the whole region, I invoke upon them the help of the Almighty, so that they may continue their efforts with the courage of peace.

5. You have also expressed, Mr. Ambassador, the desire to see your cultural institutions intensify their cooperation with the cultural institutions of the Catholic Church. I welcome these proposals all the more gladly, since the university exchanges, already begun in different circumstances, seem to me to be most desirable. This is true in a general way, for intellectual life naturally benefits from them. It is particularly opportune, inasmuch as we have an important part of our cultural roots in common, starting with the writings of the Bible, the book of books, an ever-living source. Among Jews and members of the Church, the holy books shed remarkable light on the concept of man, of his spiritual vocation, and of his morality. It can only be useful to both to share their knowledge in order to deepen their understanding of the Scriptures and to increase their knowledge of the civilizations and historical setting where they have developed over so many centuries, especially with the aid of archeology, philosophy, and the study of religious, doctrinal, and spiritual traditions.

This Ceremony Has Historical Significance

6. The particular nature of the relations between the State of Israel and the Holy See quite obviously stem from the unique character of this land which is the focus of attention for the majority of believers, Jews, Christians, and Muslims, throughout the world. This land was sanctified by the One God's revelation to men; it continues to bear the mark and does not cease to be a place of inspiration for those who can make a pilgrimage there. Most especially, believers of the great monotheistic religions turn to the Holy City of Jerusalem, which we know today is still the scene of division and conflict, but which remains a "sacred heritage for all those who believe in God" [*Apostolic Letter on the Subject of Jerusalem*, April 20, 1984] and, as its admirable name implies, a crossroads and a symbol of peace. It is also to be hoped that the unique and sacred character of this Holy City will receive international guarantees that will also ensure its access to all believers. As I had occasion to write not long ago: "I dream of the day when Jews, Christians, and Muslims will hail one another in Jerusalem with the greeting of peace" [ibid.].

7. Mr. Ambassador, you yourself have insisted on the historical significance of this ceremony, over and above the usual diplomatic conventions. Indeed, a new age is dawning in relations between the Holy See and the State of Israel, by a persevering dialogue and by active collaboration in the areas I have just mentioned. All this will help intensify the dialogue between the Catholic Church and the Jewish people of Israel and of the whole world. Important progress has already been made in mutual understanding, especially under the impetus of the Second Vatican Council [declaration *Nostra Aetate*.] I hope that these Jewish—Christian exchanges will continue and be deepened, and that they will enable both to better serve the great causes of humanity.

8. Your Excellency, you have been the spokesman for the sentiments of the president of the State of Israel and the government of the country, and of their wishes on a deeply meaningful occasion. I beg you to convey to the senior authorities of the State of Israel my gratitude for their message, and my sincere wishes for the accomplishment of their tasks in service to the harmony and peace desired by all their fellow citizens.

I also offer to you, Your Excellency, my warm wishes for the success of your mission and your stay in the city of Rome. Be assured that my assistants will always be glad to welcome you and offer you any help you may need.

As I bless the Most High who has made this historic meeting possible, I pray that he will grant you, your loved ones, and all your compatriots an abundance of his gifts.

Ambassador's Address

The ambassador's response was given in Spanish:

Your Holiness:

"*The Holy See and the State of Israel, mindful of the unique character and universal importance of the Holy Land and aware of the unique nature of the relations between the Catholic Church and the Jewish people, and of the historic process of reconciliation and growth in mutual understanding and friendship between Catholics and*

Jews. . . ." These eloquent and meaningful words introduce the preamble of the Fundamental Agreement between the Holy See and the State of Israel, which on last December 30 paved the way to the normalization of relations between the Holy See and Israel, overcoming an obstacle to progress in Jewish–Catholic *rapprochement.*

Obviously, this is not the conventional language of international diplomacy. It could not be otherwise: Our relations, despite their dramatic changes over the centuries, still retain the indelible seal of their common origin. For this reason, the signing of the Fundamental Agreement was more than a diplomatic initiative; it was a step of historical significance. A unique act, for its protagonists are unique.

I find myself here in the Holy See, representing the State of Israel, offering you the letters of credence accrediting me as Israel's first ambassador to the Holy See, a moving and immeasurable honor and privilege for the person speaking to you.

I rejoice to be here, although I still feel anxious in the face of the difficult diplomatic challenge which this appointment holds for me in all its dimensions. A challenge which definitely does not belong to the role and routine of the classical exchanges of international diplomacy.

Hence, it is perhaps needless to comment on this here, in Your Holiness's presence, since participation in this process of increasingly necessary and deeper dialogue between Catholics and Jews presents particular challenges. For this reason, I humbly recall here the words of gratitude of the prayer: *Blessed be the Creator of the universe who gave us life and allows us to experience this moment.*

We Remember Your Frequent Gestures of Fellowship

Your Holiness, centuries of misunderstandings have led to bloody and heartbreaking conflicts and to torturous and painful relations between Catholics and Jews. The establishment of diplomatic relations between the Holy See and the State of Israel is not the point of arrival, but on the contrary, a starting point, a new and constructive dimension in which to bring together in dialogue the Catholic Church and the Jewish people.

Your Holiness has given a new impetus to this creative dialogue with patience and persistence.

Actually, even without the perspective provided by time, it can be stated that Your Holiness's commitment to the Jewish—Christian dialogue has been decisive. When on February 15, 1985, you declared that relations between Christians and Jews had notably improved in recent years and, I quote you, that "where there was ignorance and therefore prejudice and stereotypes, there is now growing mutual knowledge, appreciation, and respect," Your Holiness gave public witness that a new spirit was being forged in our relations. Since then, there have been many echoes of the existence of this new spirit, which has been shown in an ongoing dialogue, in recognition of the need for combined effort.

We all remember your frequent and important declarations and gestures of fellowship. Many appreciated your words when in 1980 you declared, as I quote: "the Jewish People, since the tragic experiences associated with the extermination of many of its sons and daughters, motivated by the desire for security, established the State of Israel." Or, when, in 1984, you demanded for the Jewish people in Israel "the desired security and tranquility which are the prerogative of every nation, as well as the living conditions and progress of every society"; and in 1987, when you declared that: "The Jews have a right to their homeland, like all peoples, in accordance with international law."

It is certain, as Your Holiness clearly demonstrated in your historic and inspiring visit to the Great Synagogue of Rome in April 1986, that the way undertaken is only in its early stages, and that sufficient time is needed to be rid of prejudices and to adapt every form of expression. But it is also very clear that there is a sincere wish for reconciliation. We must all seek greater mutual understanding with patience and persistence. This long-delayed challenge is already being taken up by many good Catholics and Jews.

The Fundamental Agreement between the Holy See and the State of Israel will enable my country to take an active part in this mission. It will be one of our great challenges, which we accept during these years of transition towards the third millennium of our common history.

But there is something more, which is just as important: this new era in relations between the Holy See and Israel will have a constructive effect on the peace process in the Middle East. We have embarked on the irreversible road to peace. The inspiring words of the Prophet Isaiah are those which today guide many good Christians, Muslims, and Jews:

"The Lord . . . shall judge between the nations and impose terms on many peoples. They shall beat their swords into ploughshares, and their spears into pruning hooks; one nation shall not raise the sword against another, nor shall they train for war again" [Isa. 2:4].

We Are Grateful for Your Contribution of Deep Spirituality

In the Fundamental Agreement the Holy See and the State of Israel are committed to promoting a peaceful resolution of the conflicts between states and nations and to eliminating violence and terror from international life.

Israel aspires to make a contribution to peace not only in our afflicted region but throughout the world, a peace which men and women of goodwill desire. Hence on this occasion, my country wishes expressly to show its sentiments of sincere gratitude to Your Holiness for your tireless struggle, to the point of personal suffering, for a peace that respects human dignity and basic values. May God always preserve the renewed determination with which you champion freedom and justice at every moment. History will be able to judge your extraordinary contribution to world peace.

We would like these new relations to be the first steps in the promotion of sincere and generous cooperation, which will allow everyone to advance on the broad and difficult way to peace throughout the Middle East and particularly in the Holy Land. We cherish the hope that Your Holiness, with your high moral authority, will in the future continue to transmit your message of love and hope without faltering. The State of Israel, its Government, and all its citizens, Jews, Christians and Muslims, whom I have the honor of representing to the Holy See, are grateful to Your Holiness for your contribution of deep spirituality and lofty human fellowship.

We know that one of your greatest wishes is to make a pilgrimage to the Holy Land. I can assure you that this visit will have an immense spiritual significance for us all. However, it will above all help reinforce the foundations of the peace we are seeking to build stone by stone. The age-old Hebrew greeting and wish, "*Leshana habaa be Yerushalaim*" [Next year in Jerusalem], is here extended again to Your Holiness on behalf of all Israelis, Jews, Christians, and Muslims.

Israel will measure up to history. It has made a pledge of peace and will fulfil its commitment so that "the star of peace which once shone in Bethlehem, will return to brighten this region," as Your Holiness proclaimed in January 1991. We hope and wish that, as soon as possible, dialogue, reason, and right will prevail in the Middle East over terror and violence.

In its wording and in its spirit, our Fundamental Agreement calls for close cooperation in the struggle for the peace we are continuing tenaciously to seek. It also expresses the parties' will to resolve the sensitive bilateral disagreements that remain, with regard to their obligations and their rights. Cooperation in this regard is already under way. Negotiations in good faith will, we are certain, contribute to formalizing relations between the State of Israel and the Catholic Church, to the parties' satisfaction. In the meantime, the situation with regard to all that concerns the rights of Catholic institutions in Israel will be respected, and the proper nature of the Catholic holy places will continue to be respected and protected, as will the freedom to practice the Catholic religion.

The Holy See and the State of Israel have likewise recognized that they have a common interest in promoting and guiding the cultural exchanges between Catholic institutions throughout the world and Israel's institutions. It is our desire that Your Holiness, with your contagious enthusiasm, should give an impetus to these cultural exchanges. We do not only have common interests, but cultures that share common roots. The cultural dialogue will open new horizons in this understanding between the monotheistic religions, an understanding tenaciously pursued by us all. It will be our modest contribution to the creation of a new humanism centered on human beings as its principal objective.

There have been many echoes of Your Holiness's message and of your struggle to encourage the enforcement of human rights. But those of us who were present at the concert in the Vatican to commemorate the Holocaust, did so moved by the emotion of your heartfelt message on that occasion, which stressed the implications of the Holocaust, and by your appeal to remember and to give witness. We feel the deep need to be grateful for this action.

Holy See and Israel Will Fight All Forms of Anti-Semitism

We appreciate your tireless activity on behalf of humanity. Wherever there is suffering, Your Holiness has never ceased to be present. We appreciate, in particular, the innumerable signs of your rejection of racism and anti-Semitism. "We will risk making the victims of the most atrocious deaths die again, if we do not have the passion of justice," you said on that unforgettable commemoration which we just mentioned.

According to the Fundamental Agreement, the Holy See and the State of Israel are committed to working together to combat all forms of anti-Semitism and other forms of racism and religious intolerance. We are hopeful that together we shall be able to transmit a message of peace, fellowship, and justice. Christians and Jews must understand that the moment has come when their mission is to cooperate in carrying out the basic commandments at the heart of their beliefs, expressing them in constructive deeds. "Anti-Semitism is a sin against God and against humanity," Your Holiness declared in November 1992.

During your Pontificate, the Holy See has seen its moral authority increase. May God continue to enlighten you and may you continue to fulfill your sublime mission. May your spiritual guidance be duly followed throughout the world.

Your Holiness, in conveying the warmest greetings of the president and the government of Israel, together with their best wishes, I am pleased to recall, in their name, Your Holiness's recent words. "It is necessary to understand that the Jews, who for two thousand years were dispersed throughout the world, have decided to return to the land of their ancestors. It is their right."

Israel, a millennia-old people, as a member of the great family of humanity, preserved its spiritual wealth and best traditions for centuries without renouncing their land, until their desire to return was realized.

Therefore, to represent the State of Israel will be the greatest honor, but also a challenge. I will do all I can to make my modest contribution to relations between the Holy See and Israel. The diplomatic dialogue with the Holy See will go far beyond the usual diplomatic exchanges, considering its unique subject matter. It will certainly be a gratifying experience.

I trust, Your Holiness, that the words of Psalm 133, "Behold how good it is and how pleasant, where brethren dwell as one," will inspire my work. With this hope, I would like to close, repeating our best and most sincere wish: *Shalom.*

Audience with the Delegation of the Anti-Defamation League

September 29, 1994

On September 29, Pope John Paul II received a delegation from the Anti-Defamation League at his summer residence at Castel Gandolfo. Their visit immediately followed the presentation of credentials by the first ambassador of Israel to the Vatican. David H. Strassler, ADL National Chairman, addressed His Holiness, who then responded.

Address by David H. Strassler, ADL National Chairman

Your Holiness:

Today we are the envy of countless millions of Americans who had hoped to share in the glorious moments of your visit to our country next month. *They* will have to wait until next year. We are aware of the circumstances surrounding the postponement of your visit . . . and so we treasure even more the time you have given us today.

Joining me today is our national director, Abraham Foxman, and a leadership delegation of the Anti-Defamation League. Ours is a pilgrimage of friendship and peace . . . a pilgrimage by Jewish leaders dedicated to strengthening and expanding the relationship between. Christians and Jews. Jewish leaders who were encouraged by the Second Vatican Council's historic *Nostra Aetate* document repudiating anti-Semitism and religious persecution and dismissing the accusations of deicide against Jews. That declaration was issued nearly thirty years ago, and much has changed since.

Your historic visit to the synagogue in Rome and your reaching out to Jews as "our dearly beloved older brothers" in your unforgotten address eight years ago sent a message to Jews everywhere that a new phase in Catholic—Jewish relations had indeed begun.

The Jews of the Diaspora and the people of Israel have been moved by your many heartfelt references to the Holocaust and your proclamation that "anti-Semitism is a sin" not only against man but "against God himself."

We are delighted that with us today are Gianfranco Svidercoschi, author of *Letter to a Jewish Friend*;[1] Jerzy Kluger, your lifelong friend and subject of the book; and Professor Shiloni, the translator of the book. We are very pleased to present you with the manuscript of the Hebrew translation and tell you that this Hebrew version of *Letter to a Jewish Friend* will be distributed in Israel as well as the United States by the Anti-Defamation League. The League was also involved in the editing of the Spanish version, and we are delighted to report that an edition will be appearing in Buenos Aires in November.

It is a sad commentary, in a way, that a friendship between two young Polish boys that crossed social and religious boundaries could not have been accepted as perfectly normal. Ironically, it is because such a friendship was not commonplace that this book

---

1. Gianfranco Svidercoschi, *Letter to a Jewish Friend* (New York: Crossroad, 1994).

is so special and so important. Its description of the strength and beauty of a friendship between two boys—Catholic and Jewish— and the contribution their relationship makes, sets an example for others. This plain and simple story, we hope, will help in the creation of a better world in which every human being may enjoy the respect he or she deserves.

The story seems almost to be a parable, for it has the power to dissipate the stereotypes and prejudices that serve as an obstacle to human relations, particularly between the Christian and Jewish communities of the world. The young Catholic boy became a priest serving his Church and humanity and eventually rose through the hierarchy of the Church, becoming Pope John Paul II. Meanwhile, his Polish, Jewish friend, Jerzy Kluger, came to live in Rome, where the two have renewed their extraordinary friendship.

The significance of the book also lies in the historical context in which it was written: the Holocaust, an event which you have rightly called "the greatest tragedy of our century: the greatest trauma." World War II was a monstrous tragedy that eliminated one-third of the Jews on this planet as well as millions of other innocent human beings.

It is only natural that the Anti-Defamation League, an organization founded more than eighty years ago to counteract anti-Semitism, bigotry, and discrimination, should want to sponsor the translation of this book into Hebrew and be gratified to oversee its distribution in Israel and the United States. The story told in this book is deeply inspiring. Its values of mutual respect and its exemplary tale of extraordinary friendship can help us in moving closer to our aims of creating a better society, based on the equal dignity of all human beings.

Our sponsorship of this book is but a small token of our appreciation for the contributions made by Your Holiness toward the ideals of reciprocal respect between those of all religious beliefs.

Yours has been a distinguished record of enlightenment. We believe that history will say that one of the crowning achievements of Pope John Paul II was the establishment of full diplomatic relations between the Holy See and the State of Israel. This recognition will not affect only the people of Israel; it is a covenant whose scope is global, and it sets a moral tone for the rest of the world.

The specters of fratricide, of pseudo-religious fanaticism, and ethnic cleansing rise from the ashes of the former Communist world. We believe your embrace of the Jewish people and your outreach to all humanity will give increased impetus to the struggle of all people of good faith to stem this delirium of self-destruction of the human race. We wish to join our forces with you in combating racism and anti-Semitism in all the lands where the flames of historic hate and intolerance have ignited once again.

Your words and deeds will do more than you ever may have imagined to ensure the success of the new relations between the Church and the Jewish people and to further the peace process between Israel, its neighbors, and the other nations of the world.

You have our thanks and good wishes for the future as we proceed on the road to Jerusalem.

Shalom.

The Pope's Response

Dear Friends:

I am very pleased to welcome the representatives of the Anti-Defamation League. It is with great joy that I greet you.

In your kind words, Mr. Chairman, you have spoken of friendship and its unifying force in our lives. Friendship is a great gift from God and is a blessing for everyone who experiences it. Genuine friendship has a strength which is capable of building indestructible bridges, resisting many evils, and overcoming all kinds of difficulties. At the same time, it poses a constant challenge to those who seek to be friends.

These convictions lie behind the following words which I wrote on the occasion of the Commemoration of the Fiftieth Anniversary of the Uprising in the Warsaw Ghetto: "As Christians and Jews, following the example of the faith of Abraham, we are called to be a blessing for the world [cf. Gen. 12:2]. This is the common task awaiting us. It is therefore necessary for us, Christians and Jews, to be first a blessing to one another. This will effectively occur if we are united in the face of evils which are still threatening: indifference and prejudice, as well as displays of anti-Semitism" [April 21, 1993].

Was it not the bond of friendship which in many cases during the terrible days of the past inspired the courage of Christians who helped their Jewish brothers and sisters, even at the cost of their own lives? Truly, nobody has greater love than the one who lays down his life for his friends [cf. John 15:13]. Friendship stands against exclusion and makes people stand together in the face of threat.

Let our friendship, strengthened by our respect for divine providence, bring us ever closer, for the good of the whole world.

Fundamental Agreement Between the Holy See and the State of Israel

Preamble

The Holy See and the State of Israel,

Mindful of the singular character and universal significance of the Holy Land;

Aware of the unique nature of the relationship between the Catholic Church and the Jewish people, and of the historic process of reconciliation and growth in mutual understanding and friendship between Catholics and Jews;

Having decided on July 29, 1992 to establish a "Bilateral Permanent Working Commission," in order to study and define together issues of common interest, and in view of normalizing their relations;

Recognizing that the work of the aforementioned commission has produced sufficient material for a first and Fundamental Agreement;

Realizing that such Agreement will provide a sound and lasting basis for the continued development of their present and future relations and for the furtherance of the commission's task,

Agree upon the following articles:

Article 1

§ 1. The State of Israel, recalling its Declaration of Independence, affirms its continuing commitment to uphold and observe the human right to freedom of religion and conscience, as set forth in the Universal Declaration of Human Rights and in other international instruments to which it is a party.

§ 2. The Holy See, recalling the Declaration of Religious Freedom of the Second Vatican Ecumenical Council, *Dignitatis Humanae*, affirms the Catholic Church's commitment to uphold the human right to freedom of religion and conscience, as set forth in the Universal Declaration of Human Rights and in other international instruments to which it is a party. The Holy See wishes to affirm as well the Catholic Church's respect for other religions and their followers as solemnly stated by the Second Vatican Ecumenical Council in its Declaration on the Relations of the Church to Non-Christian Religions, *Nostra Aetate*.

Article 2

§ 1. The Holy See and the State of Israel are committed to appropriate cooperation in combating all forms of anti-Semitism and all kinds of racism and of religious intolerance, and in promoting mutual understanding among nations, tolerance among communities, and respect for human life and dignity.

§ 2. The Holy See takes this occasion to reiterate its condemnation of hatred, persecution, and all other manifestations of anti-Semitism directed against the Jewish people and individual Jews anywhere, at any time and by anyone. In particular, the Holy See deplores attacks on Jews and desecration of Jewish synagogues and cemeteries, acts which offend the memory of the victims of the Holocaust, especially when they occur in the same places which witnessed it.

Article 3

§ 1. The Holy See and the State of Israel recognize that both are free in the exercise of their respective rights and powers, and commit themselves to respect this principle in their mutual relations and in their cooperation for the good of the people.

§ 2. The State of Israel recognizes the right of the Catholic Church to carry out its religious, moral, educational, and charitable functions, and to have its own institutions, and to train, appoint, and deploy its own personnel in the said institutions or for the said functions to these ends. The Church recognizes the right of the State to carry out its functions, such as promoting and protecting the welfare and the safety of the people. Both the State and the Church recognize the need for dialogue and cooperation in such matters as by their nature call for it.

§ 3. Concerning Catholic legal personality at canon Law the Holy See and the State of Israel will negotiate on giving it full effect in Israeli law, following a report from a joint subcommission of experts.

Article 4

§ 1. The State of Israel affirms its continuing commitment to maintain and respect the status quo in the Christian holy places to which it applies and the respective rights of the Christian communities thereunder. The Holy See affirms the Catholic Church's continuing commitment to respect the aforementioned status quo and the said rights.

§ 2. The above shall apply notwithstanding an interpretation to the contrary of any article in this Fundamental Agreement.

§ 3. The State of Israel agrees with the Holy See on the obligation of continuing respect for and protection of the character proper to Catholic sacred places, such as churches, monasteries, convents, cemeteries, and their like.

§ 4. The State of Israel agrees with the Holy See on the continuing guarantee of the freedom of Catholic worship.

Article 5

§ 1. The Holy See and the State of Israel recognize that both have an interest in favoring Christian pilgrimages to the Holy Land. Whenever the need for coordination arises, the proper agencies of the Church and of the State will consult and cooperate as required.

§ 2. The State of Israel and the Holy See express the hope that such pilgrimages will provide an occasion for better understanding between the pilgrims and the people and religions in Israel.

Article 6

The Holy See and the State of Israel jointly reaffirm the right of the Catholic Church to establish, maintain, and direct schools and institutes of study at all levels; this right being exercised in harmony with the rights of the State in the field of education.

Article 7

The Holy See and the State of Israel recognize a common interest in promoting and encouraging cultural exchanges between Catholic institutions worldwide, and educational, cultural, and research institutions in Israel, and in facilitating access to manuscripts, historical documents, and similar source materials, in conformity with applicable laws and regulations.

Article 8

The State of Israel recognizes that the right of the Catholic Church to freedom of expression in the carrying out of its functions is exercised also through the Church's own communications media; this right being exercised in harmony with the rights of the State in the field of communications media.

Article 9

The Holy See and the State of Israel jointly reaffirm the right of the Catholic Church to carry out its charitable functions through its health care and social welfare institutions; this right being exercised in harmony with the rights of the State in this field.

Article 10

§ 1. The Holy See and the State of Israel jointly reaffirm the right of the Catholic Church to property.

§ 2. Without prejudice to rights relied upon by the parties:

(a) The Holy See and the State of Israel will negotiate in good faith a comprehensive agreement, containing solutions acceptable to both parties, on unclear, unsettled, and disputed issues, concerning property, economic, and fiscal matters relating to the Catholic Church generally, or to specific Catholic communities or institutions.

(b) For the purpose of the said negotiations, the Permanent Bilateral Working Commission will appoint one or more bilateral subcommissions of experts to study the issues and make proposals.

(c) The parties intend to commence the aforementioned negotiations within three months of entry into force of the present agreement, and aim to reach agreement within two years from the beginning of the negotiations.

(d) During the period of these negotiations, actions incompatible with these commitments shall be avoided.

Article 11

§ 1. The Holy See and the State of Israel declare their respective commitment to the promotion of the peaceful resolution of conflicts among States and nations, excluding violence and terror from international life.

§ 2. The Holy See, while maintaining in every case the right to exercise its moral and spiritual teaching-office, deems it opportune to recall that, owing to its own character, it is solemnly committed to remaining a stranger to all merely temporal conflicts, which principle applies specifically to disputed territories and unsettled borders.

Article 12

The Holy See and the State of Israel will continue to negotiate in good faith in pursuance of the agenda agreed upon in Jerusalem, on July 15, 1992, and confirmed at the Vatican, on July 29, 1992; likewise on issues arising from articles of the present agreement, as well as on other issues bilaterally agreed upon as objects of negotiation.

Article 13

§ 1. In this agreement the parties use these terms in the following sense:

(a) The Catholic Church and the Church—including, *interalia*, its communities and institutions;
(b) Communities of the Catholic Church—meaning the Catholic religious entities considered by the Holy See as Churches *sui iuris* and by the State of Israel as recognized religious communities;
(c) The State of Israel and the State—including, *inter alia*, its authorities established by law.

§ 2. Notwithstanding the validity of this agreement as between the parties, and without detracting from the generality of any applicable rule of law with reference to treaties, the parties agree that this agreement does not prejudice rights and obligations arising from existing treaties between either party and a state or states, which are known and in fact available to both parties at the time of the signature of this agreement.

Article 14

§ 1. Upon signature of the present Fundamental Agreement and in preparation for the establishment of full diplomatic relations, the Holy See and the State of Israel exchange special representatives, whose rank and privileges are specified in an additional protocol.

§ 2. Following the entry into force and immediately upon the beginning of the implementation of the present Fundamental Agreement, the Holy See and the State of Israel will establish full diplomatic relations at the level of apostolic nunciature, on the part of the Holy See, and embassy, on the part of the State of Israel.

Article 15

This agreement shall enter into force on the date of the latter notification of ratification by a party.

Done in two original copies in the English and Hebrew languages, both texts being equally authentic. In case of divergency, the English text shall prevail.

Signed in Jerusalem, this thirtieth day of the month of December, in the year 1993, which corresponds to the sixteenth day of the month of Tevet, in the year 5754.

For the Government
The State of Israel
For the Holy See

Apostolic Letter Tertio Millennio Adveniente of His Holiness Pope John Paul II to the Bishops, Clergy and Lay Faithful on Preparation: For the Jubilee of the Year 2000

November 10, 1994

18. From this point of view we can affirm that *the Second Vatican Council was a providential event, whereby the Church began the more immediate preparation* for the Jubilee of the Second Millennium. It was a Council similar to earlier ones, yet very different; it was a Council *focused on the mystery of Christ and his Church and at the same time open to the world* . . . 19. On the basis of this profound renewal, the Council opened itself to Christians of other denominations, to the followers of other religions and to all the people of our time. No Council had ever spoken so clearly about Christian unity, about dialogue with non-Christian religions, about the specific meaning of the Old Covenant and of Israel, about the dignity of each person's conscience, about the principle of religious liberty . . .

24. *Papal Journeys* have become an important element in the work of implementing the Second Vatican Council. Begun by John XXIII on the eve of the Council with a memorable pilgrimage to Loreto and Assisi (1962), they notably increased under Paul VI who, after first visiting the Holy Land (1964), undertook nine other great apostolic journeys which brought him into direct contact with the peoples of the different continents.

The current Pontificate has widened this programme of travels even further . . . At present, it is my fervent wish to visit Sarajevo in Bosnia-Hercegovina and the Middle East: Lebanon, Jerusalem and the Holy Land. It would be very significant if in the Year 2000 it were possible to visit the *places on the road taken by the People of God of the Old Covenant,* starting from the places associated with Abraham and Moses, through Egypt and Mount Sinai, as far as Damascus, the city which witnessed the conversion of Saint Paul.

33. Hence it is appropriate that, as the Second Millennium of Christianity draws to a close, the Church should become more fully conscious of the sinfulness of her children, recalling all those times in history when they departed from the spirit of Christ and his Gospel and, instead of offering to the world the witness of a life inspired by the values of faith, indulged in ways of thinking and acting which were truly *forms of counter-witness and scandal.*

53. On the other hand, as far as the field of religious awareness is concerned, the eve of the Year 2000 will provide a great opportunity, especially in view of the events of recent decades, for *interreligious dialogue,* in accordance with the specific guidelines set down by the Second Vatican Council in its Declaration *Nostra Aetate* on the relationship of the Church to non-Christian religions.

In this dialogue the Jews and the Muslims ought to have a pre-eminent place. God grant that as a confirmation of these intentions it may also be possible to hold *joint meetings* in places of significance for the great monotheistic religions.

In this regard, attention is being given to finding ways of arranging historic meetings in places of exceptional symbolic importance like Bethlehem, Jerusalem and Mount Sinai as a means of furthering dialogue with Jews and the followers of Islam, and to arranging similar meetings elsewhere with the leaders of the great world religions.

1995

No More Anti-Semitism or Arrogant Nationalism!

January 29, 1995

Before praying the Angelus on Sunday, January 29, the Holy Father spoke briefly about the four servants of God he had just beatified in St. Peter's Basilica, and, on the occasion of the fiftieth anniversary of the release of prisoners from the concentration camp of Auschwitz, he also referred to "one of the darkest and most tragic moments in history." Here is an excerpt of a translation of the pope's reflection, which was given in Italian.

3. The fiftieth anniversary of the liberation of the prisoners of Auschwitz reminds us of one of the darkest and most tragic moments in history. At Auschwitz, as in other concentration camps, innocent people of various nationalities died in great numbers. In particular, the children of the Jewish people, whose extermination had been planned by the Nazi regime, suffered the tragic experience of the Holocaust. It was a darkening of reason, conscience, and the heart. Recalling the triumph of evil cannot fail to fill us with deep sorrow, in fraternal solidarity with all who bear the indelible scars of those tragedies.

Unfortunately, however, our days continue to be marked by great violence. God forbid that tomorrow we will have to weep over other Auschwitzes of our time.

Let us pray and work that this may not happen. Never again anti-Semitism! Never again the arrogance of nationalism! Never again genocide! May the third millennium usher in a season of peace and mutual respect among peoples.

Address to Roman Clergy

March 2, 1995

. . . In the Apostolic Letter *Tertio millenio adveniente,* I stressed among other things the *forthcoming Jubilee's ecumenical and inter-religious dimension.* With regard to these two aspects, the Church in Rome is also entrusted with a special mission. She who, among Catholics, presides over the unity of her Sister Churches must give the example of great solicitude on the way towards the full union of all Christ's disciples. The diocesan Synod, with the participation of the fraternal delegates of the other Christian denominations, represented a further important stage of promising development on the way towards full communion. It is now necessary to continue tirelessly to place the *commitment to ecumenism among the Diocese's pastoral priorities* and to help mature the seeds of hope that have already been sown.

Relations with our Jewish brothers and sisters, who can boast that they have been present in Rome longer than Christians, must be strongly emphasized in this Jubilee so that the celebrations in Rome suitably reflect those in the Holy Land. (L'Osservartore Romano English Weekly Edition [ORE], March 8, 1995)

Apostolic Journey to the United States of America

October 4–9, 1995

Address on Arrival, October 4, 1995 (*Yom Kippur*).

To the members of the Jewish faith I extend a very cordial greeting and my respectful best wishes on this day of special significance for them.

Visit to Cathedral in Baltimore

October 8, 1995

. . . I greet the whole Catholic community. I extend the hand of friendship to the members of other Christian communities and to the Jewish and Muslim guests, as well as to the representatives of the universities and colleges in the Baltimore area, and to the federal, state, and local public officials present.

2. Maryland holds a special place in the history of American Catholicism, indeed in the religious history of the nation. It was here that religious freedom and civic tolerance were enshrined in the American experience, just as in recent times Maryland has been a pioneering area in ecumenical and interreligious dialogue. (L'Osservartore Romano English Weekly Edition [ORE], October 11, 1995)

General Audience

October 18, 1995

In Baltimore I celebrated a solemn Eucharistic liturgy and was able to share a meal with the guests at "Our Daily Bread". I had the opportunity, in the cathedral dedicated to Mary Our Queen, to confirm the Catholic Church's commitment to dialogue with other Christians and with representatives of Judaism and Islam.

ORE, October 25, 1995

Letter to Cardinal Cassidy

October 20, 1995

To my Venerable Brother
Cardinal Edward Idris Cassidy
President of the Pontifical Council for Promoting Christian Unity

I am particularly pleased to convey a cordial greeting through you to the distinguished representatives of the Christian Churches and Communities and the great world religions, who have gathered in Florence for the international prayer meeting: "*Lands and skies of peace*". It is a continuation of the meetings that have taken place over the past few years in various cities of the world, the spirit of that memorable gathering in Assisi on 27 October 1986, when, for the first time in history, men and women of different religions met to invoke peace in our world threatened by serious tensions and terrible weapons. I hoped on that occasion that the "Assisi spirit" would not be extinguished but, on the contrary, that its influence on consciences would spread. And the *Men and Religions* assemblies, held every year since then as a sort of pilgrimage of peace across the globe, show that the hope was welcomed and shared. In this regard, I express my gratitude to the Sant'Egidio Community, which enthusiastically promoted these important spiritual meetings.

This year, after significant stages this August in Jerusalem and Hiroshima, the journey has continued to Florence where, with his characteristic Gospel insight, Giorgio La Pira several times brought together in dialogue the leaders of different world religions. With these efforts he anticipated what the Second Vatican Ecumenical Council was to formulate in the Declaration *Nostra Aetate* on relations between the Church and non-Christian religions. With this document, whose 30th anniversary occurs this year, the Catholic Church pledged to seek understanding with other religious communities, without facile irenicism and in a spirit of respect, friendship and solidarity with regard to basic human values. Indeed, genuine religious experience is frequently accompanies by a yearning for universal brotherhood, which today must be put to good use and made manifest.

Coming together to pray for peace represents the promise of a new age, the dawn of a new era. Being close to one another even in diversity is also a visible expression of that unity of the human family for which we all hope, that unity which the Second Vatican Council intended to foster, in accordance with the inspiration of the man who convoked it, the Servant of God Pope John XXIII. If we are all called to co-operate in this plan, religions are so in particular, and moments of prayer are a privileged means for this task.

1996

Angelus

January 14, 1996

... 2. The Declaration devotes special attention to our *Jewish brethren*, with whom Christianity has a particularly close relationship. Indeed, Christian faith had its beginnings in the religious experience of the Jewish people from whom Christ came according to the flesh. Sharing with Jews the part of Scripture called the Old Testament, the Church continues to take life from *that same patrimony of faith*, rereading it *in the light of Christ*. The inauguration of the times, accomplished by him with the new and eternal Covenant, did not destroy the ancient root but opens it to a universal fruitfulness. In consideration of this fact, *the memory of the tensions* which have so frequently marked Christian-Jewish relations cannot fail to cause great sorrow. Today too, let us then make our own the voice of the Council, which firmly deplored "all hatreds, persecutions, displays of anti-Semitism leveled at any time or from any source against the Jews." (*Nostra Aetate, no. 4*) (L'Osservartore Romano English Weekly Edition [ORE], October 11, 1995).

Address of His Holiness John Paul II to a Group of Representatives of the "B'nai B'rith International"

March 11, 1996

Dear Friends,

I am pleased to welcome once more a group of *representatives of B nai B'rith International.* The significance of your visit lies in the fact that it is an opportunity for us all to re-commit ourselves to the joint efforts needed to build ever greater understanding and solidarity between Catholics and Jews. At a time when hopes for peace have again been jeopardized by recent terrorist attacks in Jerusalem and Tel-Aviv, we must renew our prayer and our efforts to insist on what unites rather than on what divides and separates.

An essential tool for advancing mutual understanding and creating an ever closer rapport between Catholics and Jews is education. In this education, an essential element from both of our traditions is memory. The memory of our respective traditions, of the good and the bad of past relations, should teach us humble faith and trusting hope. It should guide us as we seek "to do justice, and to love kindness, and to walk humbly with our God" (Cf. Mic. 6, 8). It will strengthen our responsibility and commitment.

This is the path to which we are committed, and I pray that the Almighty, the Creator of heaven and earth, will grant us his bounteous mercy and grace so that we may truly progress down this path together. Upon all of you I invoke abundant divine blessings.

To the Chief Rabbi of Rome

April 15, 1996

1. I am pleased to address my cordial greetings to you, the Chief Rabbi of Rome, to the distinguished representatives of the Jewish community who have accompanied you and to you all, dear friends. I am grateful for this visit, which deeply moves me. Together let us give thanks and praise to the Almighty who has granted us to experience this blessed moment.

Ten years ago, when I had the joy of going to visit the Jewish community of this beloved city, gathered around you, Prof. Elio Toaff, in the Great Temple, I received a welcome and hospitality marked by that concern for others which can only stem from a predisposition of the heart. Today, your visit enables me to relive the same experience, permitting me to welcome you in my home as you welcomed me in yours; thus I can open my heart to you and extend my sentiments of joy to the entire Jewish community of Rome, and to the Jewish community throughout the world. (L'Osservartore Romano English Weekly Edition [ORE], May 1, 1996)

Contacts during Pastoral Visit to Germany

June 21–23, 1996

Gentlemen, Dear Brothers,

1. With joy and gratitude I take this opportunity to meet you during my third visit to Germany. Our meeting today is taking place in

Berlin. In this city, which the Nazis made the headquarters of their criminal dictatorship and which has deeply suffered its consequences until quite recently, our gathering has particular significance.

Precisely Berlin's Jewish community, which has left such a great mark on the cultural and scientific life of this city, had to pay a heavy toll in blood and became very small in the dark period of Nazism. Nevertheless, it is very much alive today and a sign of unmistakable hope.

2. By their vocation and history, the Jewish people were chosen in a special way to proclaim God's saving will to the entire human race (cf. *Dei Verbum*, n. 14). Your people's inconceivable suffering has emphasized in a most dreadful way the disasters that can occur wherever man distances himself with high-handed presumption and arrogance from his God and from the latter's commandments. Christianity shares with the Jewish people the belief that God is the Creator of the world and Lord of history, and that man was created in his image, as the first book of the Bible states: "So God created man in his own image, in the image of God he created him; male and female he created them" (*Gn* 1:27).

This likeness to God is the basis of man's inviolable dignity and the rights that derive from it. Respect for God and human dignity are closely linked. The frightful experience of the Nazi regime of terror has shown that without respect for God respect for human dignity is also lost. In the face of that reign of terror, many wondered about God, who allowed this terrible disaster, but even more crucial is the realization of what human beings who have lost their respect for God can do, and of the face that a godless humanism can assume.

3. Today the Church honours two priests, Karl Leisner and Bernhard Lichtenberg, who represent many others. By virtue of their faith they opposed the inhuman ideology of Nazism and therefore sacrificed their lives. The provost Bernhard Lichtenberg, in particular, became a witness to the dignity God has given all men. In their witness we perceive the strength of what appears to be lack of strength, the strength of those who know God and whom God knows. Perceiving the sufferings of his chosen people in slavery, God said: "I know their sufferings" (*Ex* 3:7). In their witness we discover the deep meaning of the expression, *Victor in vinculis*,

victorious in chains, which is applicable to both, and we understand what Karl Leisner wrote in his diary: "If I can withstand the clear gaze of God's judgement, what can men do to me?".

The provost Bernhard Lichtenberg saw with his own eyes what men can do to their fellowmen when on 9 and 10 November 1938 he witnessed the terrible prelude to the pogrom. That evening, from the pulpit in St. Hedwig's Cathedral he said: "Outside, the temple is burning; that too is a house of God". He started to pray publicly in the cathedral every evening "for the persecuted non Aryan Christians, for the Jews". In the following years he also extended his prayers to include "the prisoners in concentration camps, the millions of refugees, without name or country, the soldiers, wounded and dying and those fighting on both sides, the bombarded cities in allied and enemy territory" (*Interrogation Report*, 25 October 1941). Denounced for these prayers, he was arrested on 23 October 1941. Two years later he died while being taken to the concentration camp in Dachau.

4. Among all the memories that weigh heavily on us today, the precious historical fact that Bernard Lichtenberg was not alone in his commitment to those persecuted by the Nazi regime comes to mind. This shows the involvement of many Catholics, alone or in groups and at the cost of their life, who offered their active assistance, often secretly. The efforts of the ecclesiastical hierarchy to stop the terrible acts of that inhuman system with protests and pastoral letters should also remind us of this commitment.

As representatives of those who opposed it and offered their help, we recall in this city Margarete Sommer, who endeavoured through the "Non-Aryan Relief Service" to stand up for her fellow citizens persecuted by the Nazi attacks; the great Bishop of Berlin, Cardinal Konrad von Preysing, who did all he could to support the opposition to Hitler's regime; and Maria Terwiel, a young woman who helped her Jewish fellow citizens by providing them with personal documents and ration cards, and who was condemned to death for "aiding and abetting the enemy."

Even if, as historians have shown, many priests and lay people were opposed to that regime of terror, and encouraged many forms of resistance in daily life, this was still insufficient. We express our gratitude and our esteem to them today. Their example and their memory are not only an everlasting model for us. They are also an appeal to Christians and Jews to work together for the dignity of all men wherever it is still threatened today or threatened again. This includes, in particular, action against any form of anti-Semitism so that events such as the Shoah will never happen again.

5. On the occasion of my visit to Rome's Synagogue on 13 April 1986, I stressed that "the Church of Christ should discover her 'bond' with Judaism, by searching into her own mystery. The Jewish religion is not 'extrinsic' to us, but in a certain way is 'intrinsic' to our own religion. With Judaism therefore we have a relationship which we do not have with any other religion" (*L'Osservatore Romano* English edition 21 April 1986, p. 6). Further to deepen these relations is one of the Church's important projects. The Second Vatican Council already called for an intense dialogue between the two religions, one which should "promote mutual knowledge and respect". This dialogue must take place through a "'dialogue of life', through which believers . . . bear witness before each other in daily life to their own human and spiritual values, and help each other to live according to those values in order to build a more just and fraternal society" (*Redemptoris missio*, n. 57). The Church in Berlin and in Germany will be especially committed to this dialogue. Through numerous activities, she has also shown how much she takes this dialogue to heart. She can joyfully say that her efforts are not only accepted willingly by the Jewish communities but have also been supported with sincere kindness.

6. From this city a message of life is proclaimed today, calling for Jews and Christians to live together in a climate of peace and mutual understanding without excluding persons of different beliefs. At the same time we must take joint responsibility for giving the future a human face.

Today we praise and thank God. But we also pray that he will bless our common progress and our efforts. May Germany and Europe oppose the powers of death; may they be open to the message of life and continue on their way towards the third millennium under the banner of new hope!

Shalom!
ORE, July 10, 1996

Prayer at Visit to Blessed Bernhard's Tomb

June 23, 1996

God, our Father,
in Jesus your Son,
you accepted all men as your children.
He became a brother and friend
for all especially the poor and the marginalized.
Turn your gaze to the many people
everywhere in the world who are
despised;
look at the many
who are forced to live in conditions
unworthy of human beings.
Your servant Bernard Lichtenberg
worked in this city as a witness
to faith and love.

He suffered greatly,
to help people in their physical
and spiritual needs
He risked his freedom and his life,
defending those persecuted by the
Nazi regime,
in particular the Jews.
We beg you, Father of all men,
free the world from the evil of selfishness and violence.
Help us to follow the example of
Bernhard Lichtenberg and to love
all men as you love them:
unconditionally and without limits.

Hear our prayer
Through Jesus Christ, your Son,
our Lord and God,
who lives and reigns with you
in the unity of the Holy Spirit,
for ever and ever.
Amen.

(L'Osservartore Romano English Weekly Edition [ORE], July 10, 1996)

Homily at Beatification of Bernhard Lichtenberg and Karl Leisner

June 23, 1996

. . . 4. Christ is the Truth. Bernhard Lichtenberg bore witness to that to his last breath. Against the lies of Nazi ideology Lichtenberg courageously confessed: "My *Führer* is Christ!". Every day during the intercessions at Vespers he prayed "for the oppressed non-Aryan Christians, for the persecuted Jews, and for prisoners in concentration camps . . .".

The fact that our new blessed was a saint of intercessory prayers is apparent not only in his prayer for Jews and prisoners in concentration camps, but is also shown in his prayer for ecclesial vocations.

. . . Bernhard Lichtenberg knew quite well that wherever God's truth is no longer heeded, human dignity also suffers. Wherever falsehood reigns, false and evil behavior also rules. "A person's actions are the consequences of his principles. When his principles are false, his actions will not be correct. . . . I fight against false principles, which necessarily give rise to false actions", he wrote in the minutes of his first appearance before the Nazi judges. And he clearly and emphatically called some of these false principles by name: "The elimination of religious instruction in the schools; struggle against the Cross; the secularization of marriage; deliberate killing of those whose lives were supposedly not worth living (euthanasia), persecution of the Jews . . .". (L'Osservartore Romano English Weekly Edition [ORE], June 26, 1996)

1997

Address of His Holiness Pope John Paul II to a Group of Jews and Christians from Boston, USA

March 6, 1997

Dear Friends,

It is a pleasure for me to welcome you, *Jews and Christians from the Boston area* actively involved in improving relations between the followers of both our traditions. The aim which you have set yourselves, of fostering mutual knowledge and understanding, and of increasing respect and co-operation between us, is very close to my heart. I earnestly encourage all such efforts, especially when they seek to strengthen the close spiritual bonds linking the children of Abraham and the followers of Jesus of Nazareth (cf. *Nostra Aetate*, n. 4).

I thank you for your generous support of the *Holy See's Commission for Religious Relations with Jews*. Since its establishment as a result of the Second Vatican Council, the Commission has served as a meeting point for all who recognize that the divine will urges us to overcome every form of discrimination and religious intolerance. May the Lord bless you all in this work.

Address of John Paul II to H.E. Mr. Aharon Lopez, Ambassador of the State of Israel to the Holy See

April 10, 1997

Mr Ambassador,

I am pleased to welcome you to the Vatican and to accept the Letters accrediting you as Ambassador Extraordinary and Plenipotentiary of the State of Israel to the Holy See. On this auspicious occasion I express my gratitude for the greetings which you have brought from President Ezer Weizman and which I cordially reciprocate. I ask you to convey my good wishes and assure him of my prayers for your country and for all the peoples of the Holy Land.

The diplomatic relations established in 1994 between the Holy See and the State of Israel represent an important step in the continuing process of normalization which we have undertaken. These diplomatic ties cannot however be considered an end in themselves, for their purpose is to help achieve the even greater goals spelled out in the *Fundamental Agreement* signed at the end of 1993. The spirit of that *Agreement*, the good faith and the commitment expressed therein, must be constantly at the forefront of all our efforts as we continue to travel together the road of mutual understanding, friendship and cooperation.

Much has already been done to implement the different Articles of the *Fundamental Agreement*, and I acknowledge with pleasure Your Excellency's reference to the "Legal Agreement" which will soon be brought before the Israeli Government for approval and implementation. We must be grateful to all those on both sides whose untiring efforts have enabled us to reach this point. It is my hope that the "Legal Agreement" will be signed and ratified as soon as possible, since it represents a most significant juridical instrument for the life of the Catholic Church in Israel and for the Catholic faithful who are Israeli citizens. Moreover, we are speaking here of an important step in helping all the people of Israel, regardless of religious faith or cultural differences, to work together as equal partners in the building up of Israeli society. This involves nothing less than firmly placing our hope in the Creator and in the ability he has given man to respond to what is asked of him: "What does the Lord require of you but to do justice, and to love kindness, and to walk humbly with your God?" (Mic 6:8).

This brings us to what you have rightly identified as one of the challenges—indeed the great challenge—facing the peoples of the Middle East: the quest for peace. As you have pointed out, progress has been made, and the Holy See, ever an active supporter of the peace process, is pleased whenever positive results are forthcoming. However, difficulties and crises are not lacking, which even now threaten to shatter the fragile optimism that has been growing. In this regard, I renew the expression of the grave concern with which the Holy See and the entire international community has noted the recent heightening of tensions in an already delicate and volatile situation. There are serious problems which daily touch upon the physical safety of individuals, both Israelis and Palestinians, and which threaten the possibility of release from the seemingly endless spiral of action, reaction and counter-reaction. This is in fact a vicious circle from which there can be no escape unless all parties act with genuine goodwill and solidarity. As I remarked earlier this year: "All people together, Jews, Christians and Muslims, Israelis and Arabs, believers and non-believers, must create and reinforce peace"; this peace "rests on sincere dialogue between equal partners, with respect for each other's identity and history, . . . on the right of peoples to the free determination of their own destiny, upon their independence and security" (*Address to the Diplomatic Corps accredited to the Holy See*, 13 January 1997, No. 3).

In this context I cannot fail to mention, if only briefly, the unique character of Jerusalem. The Holy City, the City of Peace, remains part of the common patrimony of the whole of humanity, and must be preserved and safeguarded for all generations. Different peoples identify with the words of the Psalm: "Pray for the peace of Jerusalem!" (Psalm 122:6). The Catholic Church will continue to do her part in fostering the vocation and mission which the God of Revelation himself has entrusted to the Holy City in its complex and varied history. And when we think about the peace which God desires, we cannot forget that it involves justice, respect for every person's dignity and a willingness to understand others.

The Holy See and the Catholic Church as a whole are deeply committed to cooperating with the State of Israel "in combatting all forms of anti-Semitism and all kinds of racism and of religious intolerance, and in promoting mutual understanding among nations, tolerance among communities and respect for human life and dignity" (*Fundamental Agreement*, Article 2 SS 1). There can be no question that in these areas more can be done and must be done. It is precisely such renewed efforts that will give to the Great Jubilee of the Year 2000 a truly universal significance, not limited to Catholics or Christians but embracing all peoples in every part of the world. I am confident that the Israeli authorities, and their Palestinian counterparts, will do all they can to ensure that those who come to visit the historic and holy places connected with the three great monotheistic faiths will be welcomed in a spirit of respect and friendship. It is my own fervent hope to be among those making such a pilgrimage, and I am grateful for the kind invitations which I continue to receive.

Mr Ambassador, I wish you success in your mission as your country's Representative to the Holy See, and I assure you of the cooperation of the various offices of the Roman Curia as you discharge your high duties. For you and your country I make my own the prayer of the ancient Biblical author: "The Lord lift up his countenance upon you, and give you peace!" (Num 6:26).

Address of His Holiness Pope John Paul II to Members of the Pontifical Biblical Commission

April 11, 1997

1. Your Eminence, I cordially thank you for the sentiments you have just expressed in presenting to me the Pontifical Biblical Commission at the beginning of its mandate. I cordially greet the old and new members of the Commission attending this audience. I greet the "old" members with warm gratitude for the tasks already completed and the "new" members with special joy inspired by hope. I am pleased to have this opportunity to meet you all personally and to say again to each of you how much I appreciate the generosity with which you put your competence as exegetes at the service of the Word of God and the Church's Magisterium.

The theme you have begun to study at this plenary session is of enormous importance: it is, in fact, fundamental for a correct understanding of the mystery of Christ and Christian identity. I would first like to emphasize this usefulness, which we could call *ad intra*. It is also inevitably reflected in a usefulness, so to speak, *ad extra*, since awareness of one's own identity determines the nature of one's relations with others. In this case it determines the nature of the relations between Christians and Jews.

2. Since the second century A.D., the Church has been faced with the temptation to separate the New Testament completely from the Old, and to oppose one to the other, attributing to them two different origins. The Old Testament, according to Marcion, came from a god unworthy of the name because he was vindictive and bloodthirsty, while the New Testament revealed a God of reconciliation and generosity. The Church firmly rejected this error,

reminding all that God's tenderness was already revealed in the Old Testament. Unfortunately the Marcionite temptation is making its appearance again in our time. However what occurs most frequently is an ignorance of the deep ties linking the New Testament to the Old, an ignorance that gives some people the impression that Christians have nothing in common with Jews.

Centuries of reciprocal prejudice and opposition have created a deep divide which the Church is now endeavouring to bridge, spurred to do so by the Second Vatican Council's position. The new liturgical Lectionaries have given more space to Old Testament texts, and the *Catechism of the Catholic Church* has been concerned to draw constantly from the treasures of Sacred Scripture.

3. Actually, it is impossible fully to express the mystery of Christ without reference to the Old Testament. Jesus' human identity is determined on the basis of his bond with the people of Israel, with the dynasty of David and his descent from Abraham. And this does not mean only a physical belonging. By taking part in the synagogue celebrations where the Old Testament texts were read and commented on, Jesus also came humanly to know these texts; he nourished his mind and heart with them, using them then in prayer and as an inspiration for his actions.

Thus he became an authentic son of Israel, deeply rooted in his own people's long history. When he began to preach and teach, he drew abundantly from the treasure of Scripture, enriching this treasure with new inspirations and unexpected initiatives. These—let us note—did not aim at abolishing the old revelation but, on the contrary, at bringing it to its complete fulfillment. Jesus understood the increasing opposition he had to face on the way to Calvary in the light of the Old Testament, which revealed to him the destiny reserved for the prophets. He also knew from the Old Testament that in the end God's love always triumphs.

To deprive Christ of his relationship with the Old Testament is therefore to detach him from his roots and to empty his mystery of all meaning. Indeed, to be meaningful, the Incarnation had to be rooted in centuries of preparation. Christ would otherwise have been like a meteor that falls by chance to the earth and is devoid of any connection with human history.

4. From her origins, the Church has well understood that the Incarnation is rooted in history and, consequently, she has fully accepted Christ's insertion into the history of the People of Israel. She has regarded the Hebrew Scriptures as the perennially valid Word of God addressed to her as well as to the children of Israel. It is of primary importance to preserve and renew this ecclesial awareness of the essential relationship to the Old Testament. I am certain that your work will make an excellent contribution in this regard; I am delighted with it and deeply grateful to you.

You are called to help Christians have a good understanding of their identity, an identity that is defined first and foremost by faith in Christ, the Son of God. But this faith is inseparable from its relationship to the Old Testament, since it is faith in Christ who "died for our sins, *according to the Scriptures*" and "was raised . . . *in accordance with the Scriptures*" (1 Cor 15:3–4). The Christian must know that by belonging to Christ he has become "Abraham's offspring" (Gal 3:29) and has been grafted onto a cultivated olive tree (cf. Rom 11:17–24), that is, included among the People of Israel, to "share the richness of the olive tree" (Rom 11:17). If he has this firm conviction, he can no longer allow for Jews as such to be despised, or worse, ill-treated.

5. In saying this I do not mean to disregard the fact that the New Testament preserves traces of obvious tension between the early Christian communities and some groups of non-Christian Jews. St Paul himself testifies in his Letters that as a non-Christian Jew he had proudly persecuted the Church of God (cf. Gal 1:13; 1 Cor 15:9; Phil 3:6). These painful memories must be overcome in charity, in accordance with Christ's command. Exegesis must always seek to advance in this direction and thereby help to decrease tensions and clear up misunderstandings.

Precisely in the light of all this, the work you have begun is highly important and deserves to be carried out with care and commitment. It involves certain difficult aspects and delicate points, but it is very promising and full of great hope. I trust it will be very fruitful for the glory of God. With this wish, I assure you of a constant remembrance in prayer and I cordially impart a special Apostolic Blessing to you all.

Pope John Paul II General Audience

September 10, 1997

To the English-speaking pilgrims and visitors the Holy Father said:

I am pleased to greet the participants in the Colloquium sponsored by the International Council of Christians and Jews: may your discussions and reflections lead to ever greater understanding, respect and co-operation between the followers of the Jewish and Christian faiths. Upon all the English-speaking pilgrims, especially those from England, South Africa, Australia, Japan, Canada and the United States, I invoke the joy and peace of our Lord Jesus Christ.

Address of His Holiness Pope John Paul II to a Symposium on the Roots of Anti-Judaism

October 31, 1997

Your Eminences,
Dear Brothers in the Episcopate,
Dear Friends,

1. I am pleased to receive you during your symposium on the roots of anti-Judaism. I especially greet Cardinal Roger Etchegaray, President of the Committee for the Great Jubilee of the Year 2000,

who is presiding over your work. I thank you for having devoted these days to a theological study of great importance.

Your colloquium is in keeping with preparations for the Great Jubilee, for which I have invited the sons and daughters of the Church to assess the past millennium, especially our century, in the spirit of a necessary "examination of conscience", on the threshold of what should be a time of conversion and reconciliation (cf. *Tertio millennio adveniente,* nn. 27–35).

The subject of your symposium is the correct theological interpretation of the relations between the Church of Christ and the Jewish people. The Council's Declaration *Nostra Aetate* laid the foundations for this and I myself, in exercising my Magisterium, have had occasion several times to speak on them. In fact, in the Christian world—I do not say on the part of the Church as such—erroneous and unjust interpretations of the New Testament regarding the Jewish people and their alleged culpability have circulated for too long, engendering feelings of hostility towards this people. They contributed to the lulling of consciences, so that when the wave of persecutions inspired by a pagan anti-Semitism, which in essence is equivalent to an anti-Christianity, swept across Europe, alongside Christians who did everything to save the persecuted even at the risk of their lives, the spiritual resistance of many was not what humanity rightfully expected from the disciples of Christ. Your lucid examination of the past, in view of a purification of memory, is particularly appropriate for clearly showing that anti-Semitism has no justification and is absolutely reprehensible.

Your work complements the reflection conducted particularly by the *Commission for Religious Relations with Jews,* expressed, among other ways, in the *Guidelines of 1 December 1974* (*L'Osservatore Romano* English edition, 16 January 1975, pp. 3–4) and in the *Notes on the Correct Way to Present the Jews and Judaism in Preaching and Catechesis in the Roman Catholic Church* of 24 June 1985 (*L'Osservatore Romano* English edition, 24 June 1985, pp. 6–7). I appreciate the fact that your symposium intends to conduct its theological research with great scholarly rigour, in the conviction that to serve the truth is to serve Christ himself and his Church.

2. In the closing chapters of his *Letter to the Romans* (ch. 9–11), in which he gives us crucial insights into the destiny of Israel according to God's plan, the Apostle Paul raises a resounding song of adoration: "O the depth of the riches and wisdom and knowledge of God!" (Rom 11:33). In Paul's ardent soul, this hymn echoes the principle he had just stated and which is in a way the central theme of the whole Epistle: "For God has consigned all men to disobedience, that he may have mercy upon all" (ibid., 11:32). Salvation history, even when its events seem disconcerting to us, is guided by the mercy of the One who came to save what was lost. An attitude of adoration before the unfathomable depths of God's loving Providence allows only a glimpse of what is a mystery of faith.

3. The fact of divine election is at the origin of this small people situated between the great pagan empires whose brilliant culture overshadowed them. This people was gathered together and led by God, the Creator of heaven and earth. Thus its existence is not a mere fact of nature or culture, in the sense that through culture man displays the resources of his own nature. It is a supernatural fact. This people perseveres in spite of everything because they are the people of the Covenant, and despite human infidelities, the Lord is faithful to his Covenant. To ignore this primary fact is to embark on the way of a Marcionism against which the Church immediately and vigorously reacted, in the awareness of her vital link with the Old Testament, without which the New Testament itself would be emptied of its meaning. The Scriptures cannot be separated from the people and its history, which leads to Christ, the promised and awaited Messiah, the Son of God made man. The Church ceaselessly confesses this fact, when in her liturgy she recites the psalms each day, as well as the canticles of Zechariah, the Virgin Mary and Simeon (cf. Ps 132:17; Lk 1:46–55; 1:68–79; 2:29–32).

That is why those who regard the fact that Jesus was a Jew and that his milieu was the Jewish world as mere cultural accidents, for which one could substitute another religious tradition from which the Lord's person could be separated without losing its identity, not only ignore the meaning of salvation history, but more radically challenge the very truth of the Incarnation and make a genuine concept of inculturation impossible.

4. On the basis of what has just been said, we can draw some conclusions for guiding the attitude of Christians and the work of theologians. The Church firmly condemns all forms of genocide, as well as the racist theories that have inspired them and have claimed to justify them. One may recall Pius XI's Encyclical *Mit brennender Sorge* (1937) and Pius XII's *Summi Pontificatus* (1939); the latter cited the law of human solidarity and of charity towards every individual, regardless of the people to which he belongs. Racism is thus a negation of the deepest identity of the human being, who is a person created in the image and likeness of God. To the moral evil of any genocide the *Shoah* adds the evil of a hatred that attacks God's saving plan for history. The Church knows that this hatred is also aimed directly at her.

From St Paul's teaching in the *Letter to the Romans* we learn those fraternal sentiments, rooted in faith, that we must feel towards the children of Israel (cf. Rom 9:4–5). The Apostle stresses: "For the sake of their forefathers," they are beloved of God, whose gifts and call are irrevocable (cf. Rom 11:28–29).

5. Be assured of my gratitude for the work you are doing on a very important theme that deeply concerns me. You are thus helping to further the dialogue between Catholics and Jews, which we are pleased to note has taken a new, positive direction in recent decades.

I express my best wishes to you and your loved ones, and I willingly grant you my Apostolic Blessing.

Letter to the Latin-Rite Diocese of Jerusalem

November 28, 1997

. . . By its presence in the same territory as the Islamic and Jewish communities and through the exchanges it has with them, the Latin community has been prepared over time to understand the importance of interreligious dialogues in the spirit desired and recommended by the Second Vatican Ecumenical Council. Daily life presupposes continuous contact with believers of other religious traditions, for the human, spiritual and moral development of peoples. It is obvious that respectful dialogue and joint, fraternal collaboration among all society's members can be a vigorous appeal for this same understanding to be achieved in other countries.

. . . Regarding the ties with those who belong to the Jewish religion, it should be recalled that Jews and Christians have a common heritage which links them spiritually (cf. *Nostra Aetate, n. 4*). Both are a blessing for the world (cf. Gn 12:2–3), to the extent that they work together so that peace and justice prevail among all people and all individuals and do so in fullness and depth, according to the divine plan and in the spirit of sacrifice which this noble project can demand.

They are all called to be conscious of this sacred duty and to fulfill it, through honest and friendly dialogue and by collaboration for the benefit of man and society; I am certain that this readiness to do God's will for the world will also be a blessing for our different communities and unable us to cry out with the psalmist: "Steadfast love and faithfulness will meet; righteousness and peace will kiss each other. Faithfulness will spring up from the ground, and righteousness will look down from the sky" (*Ps* 85 [84]: 10–11). (L'Osservartore Romano English Weekly Edition [ORE], January 21, 1998)

Commission for Religious Relations with the Jews

March 12, 1998

We Remember: A Reflection on the Shoah Letter of Pope John Paul II

To my Venerable Brother
Cardinal Edward Idris Cassidy

On numerous occasions during my Pontificate I have recalled with a sense of deep sorrow the sufferings of the Jewish people during the Second World War. The crime which has become known as the *Shoah* remains an indelible stain on the history of the century that is coming to a close.

As we prepare for the beginning of the Third Millennium of Christianity, the Church is aware that the joy of a Jubilee is above all the joy that is based on the forgiveness of sins and reconciliation with God and neighbor. Therefore she encourages her sons and daughters to purify their hearts, through repentance of past errors and infidelities. She calls them to place themselves humbly before the Lord and examine themselves on the responsibility which they too have for the evils of our time.

It is my fervent hope that the document: *We Remember: A Reflection on the Shoah*, which the Commission for Religious Relations with the Jews has prepared under your direction, will indeed help to heal the wounds of past misunderstandings and injustices. May it enable memory to play its necessary part in the process of shaping a future in which the unspeakable iniquity of the *Shoah* will never again be possible. May the Lord of history guide the efforts of Catholics and Jews and all men and women of good will as they work together for a world of true respect for the life and dignity of every human being, for all have been created in the image and likeness of God.

From the Vatican, 12 March 1998.
John Paul II

1998

Apostolic Journey of His Holiness John Paul II to Cuba (January 21–26, 1998), Meeting with Other Christian Communities, Message of John Paul II

January 25, 1998

4. I also wish to address a particular greeting to the Jewish community represented here. Your presence is an eloquent expression of the fraternal dialogue aimed at a better understanding between Jews and Catholics, and which, promoted by the Second Vatican Council, continues to be ever more widespread. With you we share a common spiritual patrimony, firmly rooted in the Sacred Scriptures. May God, the Creator and Saviour, sustain our efforts to walk together and, encouraged by the divine word, may we grow in worship and fervent love of him. May all of this ever find expression in effective action for the benefit of each and every person.

Address of the Holy Father Pope John Paul II to the Members of the International Catholic-Jewish Liaison Committee

March 26, 1998

Dear Friends,

With pleasure I welcome the members of the International Catholic-Jewish Liaison Committee as you gather in Rome for your sixteenth meeting. Your Committee has contributed much to improving relations between our two communities by fostering theological reflection and dialogue on significant religious and social issues. The Joint Declaration issued as a result of your last session noted important convergences in Catholic and Jewish understandings of the family, the foundation of society. You have explored the biblical vision of God's creation, with its consequences for an appreciation of the dignity of the human person and of our responsibility for the natural environment.

The progress which you have already made shows the immense promise held out by continuing dialogue between Jews and Catholics. But your work is also an impressive sign of hope to a world marked by conflict and division, all too often fomented in the name of economic or political gain. A commitment to authentic dialogue, rooted in a sincere love of truth and an openness to all the members of the human family, remains the first and indispensable path to the reconciliation and peace which the world needs. When believers look at events in the conviction that all things are ultimately governed by Divine Providence, they will surely grow closer in that blessed harmony which the Psalmist likens to the precious oil poured out on the head of Aaron, or the dew which falls on the mountains of Zion (cf. Ps 133).

Dear friends, may your present meeting discover ever more effective ways to make known and appreciated by Catholics and Jews alike the significant advances in mutual understanding and cooperation which have taken place between our two communities. Upon you and your important work I cordially invoke abundant divine blessings.

Prayer for the Jewish People, for Use in Poland

December 24, 1998

God of Abraham, the prophets, Jesus Christ, in You everything is embraced, toward You everything moves, You are the end of all things.

Hear the prayers we extend for the Jewish nation which—thanks to its forefathers—is still very dear to you.

Instill within it a constant, ever livelier desire to deepen your truth and love.

Help it, as it yearns for peace and justice, that it may reveal to the world the might of your blessing.

Succor it, that it may obtain respect and love from the side of those who do not yet understand the greatness of suffering it has borne, and those who, in solidarity and a sense of mutual care, experience together the pain of wounds inflicted upon it.

Remember the new generations of youth and children, that they may, unchangeably faithful to you, uphold what remains the particular mystery of their vocation.

Strengthen all generations, that, thanks to their testimony, humanity will understand that your salvific intention extends over all humankind, and that you, God, are for all nations the beginning and the final end. Amen

1999

International Theological Commission, Memory and Reconciliation: The Church and the Faults of the Past

December 1999

The present text was approved in *forma specifica* by the International Theological Commission, by written vote, and was then submitted to the President, Cardinal Ratzinger, Prefect of the Congregation for the Doctrine of the Faith, who gave his approval for its publication.

---

(83) This is the judgement of the recent document of the Commission for Religious Relations with the Jews, *We Remember: A Reflection on the Shoah*, Rome (March 16, 1998), III, in *Information Service* of the Pontifical Council for Promoting Christian Unity, n. 97, 19.

(84) *Ibid.*, V, 22.

(85) *Ibid.*, IV, 20, 21.

(86) *Ibid.*, IV, 21.

(87) *Ibid.*, V, 22.

5.4. Christians and Jews

The relationship between Christians and Jews is one of the areas requiring a special examination of conscience.(81) "The Church's relationship to the Jewish people is unlike the one she shares with any other religion."(82) Nevertheless, "the history of the relations between Jews and Christians is a tormented one . . . In effect, the balance of these relations over two thousand years has been quite negative."(83) The hostility or diffidence of numerous Christians toward Jews in the course of time is a sad historical fact and is the cause of profound remorse for Christians aware of the fact that "Jesus was a descendent of David; that the Virgin Mary and the Apostles belonged to the Jewish people; that the Church draws sustenance from the root of that good olive tree onto which have been grafted the wild olive branches of the Gentiles (cf. *Rom* 11:17–24); that the Jews are our dearly beloved brothers, indeed in a certain sense they are 'our elder brothers.'"(84)

The Shoah was certainly the result of the pagan ideology that was Nazism, animated by a merciless anti-Semitism that not only despised the faith of the Jewish people, but also denied their very human dignity. Nevertheless, "it may be asked whether the Nazi persecution of the Jews was not made easier by the anti-Jewish prejudices imbedded in some Christian minds and hearts . . . Did Christians give every possible assistance to those being persecuted, and in particular to the persecuted Jews?"(85) There is no doubt that there were many Christians who risked their lives to save and to help their Jewish neighbors. It seems, however, also true that "alongside such courageous men and women, the spiritual resistance and concrete action of other Christians was not that which might have been expected from Christ's followers."(86) This fact constitutes a call to the consciences of all Christians today, so as to require "an act of repentance (*teshuva*),"(87) and to be a stimulus to increase efforts to be "transformed by renewal of your mind" (*Rom* 12:2), as well as to keep a "moral and religious memory" of the injury inflicted on the Jews. In this area, much has already been done, but this should be confirmed and deepened.

John Paul II General Audience

April 28, 1999

Dear Brothers and Sisters,

1. The interreligious dialogue which the Apostolic Letter *Tertio millennio adveniente* encourages as a characteristic feature of this year particularly dedicated to God the Father (cf. nn. 52–53) first of all concerns Jews, our "elder brothers," as I called them on the occasion of my memorable meeting with the Jewish community of Rome on 13 April 1986 (*L'Osservatore Romano* English edition, 21 April 1986, p. 6). Reflecting on the spiritual patrimony we share, the Second Vatican Council, especially in the Declaration *Nostra Aetate*, gave a new direction to our relationship with the Jewish religion. We must reflect ever more deeply on that teaching, and the Jubilee of the Year 2000 can be a magnificent occasion to meet, possibly, in places of significance for the great monotheistic religions (cf. *Tertio millennio adveniente*, n. 53).

We know that, from the beginnings of the Church down to our century, relations with our Jewish brothers and sisters have unfortunately been difficult. However, throughout this long and tormented history there have been occasions of peaceful and constructive dialogue. We should recall in this regard that the first theological work entitled "Dialogue" was significantly dedicated by the philosopher and martyr Justin to his encounter with Trypho the Jew in the second century. Also of note is the vivid dialogical dimension strongly present in contemporary neo-Jewish literature, which has deeply influenced the philosophical and theological thought of the 20th-century.

2. This dialogical attitude between Christians and Jews not only expresses the general value of interreligious dialogue, but also the long journey they share leading from the Old to the New Testament. There is a long period of salvation history which Christians and Jews can view together. "The Jewish faith," in fact, "unlike

other non-Christian religions, is already a response to God's revelation in the Old Covenant" (*CCC*, n. 839). This history is illumined by an immense group of holy people whose lives testify to the possession, in faith, of what they hoped for. Indeed, the Letter to the Hebrews emphasizes this response of faith throughout the history of salvation (cf. *Heb* 11).

Today the courageous witness of faith should also mark the collaboration of Christians and Jews in proclaiming and realizing God's saving plan for all humanity. If his plan is interpreted in a different way regarding the acceptance of Christ, this obviously involves a crucial difference which is at the very origin of Christianity itself, but does not change the fact that there are still many elements in common.

It still is our duty to work together in promoting a human condition that more closely conforms to God's plan. The Great Jubilee of the Year 2000, which refers precisely to the Jewish tradition of jubilee years, points to the urgent need for this common effort to restore peace and social justice. Recognizing God's dominion over all creation, particularly the earth (*Lv* 25), all believers are called to translate their faith into a practical commitment to protecting the sacredness of human life in all its forms and to defending the dignity of every brother and sister.

3. In meditating on the mystery of Israel and its "irrevocable calling" (cf. *Insegnamenti* IX/1 [1986], p. 1028), Christians also explore the mystery of their own roots. In the biblical sources they share with their Jewish brothers and sisters, they find the indispensable elements for living and deepening their own faith.

This can be seen, for example, in the liturgy. Like Jesus, whom Luke shows us as he opens the book of the prophet Isaiah in the synagogue of Nazareth (cf. *Lk* 4:16ff.), the Church draws from the liturgical wealth of the Jewish people. She arranges the liturgy of the hours, the liturgy of the word and even the structure of her Eucharistic prayers according to the models of the Jewish tradition. A few great feasts like Easter and Pentecost recall the Jewish liturgical year and are excellent occasions for remembering in prayer the people God chose and loves (cf. *Rom* 11:2). Today dialogue means that Christians should be more aware of these elements which bring us closer together. Just as we take note of the "covenant never revoked by God" (cf. *Insegnamenti*, 1980, [III/2], pp. 1272–1276), so we should consider the intrinsic value of the Old Testament (cf. *Dei Verbum*, n. 3), even if this only acquires its full meaning in the light of the New Testament and contains promises that are fulfilled in Jesus. Was it not Jesus' interpretation of the Hebrew Scriptures which made the hearts of the disciples "burn within" them on the road to Emmaus (*Lk* 24:32), enabling them to recognize the risen Christ as he broke bread?

4. Not only the shared history of Christians and Jews, but especially their dialogue must look to the future (cf. *CCC*, n. 840), becoming as it were a *"memoria futuri"* (*We Remember: A Reflection on the "Shoah"; L'Osservatore Romano* English edition, 18 March 1998, p. 6). The memory of these sorrowful and tragic events of the past can open the way to a renewed sense of brotherhood, the fruit of God's grace, and to working so that the seeds infected with anti-Judaism and anti-Semitism will never again take root in human hearts.

Israel, a people who build their faith on the promise God made to Abraham: "You shall be the father of a multitude of nations" (*Gn* 17:4; *Rom* 4:17), shows Jerusalem to the world as the symbolic place of the eschatological pilgrimage of peoples united in their praise of the Most High. I hope that at the dawn of the third millennium sincere dialogue between Christians and Jews will help create a new civilization founded on the one, holy and merciful God, and fostering a humanity reconciled in love.

Pope John Paul II Apostolic Letter Issued *Motu Proprio*, Proclaiming Saint Bridget of Sweden, Saint Catherine of Siena, and Saint Teresa Benedicta of the Cross Co- Patronesses of Europe, His Holiness Pope John Paul II for Perpetual Remembrance

October 1, 1999

The real reason then which led me to these three particular women can be found in their lives. Their holiness was demonstrated in historical circumstances and in geographical settings which make them especially significant for the Continent of Europe. Saint Bridget brings us to the extreme north of Europe, where the Continent in some way stretches out to unity with the other parts of the world; from there she departed to make Rome her destination. Catherine of Siena is likewise well-known for the role which she played at a time when the Successor of Peter resided in Avignon; she brought to completion a spiritual work already initiated by Bridget by becoming the force behind the Pope's return to his own See at the tomb of the Prince of the Apostles. Finally, Teresa Benedicta of the Cross, recently canonized, not only lived in various countries of Europe, but by her entire life as thinker, mystic and martyr, built a kind of bridge between her Jewish roots and her commitment to Christ, taking part in the dialogue with contemporary philosophical thought with sound intuition, and in the end forcefully proclaiming by her martyrdom the ways of God and man in the horrendous atrocity of the Shoah. She has thus become the symbol of a human, cultural and religious pilgrimage which embodies the deepest tragedy and the deepest hopes of Europe.

8. With Edith Stein—Saint Teresa Benedicta of the Cross—we enter a very different historical and cultural context. For she brings us to the heart of this tormented century, pointing to the hopes which it has stirred, but also the contradictions and failures which have disfigured it. Unlike Bridget and Catherine, Edith was not from a Christian family. What we see in her is the anguish of the search and the struggle of an existential "pilgrimage." Even after she found the truth in the peace of the contemplative life, she was to live to the full the mystery of the Cross.

Edith was born in 1891 to a Jewish family of Breslau, which was then in German territory. Her interest in philosophy, and her abandonment of the religious practice which she had been taught by her mother, might have presaged not a journey of holiness but a life lived by the principles of pure "rationalism." Yet it was precisely along the byways of philosophical investigation that grace awaited her: having chosen to undertake the study of phenomenology, she became sensitive to an objective reality which, far from ultimately dissolving in the subject, both precedes the subject and becomes the measure of subjective knowledge, and thus needs to be examined with rigorous objectivity. This reality must be heeded and grasped above all in the human being, by virtue of that capacity for "empathy"—a word dear to her—which enables one in some way to appropriate the lived experience of the other (cf. Edith Stein, *The Problem of Empathy*).

It was with this listening attitude that she came face to face, on the one hand, with the testimony of Christian spiritual experience given by Teresa of Avila and the other great mystics of whom she became a disciple and an imitator, and, on the other hand, with the ancient tradition of Christian thought as consolidated in Thomistic philosophy. This path brought her first to Baptism and then to the choice of a contemplative life in the Carmelite Order. All this came about in the context of a rather turbulent personal journey, marked not only by inner searching but also by commitment to study and teaching, in which she engaged with admirable dedication. Particularly significant for her time was her struggle to promote the social status of women; and especially profound are the pages in which she explores the values of womanhood and woman's mission from the human and religious standpoint (cf. E. Stein, *Woman. Her Role According to Nature and Grace*).

9. Edith's encounter with Christianity did not lead her to reject her Jewish roots; rather it enabled her fully to rediscover them. But this did not mean that she was spared misunderstanding on the part of her family. It was especially her mother's disapproval which caused her profound pain. Her entire journey towards Christian perfection was marked not only by human solidarity with her native people but also by a true spiritual sharing in the vocation of the children of Abraham, marked by the mystery of God's call and his "irrevocable gifts" (cf. *Rom* 11:29).

In particular, Edith made her own the suffering of the Jewish people, even as this reached its apex in the barbarous Nazi persecution which remains, together with other terrible instances of totalitarianism, one of the darkest and most shameful stains on the Europe of our century. At the time, she felt that in the systematic extermination of the Jews the Cross of Christ was being laid on her people, and she herself took personal part in it by her deportation and execution in the infamous camp of Auschwitz-Birkenau. Her voice merged with the cry of all the victims of that appalling tragedy, but at the same time was joined to the cry of Christ on the Cross which gives to human suffering a mysterious and enduring fruitfulness. The image of her holiness remains for ever linked to the tragedy of her violent death, alongside all those who with her suffered the same fate. And it remains as a proclamation of the Gospel of the Cross, with which she identified herself by the very choice of her name in religion.

Today we look upon Teresa Benedicta of the Cross and, in her witness as an innocent victim, we recognize an imitation of the Sacrificial Lamb and a protest against every violation of the fundamental rights of the person. We also recognize in it the pledge of a renewed encounter between Jews and Christians which, following the desire expressed by the Second Vatican Council, is now entering upon a time of promise marked by openness on both sides. Today's proclamation of Edith Stein as a Co-Patroness of Europe is intended to raise on this Continent a banner of respect, tolerance and acceptance which invites all men and women to understand and appreciate each other, transcending their ethnic, cultural and religious differences in order to form a truly fraternal society.

2000

Homily of the Holy Father
"Day of Repentance"

March 12, 2000

3. Before Christ who, out of love, took our guilt upon himself, we are all invited to make a *profound examination of conscience.* One of the characteristic elements of the Great Jubilee is what I described as the "purification of memory" (Bull *Incarnationis mysterium,* n. 11). As the Successor of Peter, I asked that "in this year of mercy the Church, strong in the holiness which she receives from her Lord, should kneel before God and implore forgiveness for the past and present sins of her sons and daughters" (ibid.). Today, the First Sunday of Lent, seemed to me the right occasion for the Church, gathered spiritually round the Successor of Peter, to implore divine forgiveness for the sins of all believers. *Let us forgive and ask forgiveness!*

This appeal has prompted a thorough and fruitful reflection, which led to the publication several days ago of a document of the International Theological Commission, entitled: *"Memory and Reconciliation: The Church and the Faults of the Past."* I thank everyone who helped to prepare this text. It is very useful for correctly understanding and carrying out the authentic request for pardon, based on the *objective responsibility* which Christians share as members of the Mystical Body, and which spurs today's faithful to recognize, along with their own sins, the sins of yesterday's Christians, in the light of careful historical and theological discernment.

4. *Let us forgive and ask forgiveness!* While we praise God who, in his merciful love, has produced in the Church a wonderful harvest of holiness, missionary zeal, total dedication to Christ and neighbor, we cannot fail to recognize *the infidelities to the Gospel*

324

committed by some of our brethren, especially during the second millennium. Let us ask pardon for the divisions which have occurred among Christians, for the violence some have used in the service of the truth and for the distrustful and hostile attitudes sometimes taken towards the followers of other religions.

First Sunday of Lent "Day of Repentance" Presentation

Vatican Basilica, March 12, 2000

3. "The Church cannot cross the threshold of the new millennium without encouraging her children to purify themselves through repentance of past errors and instances of infidelity, inconsistency and slowness to act" (*Tertio Millennio Adveniente,* 33). Consequently, a liturgy seeking pardon from God for the sins committed by Christians down the centuries is not only legitimate; it is also the most fitting means of expressing repentance and gaining purification.

[...]

5. The reference to errors and sins in a liturgy must be frank and capable of specifying guilt; yet given the number of sins committed in the course of twenty centuries, it must necessarily be rather summary. It is also appropriate that it should take into account the admissions of sin already made both by Pope Paul VI and by Pope John Paul II himself on numerous occasions in the course of his Pontificate.

These include:

[...]

d) Confession of sins against the people of Israel (cf. JOHN PAUL II, *Mainz,* 17 November 1980; *Vatican Basilica,* 7 December 1991; *Commission for Religious Relations with the Jews,* "*We Remember,*" 16 March 1998, No. 4).

Universal Prayer, Confession of Sins and Asking for Forgiveness

IV. Confession of Sins against the People of Israel

A representative of the Roman Curia:

> *Let us pray that, in recalling the sufferings*
> *endured by the people of Israel throughout history,*
> *Christians will acknowledge the sins*
> *committed by not a few of their number*
> *against the people of the Covenant and the blessings,*
> *and in this way will purify their hearts.*

Silent prayer.

The Holy Father:

> *God of our fathers,*
> *you chose Abraham and his descendants*
> *to bring your Name to the Nations:*
> *we are deeply saddened by the behaviour of those*
> *who in the course of history*
> *have caused these children of yours to suffer,*
> *and asking your forgiveness we wish to commit ourselves*
> *to genuine brotherhood*
> *with the people of the Covenant.*
> *We ask this through Christ our Lord.*
> R. Amen

Jubilee Pilgrimage of His Holiness John Paul II to the Holy Land (March 20–26, 2000), Visit to the Chief Rabbis at Hechal Shlomo *Speech of John Paul II*

March 23, 2000

Very Reverend Chief Rabbis,

It is with deep respect that I visit you here today and thank you for receiving me at Hechal Shlomo. Truly this is a uniquely significant meeting which—I hope and pray—will lead to increasing contacts between Christians and Jews, aimed at achieving an ever deeper understanding of the historical and theological relationship between our respective religious heritages.

Personally, I have always wanted to be counted among those who work, on both sides, to overcome old prejudices and to secure ever wider and fuller recognition of the spiritual patrimony shared by Jews and Christians. I repeat what I said on the occasion of my visit to the Jewish Community in Rome, that we Christians recognize that the Jewish religious heritage is intrinsic to our own faith: "you are our elder brothers" (cf. *Address at the Synagogue of Rome*, 13 April 1986, 4). We hope that the Jewish people will acknowledge that the Church utterly condemns anti-Semitism and every form of racism as being altogether opposed to the principles of Christianity. We must work together to build a future in which there will be no more anti-Judaism among Christians or anti-Christian sentiment among Jews.

There is much that we have in common. There is so much that we can do together for peace, for justice, for a more human and fraternal world. May the Lord of heaven and earth lead us to a new and fruitful era of mutual respect and cooperation, for the benefit of all! Thank you.

Jubilee Pilgrimage of His Holiness John Paul II to the Holy Land (March 20–26, 2000), *Speech of John Paul II,* Visit to the President of Israel

March 23, 2000

Mr President,
Government Ministers,
Members of the Knesset,
Your Excellencies,

I am most grateful, Mr President, for the welcome you have given me to Israel. To this meeting we both bring long histories. You represent Jewish memory, reaching beyond the recent history of this land to your peoples unique journey through the centuries and millennia. I come as one whose Christian memory reaches back throughout the two thousand years since the birth of Jesus in this very Land.

History, as the ancients held, is the *Magistra vitae*, a teacher of how to live. This is why we must be determined to heal the wounds of the past, so that they may never be opened again. We must work for a new era of reconciliation and peace between Jews and Christians. My visit is a pledge that the Catholic Church will do everything possible to ensure that this is not just a dream but a reality.

We know that real peace in the Middle East will come only as a result of mutual understanding and respect between all the peoples of the region: Jews, Christians and Muslims. In this perspective, my pilgrimage is a journey of hope: the hope that the twenty-first century will lead to a new solidarity among the peoples of the world, in the conviction that development, justice and peace will not be attained unless they are attained for all.

Building a brighter future for the human family is a task which concerns us all. That is why I am pleased to greet you, Government Ministers, members of the Knesset and Diplomatic Representatives of many countries, who must make and implement decisions which affect the lives of people. It is my fervent hope that a genuine desire for peace will inspire your every decision. With that as my prayer, I invoke abundant divine blessings upon you, Mr President, upon your country, and upon all of you who have honoured me with your presence. Thank you.

Jubilee Pilgrimage of His Holiness John Paul II to the Holy Land (March 20–26, 2000), *Speech of John Paul II,* Visit to the Yad Vashem Museum *Jerusalem—Yad Vashem*

March 23, 2000

The words of the ancient Psalm rise from our hearts:

> *"I have become like a broken vessel.*
> *I hear the whispering of many—terror on every side!—*
> *as they scheme together against me, as they plot to take my life.*
> *But I trust in you, O Lord; I say, 'You are my God'." (Ps 31:13–*
> *15).*

1. In this place of memories, the mind and heart and soul feel an extreme need for silence. Silence in which to remember. Silence in which to try to make some sense of the memories which come flooding back. Silence because there are no words strong enough to deplore the terrible tragedy of the *Shoah.* My own personal memories are of all that happened when the Nazis occupied Poland during the War. I remember my Jewish friends and neighbors, some of whom perished, while others survived.

I have come to Yad Vashem to pay homage to the millions of Jewish people who, stripped of everything, especially of human dignity, were murdered in the Holocaust. More than half a century has passed, but the memories remain.

Here, as at Auschwitz and many other places in Europe, we are overcome by the echo of the heart-rending laments of so many. Men, women and children cry out to us from the depths of the horror that they knew. How can we fail to heed their cry? No one can forget or ignore what happened. No one can diminish its scale.

2. We wish to remember. But we wish to remember for a purpose, namely to ensure that never again will evil prevail, as it did for the millions of innocent victims of Nazism.

How could man have such utter contempt for man? Because he had reached the point of contempt for God. Only a Godless ideology could plan and carry out the extermination of a whole people.

The honour given to the "just gentiles" by the State of Israel at Yad Vashem for having acted heroically to save Jews, sometimes to the point of giving their own lives, is a recognition that not even in the darkest hour is every light extinguished. That is why the Psalms, and the entire Bible, though well aware of the human capacity for evil, also proclaims that evil will not have the last word. Out of the depths of pain and sorrow, the believer's heart cries out: "I trust in you, O Lord; I say, 'You are my God'." (*Ps* 31:14).

3. Jews and Christians share an immense spiritual patrimony, flowing from God's self-revelation. Our religious teachings and our spiritual experience demand that we overcome evil with good. We remember, but not with any desire for vengeance or as an incentive to hatred. For us, to remember is to pray for peace and justice, and to commit ourselves to their cause. Only a world at peace, with justice for all, can avoid repeating the mistakes and terrible crimes of the past.

As Bishop of Rome and Successor of the Apostle Peter, I assure the Jewish people that the Catholic Church, motivated by the Gospel law of truth and love and by no political considerations, is deeply saddened by the hatred, acts of persecution and displays of anti-Semitism directed against the Jews by Christians at any time and in any place. The Church rejects racism in any form as a denial of the image of the Creator inherent in every human being (cf. *Gen* 1:26).

4. In this place of solemn remembrance, I fervently pray that our sorrow for the tragedy which the Jewish people suffered in the

twentieth century will lead to a new relationship between Christians and Jews. Let us build a new future in which there will be no more anti-Jewish feeling among Christians or anti-Christian feeling among Jews, but rather the mutual respect required of those who adore the one Creator and Lord, and look to Abraham as our common father in faith (cf. *We Remember*, V).

The world must heed the warning that comes to us from the victims of the Holocaust and from the testimony of the survivors. Here at Yad Vashem the memory lives on, and burns itself onto our souls. It makes us cry out:

> *"I hear the whispering of many—terror on every side!—But I trust in you, O Lord; I say, 'You are my God'." (Ps 31:13–15).*

Jubilee Pilgrimage of His Holiness John Paul II to the Holy Land (March 20–26, 2000), *Address of John Paul II*, Interreligious Meeting at the Notre Dame Pontifical Institute *Jerusalem*

March 23, 2000

Distinguished Jewish, Christian and Muslim Representatives,

1. In this year of the Two Thousandth Anniversary of the Birth of Jesus Christ, I am truly happy to be able to fulfill my long-cherished wish to make a journey through the geography of salvation history.

I am deeply moved as I follow in the footsteps of the countless pilgrims who before me have prayed in the Holy Places connected with God's interventions. I am fully conscious that this Land is Holy to Jews, Christians and Muslims. Therefore my visit would have been incomplete without this meeting with you, distinguished religious leaders. Thank you for the support which your presence here this evening gives to the hope and conviction of so many people that we are indeed entering a new era of interreligious dialogue. We are conscious that closer ties among all believers are a necessary and urgent condition for securing a more just and peaceful world.

For all of us Jerusalem, as its name indicates, is the "City of Peace." Perhaps no other place in the world communicates the sense of transcendence and divine election that we perceive in her stones and monuments, and in the witness of the three religions living side by side within her walls. Not everything has been or will be easy in this co-existence. But we must find in our respective religious traditions the wisdom and the superior motivation to ensure the triumph of mutual understanding and cordial respect.

2. We all agree that religion must be genuinely centered on God, and that our first religious duty is adoration, praise and thanksgiving. The opening *sura* of the Qur'ân makes this clear: "Praise be to God, the Lord of the Universe" (*Qur'an*, 1:1). In the inspired songs of the Bible we hear this universal call: "Let everything that breathes give praise to the Lord! Alleluia!" (*Ps* 150:6). And in the Gospel we read that when Jesus was born the angels sang: "Glory to God in the highest heaven" (*Lk* 2:14). In our times, when many are tempted to run their affairs without any reference to God, the call to acknowledge the Creator of the universe and the Lord of history is essential in ensuring the well-being of individuals and the proper development of society.

3. If it is authentic, devotion to God necessarily involves attention to our fellow human beings. As members of the one human family and as God's beloved children, we have duties towards one another which, as believers, we cannot ignore. One of the first disciples of Jesus wrote: "If any one says, 'I love God', and hates his brother, he is a liar; for he who does not love his brother whom he has seen, cannot love God whom he has not seen" (*1 Jn* 4:20). Love

of our brothers and sisters involves an attitude of respect and compassion, gestures of solidarity, cooperation in service to the common good. Thus, concern for justice and peace does not lie outside the field of religion but is actually one of its essential elements.

In the Christian view it is not for religious leaders to propose technical formulas for the solution of social, economic and political problems. Theirs is, above all, the task of teaching the truths of faith and right conduct, the task of helping people—including those with responsibility in public life—to be aware of their duties and to fulfill them. As religious leaders, we help people to live integrated lives, to harmonize the vertical dimension of their relationship with God with the horizontal dimension of service to their neighbor.

4. Each of our religions knows, in some form or another, the Golden Rule: "Do unto others as you would have them do unto you." Precious as this rule is as a guide, true love of neighbor goes much further. It is based on the conviction that when we love our neighbor we are showing love for God, and when we hurt our neighbor we offend God. This means that religion is the enemy of exclusion and discrimination, of hatred and rivalry, of violence and conflict. Religion is not, and must not become, an excuse for violence, particularly when religious identity coincides with cultural and ethnic identity. Religion and peace go together! Religious belief and practice cannot be separated from the defence of the image of God in every human being.

Drawing upon the riches of our respective religious traditions, we must spread awareness that today's problems will not be solved if we remain ignorant of one another and isolated from one another. We are all aware of past misunderstandings and conflicts, and these still weigh heavily upon relationships between Jews, Christians and Muslims. We must do all we can to turn awareness of past offences and sins into a firm resolve to build a new future in which there will be nothing but respectful and fruitful cooperation between us.

The Catholic Church wishes to pursue a sincere and fruitful interreligious dialogue with the members of the Jewish faith and the followers of Islam. Such a dialogue is not an attempt to impose our views upon others. What it demands of all of us is that, holding to what we believe, we listen respectfully to one another, seek to discern all that is good and holy in each other's teachings, and cooperate in supporting everything that favours mutual understanding and peace.

5. The Jewish, Christian and Muslim children and young people present here are a sign of hope and an incentive for us. Each new generation is a divine gift to the world. If we pass on to them all that is noble and good in our traditions, they will make it blossom in more intense brotherhood and cooperation.

If the various religious communities in the Holy City and in the Holy Land succeed in living and working together in friendship and harmony, this will be of enormous benefit not only to themselves but to the whole cause of peace in this region. Jerusalem will truly be a City of Peace for all peoples. Then we will all repeat the words of the Prophet: "Come, let us go up to the mountain of the Lord . . . that he may teach us his ways and that we may walk in his paths" (*Is* 2:3).

To re-commit ourselves to such a task, and to do so in the Holy City of Jerusalem, is to ask God to look kindly on our efforts and bring them to a happy outcome. May the Almighty abundantly bless our common endeavours!

Jubilee Pilgrimage of His Holiness John Paul II to the Holy Land (March 20–26, 2000), *Prayer of the Holy Father at the Western Wall*

God of our fathers,
you chose Abraham and his descendants
to bring your Name to the Nations:
we are deeply saddened by the behaviour of those
who in the course of history
have caused these children of yours to suffer,
and asking your forgiveness we wish to commit ourselves
to genuine brotherhood
with the people of the Covenant.
R. Amen

Message of John Paul II to His Beatitude Michel Sabbah

November 6, 2000

To His Beatitude Michel Sabbah
Patriarch of Jerusalem for Latins
President of the Assembly of Catholic Ordinaries of the Holy Land
    The trials which the peoples of the Holy Land are enduring at this time are a cause of great suffering to me and I wish to express to everyone, without exception, my deepest solidarity.

Without doubt, the violent change from negotiation to confrontation represents a setback for peace, yet no one must be resigned to fatalism: the Israeli and Palestinian peoples are called by geography and history to live together.

They can achieve this in a peaceful and lasting way only if fundamental rights are guaranteed for everyone: both the Israeli and the Palestinian peoples have the right to live in their own homes in dignity and security.

Only a return to the negotiating table, on an equal footing and with respect for international law, can lead to a future of brotherhood and peace for those living in that blessed land.

Recalling my pilgrimage among you some months ago, I am deeply moved to think of all those places which speak of God's history with man and are a call to work together so that violence, hatred and suspicion may never again disfigure that part of the world.

I encourage you, the Catholic Bishops of the Holy Land, and all leaders of Christian communities to renew your efforts so that mutual respect, with humility and trust, may inspire your relations.

I also appeal to those who have the task of guiding the faithful of Judaism and Islam, that they may find in their faith all the necessary energy for the internal and external peace for which these peoples long to become a reality.

I invite the international community to continue its efforts to help both sides to find solutions that guarantee the desired security and tranquillity, which are the prerogatives of every nation and the preconditions for the life and progress of all society.

As I invoke upon all people of good will the blessing of almighty God, who proclaims peace to his people, to his faithful ones, to those who put their hope in him (cf. *Ps* 85: 9), I also impart an affectionate Apostolic Blessing to Your Beatitude, to your Brother Bishops and to all the faithful entrusted to their care.

From the Vatican, 6 November 2000.

2001

Meeting with Representatives of the All-Ukrainian Council of Churches and Religious Organizations, *Address of the Holy Father*

June 24, 2001, Kiev, National Philharmonic

5. I now greet you, the Representatives of the other Religions and Religious Organizations, who work in close cooperation with Christians in Ukraine. This is a typical quality of your land which, on account of its particular position and make-up, *is a natural bridge* not only between East and West, but also between the peoples who have been here together for several centuries. These are people who differ as regards historical origin, cultural tradition and religious belief. I wish to recall the significant presence of the Jews, who form a community which is solidly rooted in Ukrainian society and culture. They too suffered injustices and persecutions for having remained faithful to the religion of their ancestors. Who can ever forget the immense tribute of blood which they paid to the fanaticism of an ideology propounding the superiority of one race over others? Here, in Kyiv, at Babyn Yar, during the Nazi occupation countless people, including over 100,000 Jews, were killed within a few days. This is one of the most atrocious of the many crimes which the history of the last century unhappily has had to record.

May the memory of this episode of murderous frenzy be a *salutary warning to all*. What atrocities is man capable of, when he fools himself into thinking that he can do without God! The desire to set himself up in opposition to God and to combat every form of religion showed itself in an overbearing way also in atheistic and Communist totalitarianism. In this city, this memory lives on in the monuments to the victims of Holodomar, to those killed at Bykivnia, to those who died in the Afghanistan war, to mention but a few. May the memory of such painful experiences help humanity today, especially the younger generation, *to reject every form of violence* and to grow in respect for human dignity, by safeguarding the fundamental rights rooted in it, not least the right to religious freedom.

Letter of John Paul II to Cardinal Walter Kasper

To Cardinal Walter Kasper
President of the Commission for Religious Relations with the Jews
   Informed of the meeting organized on 28 and 29 January in Paris by the European Jewish Congress in which you will be taking part, together with Cardinal Jean-Marie Lustiger, Archbishop of Paris, I would like to join by prayer all those who have come together to address the question: After the Second Vatican Council and *Nostra Aetate*, Improving Relations between Jews and Catholics in Europe in the Pontificate of His Holiness John Paul II.
   I am delighted by this initiative that is called to contribute to the dialogue and draws support from the development of the Catholic Church, as the Council desired. *Shalom,* peace! With this Biblical term, I would like to greet warmly all the participants in this meeting. It is particularly timely, as a continuation of the recent *Day of Prayer for Peace in the World,* which was held in Assisi on 24 January. All the religions accepted the mission of working for peace, thus offering a sign of hope for the world and recalling that the spiritual

and transcendent dimension of man invites him to promote peace and respect for the dignity of every human person. Jews and Christians have a special relationship. The message that comes to us from the God of the Covenant with Moses, the patriarchs and the prophets, is part of our common heritage and invites us to collaborate in the life of the world, for the Most High is calling us to be holy as He is holy, and at the same time, to love our neighbor as ourselves.

Since the Conciliar Declaration *Nostra Aetate,* great progress has been made—and I am very glad of it—towards better mutual understanding and reconciliation between our two communities. A text of this kind constitutes a starting point, an anchor and a compass for future relations. After the sorrowful events that scarred Europe's history, especially in the 20th century, it is right to give fresh energy to our relations, so that the religious tradition that inspired the culture and life of the continent may continue to be part of its soul and thus enable it to serve the growth of the whole human person and the whole of mankind.

Jews and Christians are bound to one another because of their respective identity and should pursue that culture of dialogue that Martin Buber envisaged. It is our task to pass on to the new generations the treasures and values we have in common, so that never again will man despise his own brother in humanity and never again will conflicts or wars be unleashed in the name of an ideology that despises a culture or religion. On the contrary, the different religious traditions are called together to put their patrimony at the service of all, in the hope of building the common European home together, united in justice, peace, equity and solidarity. Then will begin to be realized the word of God announced by the prophet (cf. Is 11,6–9). Youth need our witness and our joint commitment if they are to believe, to sanctify God's name by their lives and to hope in a future for the world that will be rich in promise. In this way, they will be determined to affirm the ties of brotherhood to establish a renewed humanity.

I ask the Almighty to inspire the work of the Paris meeting and to make the efforts of the participants fruitful. May God's peace dwell in the heart of each one!

From the Vatican, 25 January 2002

2002

Apostolic Visit of His Holiness Pope John Paul II to Azerbaijan and Bulgaria, Arrival Ceremony, *Address of the Holy Father,* Sophia, St. Alexander Nevski Square

May 23, 2002

I greet the Christians of the *other Ecclesial Communities,* the members of the *Jewish Community* with their President, and *the followers of Islam* led by the Grand Mufti. I reaffirm here, as I did at the meeting in Assisi, my conviction that *every religion is called to promote justice and peace among peoples,* forgiveness, life and love.

Telegram of Holy Father to Chief Rabbi of Rome, Riccardo Di Segni

July 18, 2002

As soon as he learned of the deplorable desecration of the graves of the Jewish community in Rome, deeply saddened by this ignoble act, that continues the series of similar events occurring with worrisome repetition in Europe and on other continents, the Supreme Pontiff wished to convey the expression of his spiritual closeness to the families whose emotions and dignity have been offended. While firmly condemning such deplorable actions and the anti-Jewish sentiments that prompt them, he assures the families that he will remember them in prayer so that the Most High may grant comfort to all who are suffering and eternal peace to the deceased of this community that is dear to him.

Cardinal Angelo Sodano
Secretary of State of His Holiness
ORE, July 24, 2002

2003

Address of John Paul II to the Chief Rabbi of Rome, Dr. Riccardo Di Segni

February 13, 2003

Esteemed Chief Rabbi of Rome,
Dear Brothers in the faith of Abraham,

1. I am glad to meet you, esteemed Dr Riccardo Di Segni, after your election as Chief Rabbi of Rome, and I cordially greet you and the representatives who have accompanied you. I renew my congratulations to you for the important office which has been entrusted to you, and on this important occasion, I would like to recall with deep esteem your illustrious predecessor, Prof. Elio Toaff.

Today's visit allows me to emphasize the deep desire of the Catholic Church to strengthen the bonds of friendship and reciprocal collaboration with the Jewish community. Here in Rome, the Synagogue, a symbol of the faith of the children of Abraham, is very close to St Peter's Basilica, the centre of the Church, and I am grateful to God who granted me on 13 April 1986, to travel the short distance that separates these two temples. That historic and unforgettable visit was a gift from the Almighty, and an important milestone on the path of understanding between Jews and Catholics. I hope that the memory of that event may continue to exercise a beneficial influence and that the path of reciprocal confidence that has developed so far will serve to intensify relations between the Catholic community and the Jewish community of Rome, the most ancient one in Western Europe.

2. It must be recognized that in the past our two communities lived side by side, at times writing "a turbulent history," that in some cases was not free of hostility and distrust. The document *Nostra Aetate* of the Second Vatican Council, the gradual application of the conciliar directive, the gestures of friendship made by both parties have contributed in these years to guide our relations towards a greater reciprocal understanding. I hope that this effort may continue, that it may be shaped by initiatives of fruitful collaboration in the social, cultural and theological fields, and may deepen the consciousness of those spiritual bonds that unite us.

3. In these days we can hear resounding in the world dangerous shouts of war. We, Jews and Catholics, perceive the urgent mission of imploring peace from God, the Creator and Eternal One, and of being ourselves peacemakers.

Shalom! This beautiful word, so dear to you, means salvation, happiness, harmony; it highlights the fact that peace is a gift of God; a fragile gift, placed in human hands, that has to be safeguarded by the dedication of our communities.

May God make us *builders of peace,* with the consciousness that, when man works for peace, he becomes capable of making the world better.

Shalom! This is my cordial greeting to you and to the entire Jewish community of Rome. May God, in his goodness, protect and bless each one of us. May he especially bless all who forge a path of friendship and peace among the men and women of every race and culture.

Address of the Holy Father John Paul II to H.E. Mr. Oded Ben- Hur, New Ambassador of Israel to the Holy See

June 2, 2003

Mr Ambassador,

I am pleased to welcome you to the Vatican and to accept the Letters of Credence appointing you Ambassador Extraordinary and Plenipotentiary of the State of Israel to the Holy See. Your presence here today is a testimony to our common desire to work together to build a world of peace and security, not only in Israel and the Middle East, but in every part of the globe, for all peoples everywhere. This is a task which we undertake not alone but with the whole international community: indeed, perhaps unlike any time in the past, the entire human family today feels the urgent need to overcome violence and terror, to expunge intolerance and fanaticism, to usher in an era of justice, reconciliation and harmony among individuals, groups and nations.

This need is probably nowhere more acutely felt than in the Holy Land. There is absolutely no question that peoples and nations have the inherent right to live in security. This right, however, entails a corresponding duty: to respect the right of others. Therefore, just as violence and terror can never be an acceptable means for making political statements, neither can retaliation ever lead to a just and lasting peace. Acts of terrorism are always to be condemned as true crimes against humanity (cf. *Message for the 2002 World Day of Peace*, 4). Every State has the undeniable right to defend itself against terrorism, but this right must always be exercised with respect for moral and legal limits in its ends and means (cf. *ibid.*, 5).

Like other members of the international community, and fully supporting the role and efforts of the larger family of nations in helping to resolve the crisis in the Middle East, the Holy See is convinced that the present conflict will be resolved only when there are two independent and sovereign States. As I said earlier this year to the Diplomatic Corps: "Two peoples, Israeli and Palestinian, are called to live side-by-side, equally free and sovereign, in mutual respect" (*Speech to the Diplomatic Corps accredited to the Holy See*, 13 January 2003, 4). It is essential that both parties give clear signs of their determined commitment to bring this peaceful coexistence about. By doing so, a priceless contribution will be made towards the building of a relationship of mutual trust and cooperation. In this context, I am pleased to note the Israeli Government's recent vote in support of the peace process: for all involved in that process, the Government's position is a positive sign of hope and encouragement.

Of course, the many issues and difficulties raised by this crisis must be dealt with in a fair and effective manner. Questions concerning Palestinian refugees and Israeli settlements, for example, or the problem of setting territorial boundaries and defining the status of the most sacred places of the City of Jerusalem, need to be the subject of open dialogue and sincere negotiation. By no means should a decision be made unilaterally. Rather, respect, mutual understanding and solidarity demand that the path of dialogue never be abandoned. Nor should real or apparent failures lead the partners in dialogue and negotiation to be discouraged. On the contrary, it is precisely in such circumstances that "it is all the more necessary that they should consent to begin again ceaselessly to propose true dialogue, by removing obstacles and by eliminating the defects of dialogue." In this way, they will walk together the path "which leads to peace, with all its demands and conditions" (*Message for the 1983 World Day of Peace*, 5).

Mr Ambassador, as you have noted, it was ten years ago that the Fundamental Agreement between the Holy See and the State of Israel was signed. It is this Agreement that paved the way for the subsequent establishment of full diplomatic relations between us and which continues to guide us in our dialogue and mutual exchange of positions regarding many issues of importance to both of us. The fact that we have been able to reach an accord on the full recognition of the legal personality of the Church's institutions is a source of satisfaction, and I am pleased that an accord also appears close at hand regarding related fiscal and economic matters. Along these same lines, I am confident that we shall be successful in drawing up useful guidelines for future cultural exchanges between us as well.

I would further express the fervent hope that this climate of cooperation and friendship will allow us to deal effectively with other difficulties that the Catholic faithful in the Holy Land face on a daily basis. Many of these problems, such as access to Christian shrines and holy sites, the isolation and suffering of Christian communities, the dwindling of the Christian population due to emigration, are in some way connected to the current conflict, but that should not discourage us from seeking possible remedies now, from working now to meet these challenges. I am confident that the Catholic Church will be able to continue to promote good will among peoples and to advance the dignity of the human person in her schools and educational programs, and through her charitable and social institutions. Overcoming the difficulties mentioned above will serve not only to enhance the contribution that the Catholic Church makes to Israeli society, but will also strengthen the guarantees of religious freedom in your country. This in turn will reinforce the feelings of equality between citizens, and each individual, inspired by his own spiritual convictions, will thus be better enabled to build up society as a common home shared by all.

Three years ago, during my Jubilee Year pilgrimage to the Holy Land, I remarked that "real peace in the Middle East will come only as a result of mutual understanding and respect between all the peoples of the region: Jews, Christians and Muslims. In this perspective, my pilgrimage is a pilgrimage of hope: the hope that the 21st century will lead to a new solidarity among the peoples of the world, in the conviction that development, justice and peace will not be attained unless they are attained by all" (*Visit to Israeli President Ezer Weizman*, 23 March 2000). It is precisely this hope and this concept of solidarity that must ever inspire all men and women—in the Holy Land and elsewhere—in working for a new world order based on harmonious relations and effective cooperation between peoples. This is mankind's task for the new millennium, this is the only way to ensure a future of promise and light for all.

Your Excellency, I ask you kindly to convey to the President, Prime Minister, Government and People of the State of Israel the assurance of my prayers for the nation, especially at this critical moment in its history. I am certain that your term of service as representative to the Holy See will do much to strengthen the bonds of understanding and friendship between us. Wishing you every success in your mission, and assuring you of the full cooperation of the various offices of the Roman Curia in the fulfilment of your high duties, I cordially invoke upon you, your fellow citizens and all the peoples of the Holy Land an abundance of divine blessings.

2004

Address of John Paul II to the Chief Rabbinate of Israel

January 16, 2004

Distinguished Gentlemen,

I am pleased that you have come to Rome to attend the Concert of Reconciliation at the Vatican, and I am happy to extend to you today my warm and cordial greetings. In the twenty-five years of my Pontificate I have striven to promote Jewish-Catholic dialogue and to foster ever greater understanding, respect and cooperation between us. Indeed, one of the highlights of my Pontificate will always remain my Jubilee Pilgrimage to the Holy Land, which included intense moments of remembrance, reflection and prayer at the Yad Vashem Holocaust Memorial and at the Wailing Wall.

The official dialogue established between the Catholic Church and the Chief Rabbinate of Israel is a sign of great hope. We must spare no effort in working together to build a world of justice, peace and reconciliation for all peoples. May Divine Providence bless our work and crown it with success!

Address of John Paul II at the Conclusion of the Concert Dedicated to the Theme of Reconciliation among Jews, Christians, and Muslims, Paul VI Audience Hall

January 17, 2004

1. I have taken part with deep emotion in this evening's concert dedicated to the theme of reconciliation among Jews, Christians and Muslims. With deep participation I listened to the splendid musical performance that gave us all an opportunity for reflection and prayer. I greet and cordially thank the sponsors of this initiative and everyone who helped to organize it.

I greet the Presidents and the members of the Pontifical Councils that sponsored this very important event. I greet the well-known figures and representatives of various Jewish International Organizations, of the Churches and Ecclesial Communities and of Islam; they have made our meeting even more evocative with their participation. A special "thank you" goes to the Knights of Columbus who gave the concert their concrete support, and to RAI (Italian Radio and Television), represented here by the directors who have ensured its proper broadcast.

I then extend my greeting to the distinguished conductor, Maestro Gilbert Levine, the members of the "Pittsburgh Symphony Orchestra" and the choirs from Ankara, Kraków, London and Pittsburgh. The choice of pieces for this evening has brought to our attention two important points which, despite the different treatment they are given by the respective sacred texts, bind together in a certain way all those who refer to Judaism, Islam and Christianity. These two points are: veneration for the Patriarch Abraham and the resurrection of the dead. We have heard the masterly comment in the sacred motet "Abraham" by John Harbison, and in Gustav Mahler's Symphony N. 2 that was inspired by the dramatic poem "Dziady" [celebration of death] written by Adam Mickiewicz, the distinguished Polish playwright.

2. The history of relations between Jews, Christians and Muslims is marked by patches of light and shadow and has unfortunately known some painful moments. Today we are aware of the pressing need for sincere reconciliation among believers in the one God.

This evening we are gathered here to give concrete expression to this commitment to reconciliation, entrusting ourselves to the universal message of music. We have been reminded of the recommendation *"I am God Almighty; walk before me and be blameless"* (Gn 17: 1). Every human being hears these words echoing within him: he knows that one day he will have to account to that God who observes his pilgrimage on earth from on High.

The unanimous hope that we express is that people may be purified of the hatred and evil that threaten peace continuously, and be able to extend to one another hands that have never been stained by violence but are ready to offer help and comfort to those in need.

3. Jews honour the Almighty as *protector of the human person* and the God of the *promises of life*. Christians know that love is the reason why God enters into relations with human beings and that love is the response he demands of them. For Muslims, God is good and can fill the believer with his mercies. Nourished by these convictions, Jews, Christians and Muslims cannot accept that the earth be afflicted by hatred or that humanity be overwhelmed by endless wars.

Yes! We must find within us the courage for peace. We must implore from on High the gift of peace. And this peace will spread like a soothing balm if we travel non-stop on the road to reconciliation. Then the wilderness will become a garden in which justice will flourish, and the effect of justice will be peace (cf. Is 32: 15–16).

Omnia vincit amor!

Address of John Paul II to a Delegation the "American Jewish Committee"

February 5, 2004

Distinguished Friends,

With affection I greet you, the members of the American Jewish Committee as you come to the Vatican. It is with gratitude that I recall your 1985 visit to mark the twentieth anniversary of the Conciliar Declaration *Nostra Aetate,* which has so significantly contributed to the strengthening of Jewish-Catholic relations.

As we now approach the fortieth anniversary of this historic document, there is regrettably a great need to repeat our utter condemnation of racism and anti-semitism. Violence in the name of religion is always a desecration to religion. Countering this alarming trend requires that together we stress the importance of religious education which promotes respect and love towards others.

In these days our attention remains drawn to the Holy Land which continues to be afflicted by violence and suffering. It is my fervent prayer that a just solution will be found which respects the rights and security of both Israelis and Palestinians.

Upon all of you, I invoke the gift of peace. *Shalom aleichem.*

Address of John Paul II to the Members of the American Jewish Distribution Committee

March 29, 2004

Distinguished Guests,

It is a great pleasure for me to welcome you, the President and members of the American Jewish Joint Distribution Committee. Your visit is yet another sign of the bonds of friendship between the Jewish people and the Catholic Church, bonds which we hope will grow ever stronger.

God has created man in his image and has endowed human beings with the capacity to love. It is through love that we fulfill our destiny to act in the likeness of God. From this stems our duty to serve one another according to the commandment found in the Book of Leviticus: "You shall love your neighbour as yourself. I am the Lord" (19:18). We are called especially to serve those who need our help to live in security, justice and freedom.

I gladly encourage the activity of your Joint Committee. May God bless your efforts and grant you success in helping those in need.

Message of John Paul II to the Chief Rabbi of Rome, Dr Riccardo Di Segni, for the Centenary of the Great Synagogue of Rome

To the most distinguished Dr Riccardo Di Segni
Chief Rabbi of Rome
Shalom!

> *"Behold, how good and pleasant it is when brothers dwell in unity!*
> *Hinneh ma tov u-ma na"im, shevet akhim gam yakhad!" (Ps 133*
> *[132]: 1).*

1. With deep joy I join the Jewish Community of Rome which is celebrating the centenary of the Great Synagogue of Rome, a symbol and a reminder of the millennial presence in this city of the people of the Covenant of Sinai. For more than 2,000 years your community has been an integral part of life in the city; it can boast of being the most ancient Jewish Community in Western Europe and of having played an important role in spreading Judaism on this Continent. Today's commemoration, therefore, acquires a special significance for religious, cultural and social life in the capital and cannot but have a very special resonance in the heart of the Bishop of Rome! Since I am unable to attend in person, I have asked my Vicar General for the Diocese of Rome, Cardinal Camillo Ruini, to represent me; he is accompanied by Cardinal Walter Kasper, President of the Holy See's Commission for Relations with the Jews. They formally express my desire to be with you on this day.

In offering you my respectful greeting, distinguished Dr Riccardo Di Segni, I extend my cordial thoughts to all the Members of the Community, to their President, Mr Leone Elio Paserman, and to all who are gathered to witness once again to the importance and vigour of the religious patrimony that is celebrated every Saturday in the Great Synagogue of Rome. I would like to extend a special greeting to Professor Elio Toaff, Chief Rabbi emeritus; with his open and generous spirit, he welcomed me to the Synagogue when I visited it on 13 April 1986. The event lives on, engraved in my mind and heart as a symbol of new developments in relations between the Jewish people and the Catholic Church in recent decades after periods that were at times difficult and troubled.

2. Today's celebration, in whose joy we all readily join, recalls the first century of this majestic Synagogue. It stands on the banks of the Tiber, witnessing with the harmony of its architectural lines to faith and to praise of the Almighty. The Christian Community of Rome, through the Successor of Peter, joins you in thanking the Lord for this happy occasion. As I said during the Visit I mentioned, we greet you as our "beloved brothers" in the faith of Abraham, our Patriarch, of Isaac and Jacob, of Sarah and Rebecca, Rachael and Leah. In writing to the Romans (cf. Rom 11: 16–18), St Paul was already speaking of the holy root of Israel on which pagans are grafted onto Christ, "for the gifts and the call of God are irrevocable" (Rom 11: 29), and you continue to be the first-born people of the Covenant (Liturgy of Good Friday, General Intercessions, *For the Jewish People*).

You have been citizens of this City of Rome for more than 2,000 years, even before Peter the fisherman and Paul in chains came here sustained from within by the breath of the Spirit. Not only the Sacred Scriptures, in which to a large extent we share, not only the liturgy but also very ancient art forms witness to the Church's deep bond with the Synagogue; this is because of that spiritual heritage which without being divided or rejected has been made known to believers in Christ and constitutes an inseparable bond between us and you, the people of the Torah of Moses, the good olive tree onto which a new branch was grafted (cf. Rom 11: 17).

In the Middle Ages, some of your great thinkers, such as Yehuda ha-Levi and Moses Maimonides, sought to examine how it would be possible to worship the Lord and serve suffering humanity together, thereby paving the way to peace. The great philosopher and theologian, well known to St Thomas Aquinas, Maimonides of Cordoba (1138–1204), the eighth centenary of whose death we are commemorating this year, expressed the hope that better relations between Jews and Christians might lead "the whole world to unanimous adoration of God as has been said: 'I will change the speech of the peoples to a pure speech, that all of them may call on the name of the Lord and serve him with one accord' (Zep 3: 9)" (*Mishneh Torah,* Hilkhòt Melakhim XI, 4, ed. Jerusalem, Mossad Harav Kook).

3. We have covered much ground together since that 13 April 1986 when the Bishop of Rome—the first since the Apostle Peter—paid you a visit: it was the embrace of brothers who were meeting again after a long period fraught with misunderstanding, rejection and distress. With the Second Vatican Ecumenical Council inaugurated by Bl. Pope John XXIII, and especially after the publication of the Declaration *Nostra Aetate* (28 October 1965), the Catholic Church opened her arms wide to you, remembering that "Jesus was and will always remain a Jew" (Commission for Religious Relations with the Jews, *Notes on the correct way to present the Jews and Judaism in preaching and catechesis in the Roman Catholic Church* [1985]: III, 12). During the Second Vatican Council, the Church clearly and definitively reaffirmed her rejection of all expressions of anti-Semitism. However, the sincere deploration and condemnation of those hostilities directed against the Jewish people that have often marked history do not suffice; we must also develop friendship, esteem and brotherly relations with them. These friendly relations, reinforced and nurtured after the session of the Council in the last century, saw us united in commemorating the victims of the Shoah, especially those who were wrenched from their families and from your beloved Jewish Community in Rome in October 1943 and interned in Auschwitz. May their memory be blessed and induce us to work as brothers and sisters.

Moreover, it is only right to remember all those Christians, motivated by natural kindliness and an upright conscience and sustained by their faith and the teaching of the Gospel, who reacted courageously also in this city of Rome and offered the persecuted Jews practical help in the form of solidarity and assistance, sometimes even at the risk of their own lives. May their blessed memory live on, together with the certainty that for them, as for all the "just of nations," the *tzaddiqim,* a place is prepared in the future world in the resurrection of the dead. Nor can we forget, in addition to the official pronouncements, the often hidden action of the Apostolic See which went to the aid of the Jews in danger in many ways, as has been recognized by authoritative representatives of it (cf. *We remember: A reflection on the "Shoah,"* 16 March 1998).

4. With help from Heaven, in taking this road to brotherhood, the Church has not hesitated to express deep sorrow at "the failures of her sons and daughters in every age" (*ibid.*) and, in an act of repentance (*teshuvà*), has asked forgiveness for their responsibility connected in any way with the scourges of anti-Judaism and anti-Semitism (*ibid.*). During the Great Jubilee, we prayed for God's mercy in the Basilica sacred to the memory of Peter in Rome, and in Jerusalem, the city beloved by all Jews, the heart of that Land which is Holy for us all. The Successor of Peter went on pilgrimage to the hills of Judea and paid homage to the victims of the Shoah at Yad Vashem; he prayed beside you on Mount Zion at the foot of that Holy Place.

Unfortunately, the mere thought of the Holy Land gives rise in our hearts to anxiety and sorrow because of the violence that continues to stain that region and the excessive flow of innocent blood poured out by both Israelis and Palestinians that hinders peace in justice from dawning. Today, therefore, in faith and hope, we are addressing a fervent prayer to the Eternal One, to the God of *Shalom*, so that enmity and hatred may no longer overpower those who turn to our father, Abraham—Jews, Christians and Muslims—and may lead the way to a clear knowledge of the ties that bind them and the responsibilities that lie on each one's shoulders.

We still have a long way to go: the God of justice and peace, of mercy and of reconciliation calls us to collaborate without wavering in our world today which is scarred by disputes and hostilities. If we can join our hearts and hands to respond to the divine call, the light of the Eternal One will shine close to us to illumine all peoples and show us paths to peace, to *Shalom*. Let us walk them with one heart.

5. Not only in Jerusalem and in the Land of Israel but also here in Rome, we can do many things together: for those close to us who are suffering marginalization, for immigrants and foreigners, for the weak and the poverty-stricken. Sharing the values of the defence of life and the dignity of every human person, we can increase our fraternal cooperation in concrete ways.

Our meeting today is, as it were, in preparation for your imminent solemnity of *Shavu"òt* and of our Pentecost which proclaim the fullness of our respective paschal celebrations. May these feasts see us united in praying David's paschal *Hallel.*

> *"Hallelu et Adonay kol goim*
> *shabbehuHu kol ha-ummim*
> *ki gavar "alenu khasdo*
> *we-emet Adonay le-"olam."*

> *"Laudate Dominum, omnes gentes, collaudate Eum, omnes populi.*
> *Quoniam confirmata est super nos misericordia eius,*
> *et veritas Domini manet in aeternum" Hallelu-Yah (Ps 117[116]).*

From the Vatican, 22 May 2004
Ioannes Paulus II

To Members of the ADL

December 17, 2004

Distinguished Guests,

It is a pleasure for me to welcome you, members of a delegation of the Anti-Defamation League as you visit the Vatican. The Catholic Church and the Jewish People continue to enjoy close bonds of friendship. It is my fervent prayer that men and women will work together to eradicate all forms of racism in order to build a society that promotes truth, justice, love and peace. Upon all of you I invoke the divine gifts of strength and joy. *Shalom*! (L'Osservartore Romano English Weekly Edition [ORE], December 22–29, 2004)

2 0 0 5

Message of His Holiness John Paul II on the Sixtieth Anniversary of the Liberation of the Prisoners of the Auschwitz-Birkenau Death Camp

January 15, 2005

Sixty years have passed since the liberation of the prisoners of the Auschwitz-Birkenau death camp. This anniversary calls us to ponder once again the drama which took place there, the final, tragic outcome of a program of hatred. In these days we must remember the millions of persons who, through no fault of their own, were forced to endure inhuman suffering and extermination in the gas chambers and ovens. I bow my head before all those who experienced this manifestation of the *mysterium iniquitatis*.

When, as Pope, I visited the Auschwitz-Birkenau camp in 1979, I halted before the monuments dedicated to the victims. There were inscriptions in many languages: Polish, English, Bulgarian, Romani, Czech, Danish, French, Greek, Hebrew, Yiddish, Spanish, Flemish, Serbo-Croat, German, Norwegian, Russian, Romanian, Hungarian and Italian. All these languages spoke of the victims of Auschwitz: real, yet in many cases completely anonymous men, women and children.

I stood somewhat longer before the inscription written in Hebrew. I said: "This inscription invites us to remember the people whose sons and daughters were doomed to total extermination.

This people has its origin in Abraham, our father in faith (cf. *Rom* 4:11–12), as Paul of Tarsus has said. This, the very people that received from God the commandment, 'You shall not kill,' itself experienced in a special measure what killing means. No one is permitted to pass by this inscription with indifference."

Today I repeat those words. No one is permitted to pass by the tragedy of the Shoah. That attempt at the systematic destruction of an entire people falls like a shadow on the history of Europe and the whole world; it is a crime which will for ever darken the history of humanity. May it serve, today and for the future, as a warning: there must be no yielding to ideologies which justify contempt for human dignity on the basis of race, colour, language or religion. I make this appeal to everyone, and particularly to those who would resort, in the name of religion, to acts of oppression and terrorism.

These reflections have remained with me, especially when, during the Great Jubilee of the Year 2000, the Church celebrated the solemn penitential liturgy in Saint Peter's, and I journeyed as a pilgrim to the Holy Places and went up to Jerusalem. In *Yad Vashem*—the memorial to the Shoah—and at the foot of the Western Wall of the Temple I prayed in silence, begging forgiveness and the conversion of hearts.

That day in 1979, I also remember stopping to reflect before two other inscriptions, written in Russian and in Romani. The history of the Soviet Union's role in that war was complex, yet it must not be forgotten that in it the Russians had the highest number of those who tragically lost their lives. The Roma were also doomed to total extermination in Hitler's plan. One cannot underestimate the sacrifice of life which was imposed on these, our brothers and sisters in the Auschwitz-Birkenau death camp. For this reason, I insist once more that no one is permitted to pass by those inscriptions with indifference.

Finally I halted before the inscription written in Polish. There I recalled that the experience of Auschwitz represented "yet another stage in the centuries-old struggle of this nation, my nation, for its fundamental rights among the peoples of Europe. Yet another loud cry for the right to have a place of its own on the map of Europe. Yet another painful reckoning with the conscience of humanity."

The statement of this truth was nothing more or less than a call for historical justice for this nation, which had made such great sacrifices in the cause of Europe's liberation from the infamous Nazi ideology, and which had been sold into slavery to another destructive ideology: that of Soviet Communism.

Today I return to those words—without retracting them—in order to thank God that, through the persevering efforts of my countrymen, Poland has taken its proper place on the map of Europe. It is my hope that this tragic historical experience will prove to be a source of mutual spiritual enrichment for all Europeans.

During my visit to Auschwitz-Birkenau, I also said that one should halt before every one of the inscriptions. I myself did so, passing in prayerful meditation from one to the next, and commending to the Divine Mercy all the victims from all those nations which experienced the atrocities of the war. I also prayed that, through their intercession, the gift of peace would be granted to our world. I continue to pray unceasingly, trusting that everywhere, in the end, there will prevail respect for the dignity of the human person and for the right of every man and women to seek the truth in freedom, to follow the moral law, to discharge the duties imposed by justice and to lead a fully human life (Cf. JOHN XXIII, Encyclical Letter *Pacem in Terris*: AAS 55 [1963], 295–296).

In speaking of the victims of Auschwitz, I cannot fail to recall that, in the midst of that unspeakable concentration of evil, there were also heroic examples of commitment to good. Certainly there were many persons who were willing, in spiritual freedom, to endure suffering and to show love, not only for their fellow prisoners, but also for their tormentors. Many did so out of love for God and for man; others in the name of the highest spiritual values.

Their attitude bore clear witness to a truth which is often expressed in the Bible: even though man is capable of evil, and at times boundless evil, evil itself will never have the last word. In the very abyss of suffering, love can triumph. The witness to this love shown in Auschwitz must never be forgotten. It must never cease to rouse consciences, to resolve conflicts, to inspire the building of peace.

Such, then, is the deepest meaning of this anniversary celebration. We remember the tragic sufferings of the victims not for the sake of reopening painful wounds or of stirring up sentiments of hatred and revenge, but rather in order to honour the dead, to acknowledge historical reality and above all to ensure that those terrible events will serve as a summons for the men and women of today to ever greater responsibility for our common history.

Never again, in any part of the world, must others experience what was experienced by these men and women whom we have mourned for sixty years!

To those taking part in the anniversary celebrations I send my greetings, and upon all I invoke the blessings of Almighty God.

From the Vatican, 15 January 2005
John Paul II

Address of John Paul II to the Members of the "Pave the Way Foundation"

January 18, 2005

Dear Friends,

With affection I greet the members of the "Pave the Way Foundation" on your visit to the Vatican, and I thank Mr. Krupp for the kind words which he has addressed to me on your behalf.

This year we will be celebrating the fortieth anniversary of the Second Vatican Council's Declaration *Nostra Aetate*, which has significantly contributed to the strengthening of Jewish-Catholic dialogue. May this be an occasion for renewed commitment to increased understanding and cooperation in the service of building a world ever more firmly based on respect for the divine image in every human being.

Upon all of you, I invoke the abundant blessings of the Almighty and, in particular, the gift of peace. *Shalom aleichem.*

Address of His Holiness Benedict XVI to a Delegation of the International Jewish Committee on Interreligious Consultations

June 9, 2005

Our meeting takes place during this year which marks the fortieth anniversary of the Declaration *Nostra Aetate* of the Second Vatican Council, whose teaching has served as the basis of the Church's relationship with the Jewish people since then. . . .

In the years following the Council, my predecessors Pope Paul VI and, in a particular way, Pope John Paul II, took significant steps towards improving relations with the Jewish people. *It is my intention to continue on this path.*